MALAYSIA@50

ECONOMIC DEVELOPMENT, DISTRIBUTION, DISPARITIES

MALAYSIA@50

ECONOMIC DEVELOPMENT, DISTRIBUTION, DISPARITIES

Jomo Kwame Sundaram
Food and Agriculture Organization, Rome

Wee Chong hui
Universiti Teknologi Mara, Malaysia

World Scientific

NEW JERSEY · LONDON · SINGAPORE · BEIJING · SHANGHAI · HONG KONG · TAIPEI · CHENNAI

Published by

World Scientific Publishing Co. Pte. Ltd.
5 Toh Tuck Link, Singapore 596224
USA office: 27 Warren Street, Suite 401-402, Hackensack, NJ 07601
UK office: 57 Shelton Street, Covent Garden, London WC2H 9HE

British Library Cataloguing-in-Publication Data
A catalogue record for this book is available from the British Library.

This book is published and distributed worldwide by World Scientific Publishing Co Pte Ltd except Malaysia.

MALAYSIA@50: ECONOMIC DEVELOPMENT, DISTRIBUTION, DISPARITIES

ISBN 978-981-4571-38-8

In-house Editors: Dong Lixi/Sandhya Venkatesh

Typeset by Ivan Foo Ah Hiang

Printed in Singapore

Contents

List of Tables

List of Figures

Glossary

2MP	*The Second Malaysia Plan, 1971–1975*
3MP	*The Third Malaysia Plan, 1976–1980*
4MP	*The Fourth Malaysia Plan, 1981–1985*
5MP	*The Fifth Malaysia Plan, 1986–1990*
6MP	*The Sixth Malaysia Plan, 1991–1995*
7MP	*The Seventh Malaysia Plan, 1996–2000*
8MP	*The Eighth Malaysia Plan, 2001–2005*
9MP	*The Ninth Malaysia Plan, 2006–2010*
10MP	*The Tenth Malaysia Plan, 2011–2015*
ASEAN	Association of Southeast Asian Nations
BN	Barisan Nasional (National Front)
CPI	consumer price index
DAP	Democratic Action Party
EO	export-oriented
EPF	Employees Provident Fund
EPR	effective protection rate
EPU	Economic Planning Unit, Prime Minister's Department
FDI	foreign direct investment
FELDA	Federal Land Development Authority
FTKL	Federal Territory of Kuala Lumpur
FTL	Federal Territory of Labuan (Island)
FTP	Federal Territory of Putrajaya
GDP	gross domestic product
GNP	gross national product
HICOM	Heavy Industries Corporation of Malaysia
ICA	Industrial Coordination Act, 1975
ICOR	incremental capital-output ratio
ILO	International Labour Organization
IMP	The First Industrial Master Plan, 1986–1995
IMP2	The Second Industrial Master Plan, 1996–2005

IPO	initial public offer
IS	import-substituting
ISI	import-substituting industrialization
IWK	Indah Water Konsortium
KR1M	Kedai Raykat 1Malaysia
LDS	less developed state
LNG	liquefied natural gas
LTCM	Long Term Capital Management
MARA	Majlis Amanah Rakyat
MAS	Malaysia Airlines System
MASA	Malaysian Shipowners' Association
MB	Mentri Besar (Chief Minister)
MCA	Malaysian Chinese Association
MDS	more developed state
METR	marginal effective tax rate
MIC	Malaysian Indian Congress
MIDA	Malaysian Industrial Development Authority
MISC	Malaysian International Shipping Corporation
MLO	Malaysian Labour Organization
MOU	memorandum of understanding
MP	Member of Parliament
MPEN	Majlis Perundingan Ekonomi Nasional (NECC)
MTR4MP	*The Mid-Term Review of the Fourth Malaysia Plan, 1981–1985*
MTR7MP	*The Mid-Term Review of the Seventh Malaysia Plan, 1996–2000*
MTR8MP	*The Mid-Term Review of the Eighth Malaysia Plan, 2001–2005*
MTR9MP	*The Mid-Term Review of the Ninth Malaysia Plan, 2006–2010*
MTUC	Malaysian Trades Union Congress
N. Sembilan	Negri Sembilan
NECC	National Economic Consultative Council (MPEN)
NAP	National Agricultural Policy
NEP	New Economic Policy
NFC	National Finance Council
NHI	National Health Institute

NHMS1	The First National Health and Morbidity Survey
NHMS2	The Second National Health and Morbidity Survey
NIC	newly industrializing country
NIE	newly industrializing economy
NIRR	net internal rate of return
NFPE	non-financial public enterprise
OECD	Organization for Economic Co-operation and Development
OPEC	Organization of Petroleum Exporting Countries
OPP1	*First Outline Perspective Plan, 1971–1990*
OPP2	*Second Outline Perspective Plan, 1991–2000*
OPP3	*Third Outline Perspective Plan, 2001–2010*
P. Malaysia	Peninsular Malaysia
P. Pinang	Pulau Pinang (Penang)
PAP	People's Action Party
PAS	Parti Islam
PBS	Parti Bersatu Sabah
PDA	Petroleum Development Act, 1974
Pernas	Perbadanan Nasional Berhad
PETRONAS	Petroliam Nasional Berhad
PKR	Parti Keadilan Rakyat
PM	Prime Minister (Perdana Menteri)
PMP	Privatization Master Plan
QCC	quality control circle
R&D	research and development
RISDA	Rubber Industry Smallholders Development Authority
RM	ringgit Malaysia (Malaysian ringgit)
SEDC	state economic development corporation
SOCSO	Social Security Organization
SOE	state-owned enterprise
SST	sales and service tax
SUPP	Sarawak United People's Party
UMNO	United Malays National Organisation
UNIDO	United Nations Industrial Development Organization
US	United States
WB	World Bank
WTO	World Trade Organization

Preface

Peninsular Malaysia, then known as the Federation of Malaya, gained independence from Britain in 1957. An expanded federation of Malaysia was formed in September 1963 by federating the Federation of Malaya with the former Straits Settlements island colony of Singapore to the south of Malaya, Sabah (previously run by the British North Borneo Company, set up by royal charter) and the former Brooke family fiefdom of Sarawak. After the Japanese Occupation of these British controlled territories in Southeast Asia, new political arrangements were introduced to cope with the growing anti-colonial sentiments and mobilization in British Malaya (including Singapore), North Borneo, Sarawak and Brunei. Although the term Malaysia had been used to refer to different political spaces in the region for some time, the creation of the new federation only began in earnest from 1961 as the British sought to preserve their hegemony in the disparate British controlled territories in Southeast Asia in the face of internal dissent encouraged by regional rivalries supported, in turn, by external political competition (Poulgrain 1998).

The new nation of Malaysia was created in the face of opposition from two of its powerful neighbours, Indonesia and the Philippines. The sultanate of Brunei opted out of joining the new federation at the last minute. Less than two years later, in August 1965, Singapore seceded from Malaysia to become the Republic of Singapore, leaving thirteen states in Malaysia, with special terms and conditions for the Borneo states' integration into the expanded nation. Sabah and Sarawak on the island of Borneo were referred to as East Malaysia for more than half a decade until the secession of East Pakistan, comprising the former East Bengal, from Pakistan to form Bangladesh.

Half a century later, it is generally agreed that Malaysia has done well compared to most other developing countries despite its rocky start. Yet, there remains a great deal of disaffection. In May 2013, the ruling

Barisan Nasional, dominated by the United Malays National Organization (UMNO), retained control of three fifths of parliamentary seats and government despite losing the popular vote for the first time ever. Historically gerrymandered electoral constituencies, a virtual monopoly of the broadcast and print media, abuse of fiscal, police and other government resources and often blatant political patronage and corruption over decades have been effectively deployed to retain political power.

In anticipation of the golden anniversary of the formation of a nation not expected to succeed, it seems worthwhile to review several dimensions of Malaysian economic development to understand where economic growth has come from and some of the major determinants of economic distribution. Much public economic discourse about Malaysia has tended to focus on ethnic stereotypes and related distributional conflicts and presumed consequences for economic growth. While not ignoring such issues, this volume emphasizes some other distribution issues as well.

To set the stage for the rest of the book, Part One reviews Malaysian economic growth and structural change over the last half century. It emphasizes the role of government, particularly policy, planning and public finance involving the federal or central government. Malaysia's generally impressive economic development has been largely due to appropriate government interventions and reforms, which have not crowded out, but have instead induced private investments. But a successful role for government depends crucially on its responsiveness to new circumstances and challenges. Hence, this account identifies and distinguishes at least five regimes with different policy priorities in post-colonial Malaysian economic development. Of course, economic performance does not simply follow from economic policies and is profoundly influenced by other factors as well, including economic conditions, both nationally as well as internationally. Nevertheless, this interpretation is very different from the laissez faire claim that market forces alone have been responsible for the country's economic performance despite the role of government.

Part Two surveys the evidence on economic distribution in Malaysia. Malaysian social, economic and political discourse has focused on inter-ethnic disparities. As the major source of household income is from employment, the discussion reviews labour force participation and unemployment rates, education level, wage rates as well as industry, employment and occupational status. These are reviewed in terms of ethnicity (or race, the preferred term in Malaysia), gender and state or region in so far as information is available. Besides reviewing New Economic Policy (NEP) poverty reduction and wealth redistribution efforts, it also reviews other dimensions of income distribution trends.

In this context, the distributional consequences of federal government finance, including both taxation and spending, are considered in Part Three. In particular, it considers social expenditure, such as health and education spending, as well as the changing incidence and distributional impacts of various taxes. Most Malaysian government revenue is from taxation, although the revenue from state-owned enterprises — especially PETRONAS, the relatively well-run national petroleum corporation — has been very significant.

In the Malaysian federation, the central government receives at least three quarters of all government revenue and accounts for over four-fifths of all government spending. State government revenues vary significantly, largely reflecting their varied revenue streams. Consequently, state governments have to rely on federal government grants to supplement their own limited revenue sources. Thus, the federal government is able to exert considerable control over state governments.

Part Four of this book considers some consequences of expansion of the common market following the formation of Malaysia. It reviews trade between Peninsular Malaysia on the one hand and Sabah as well as Sarawak on the other. The new context has shaped the uneven nature of industrialization and development, shaping regional disparities in the new federation. The respective powers of the federal and state governments, including their respective fiscal capacities, as well as consequent federal-state financial relations are also considered. Some spatial consequences of various policies and arrangements are considered.

Part 1

Development Stages

This Part reviews Malaysia's economic growth and structural change over the last five decades since Malaya (later Peninsular Malaysia) gained independence in 1957 and Malaysia was formed six years later in 1963 with the inclusion of the Borneo states of Sabah and Sarawak. Specific emphasis is given to the economic role of government, particularly in terms of public finance and spending by the federal or central government. This should make clear that Malaysia's generally impressive post-colonial economic development has been largely due to appropriate government interventions and reforms, rather than simple reliance on market forces, as often suggested in much of the literature on the country. At least five regimes with different priorities can be distinguished in Malaysian economic development from 1957 to the end of the Mahathir era in late 2003.

Before the Japanese Occupation during the Second World War, there was no pretence of colonial government planning. In fact, before the colonial creation of the Malayan Union in 1946, there was no unified government of the peninsula. The Straits Settlements of Penang, Melaka and Singapore were outright colonies while British influence was more pronounced despite indirect rule in the Federated Malay States of Perak, Selangor, Negri Sembilan and Pahang as well as Johor compared to the other northern Unfederated Malay States of Kedah, Perlis, Kelantan and Terengganu. This changed during the Emergency authority over plan formulation and implementation rested with senior British officials mainly concerned with imperial interests and committed to protecting the predominantly British plantation and mining interests in Malaya.

The colonial bias for these interests was reflected in public development expenditure that prioritized economic infrastructure to service the primary commodity export economy. As Britain's most profitable colony, Malaya provided much of the export earnings that financed British post war reconstruction. Legal developments during this era played an important role in shaping and developing British Malaya. During the early and mid-1950s, the colonial government initiated reforms, including rural development and affirmative action efforts. (For an alternative view suggesting that colonial and post-colonial governments were mainly concerned with ensuring social and political stability, rather than advancing British corporate interests, see Drabble, 2000).

Independence in 1957 was followed by a dozen years of post-colonial economic diversification with limited government intervention. Generally laissez faire policies were pursued, with some import-substituting industrialization, agricultural diversification, rural development and ethnic affirmative action efforts. A period of growing state intervention followed the post-election race riots of May 1969. The New Economic Policy (NEP) legitimized increasing government intervention and public sector expansion for inter-ethnic redistribution and rural development to reduce poverty. Export-oriented (EO) industrialization also generated considerable employment, especially for women, while increased petroleum revenues financed rapidly growing state spending.

Malaysian economic performance has been very susceptible to changes in global economic conditions as indicated in Figure 1.1. But Malaysian economic vulnerability has changed over time. Earlier, vulnerability to commodity prices was very important, but later, changing demand for manufactured outputs has become more significant. Especially since the 1990s, the Malaysian economy has become more vulnerable to movements on the capital account, as during the 1997–1998 and 2008–2009 crises, when easily reversible portfolio capital inflows were quickly reversed with destabilizing consequences, not only for the stock market, but also for the real economy (Figure 1.1).

Expansionary public expenditure from the 1970s continued after Mahathir became Prime Minister in mid-1981. Spending was cut from

Figure 1.1 Malaysia: Economic Growth, 1970–2012 (% per annum)

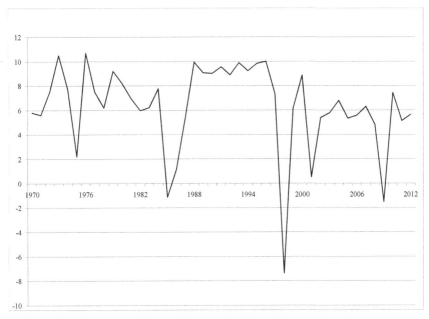

Sources: Calculated with data from Bank Negara Malaysia, *Monthly Bulletin of Statistics*, various issues.

mid-1982, but government-sponsored heavy industries grew as other foreign investments declined. Thus, the Mahathir regime had a different rationale for state intervention, shifting from interethnic redistribution to heavy industrialization. From the mid-1980s, the economic slowdown and massive foreign debt build-up from the early 1980s led to massive ringgit depreciation and economic liberalization. Liberalization was accompanied by privatization and greater government support for the private sector, including new investment incentives and regressive tax reforms. The new measures favouring private investment resulted in a decade of rapid growth until the 1997–1998 financial crisis led to renewed state intervention for crisis management and economic recovery, including currency controls and bail out facilities for the banking sector and favoured corporate interests.

In the following sections, we review the major periods of Malaysian economic development policymaking since independence in 1957 and also consider economic performance indicators over the last half century.

Needless to say, economic performance does not simply follow from economic policies and is influenced by other factors as well, including economic conditions, both nationally as well as internationally. We conclude with lessons from the Malaysian experience with economic development policies.

The eleven tables try to cover the entire period under consideration, but although Malaysia was formed in 1963 and took its current territorial boundaries in August 1965, data collection has lagged behind and generally begins from around 1970. The first two tables provide growth, inflation and other economic indicators. Table 1.3 tracks savings, investment and foreign direct investment trends which have, in turn, shaped sectoral growth trends in the following two tables. Tables 1.6 and 1.7 summarize the composition of exports and imports over this period, reflecting the changing openness of the Malaysian economy over time. The next three tables looks at sectoral employment growth while the last two tables reflect wage and household income trends.

The Alliance Era (1957–1969)

In preparing for political independence, the British had ensured that the leftist anti-colonial forces who threatened their economic interests were curbed, while ethnic elites committed to protecting their interests were cultivated to eventually inherit state office in 1957. With the attainment of independence in August 1957, the Alliance, a coalition of the political elites from the three major ethnic groups, formally took over political authority in Malaya. Not unlike other newly independent countries, the post-colonial government embarked upon a programme of economic development emphasizing economic diversification and industrialization. Otherwise, the basically laissez faire development path for newly independent Malaya was thus assured. The post-colonial government continued to promote private enterprise and encourage foreign investments inflows, while the economic interests of the ex-colonial power were protected.

The Alliance government's economic development strategy reflected the class interests represented by the major parties in the ruling coalition and the political compromise among their leaders and with the Colonial power. Consistent with this compromise, the state pursued basically laissez

Table 1.1 Malaysia: Growth and Inflation Indicators, 1971–2012

	1971–80	1981–90	1991–97	1998–2005	2006	2007	2008	2009	2010	2011	2012
GDP growth, % p. a.	7.5	6.0	9.2	5.3	5.8	6.5	4.8	-1.5	7.2	5.1	4.8
CPI inflation, % p. a.	5.9	3.8	3.6	1.9	3.6	2.0	5.4	0.6	1.7	3.2	1.9

Sources: Ministry of Finance, Malaysia, *Economic Report*, various issues.

Table 1.2 Malaysia: Economic Indicators, 1970–2012

	1970	1980	1990	1995	2005	2006	2007	2008	2009	2010	2011	2012[a]
Per capita GNP (RM)	1,071	3,734	6,513	10,710	19,951	21,826	24,073	27,094	24,879	26,969	29,783	30,856
Per capita GNP (USD)	348	1,715	2,414	4,119	5,278	6,180	7,281	7,822	7,265	8,746	9,375	10,089
Unemployment rate	2.4	5.6	6.0	2.8	3.5	3.3	3.2	3.2	3.7	3.3	3.1	3.2
CPI inflation (%)	1.9	6.7	3.1	3.4	3.0	3.6	2.0	5.4	0.6	1.7	3.2	1.9
RM/USD	3.078	2.218	2.698	2.538	3.78[b]	3.53[b]	3.31	3.46	3.42	3.08	3.18	3.06

Notes: [a] Estimates.
  [b] The ringgit was pegged at US$1 = RM3.80 from September 1998 – May 2006.
Sources: Ministry of Finance, Malaysia, *Economic Report*, various issues.

Table 1.3 Malaysia: Savings, Investment and Foreign Direct Investment, 1970–2012 (% of GNP)

	1970	1975	1980	1985	1990	1995	2000	2005	2010	2011	2012
Savings	21.6	19.2	27.6	27.2	30.5	35.6	39.1	38.5	35.4	35.7	33.1
Investment, of which:	30.1	19.4	28.5	32.1	32.7	45.8	27.5	23.3	28.3	29.6	34.9
Private investment	12.5	16.2	16.5	17.1	20.7	32.7	14.6	12.7	15.5	16.9	20.2
Public investment	17.7	3.3	12.0	15.1	12.0	13.0	12.9	10.6	12.8	12.7	14.7
Savings-investment gap	-8.5	-0.2	-0.9	-4.9	-2.2	-10.2	11.6	15.2	7.1	6.1	-1.8
Foreign direct investment	2.4	3.9	4.0	2.4	5.5	4.3	2.0	0.7	-1.8	-1.1	-2.4
Current account balance	0.2	-4.9	-1.2	-2.1	-2.2	-8.9	9.8	15.1	11.3	11.9	6.3
Overall balance of payments	0.6	0.8	1.9	4.5	4.7	-1.8	-2.6	2.6	-0.3	11.0	0.4

Sources: Calculated with data from various Malaysia plan documents; Bank Negara Malaysia, *Monthly Statistical Bulletin*, May 2012; Ministry of Finance, Malaysia, *Economic Report 2012/2013*.

Table 1.4 Malaysia: Growth by Sector, 1965–2012 (% per annum)

	1965–70[a]	1971–75	1976–80	1981–85	1986–90	1991–95	1996–2000	2001–05	2006–10	2011	2012
Agriculture, forestry & fishing	6.3	4.8	3.9	3.4	4.6	2.0	-0.3	3.0	2.7	5.8	1.0
Mining & quarrying	1.1	0.4	8.9	6.0	5.2	2.9	0.7	2.6	-1.5	-5.5	1.4
Manufacturing	9.9	11.6	13.5	4.6	13.7	13.3	7.0	4.1	2.6	4.7	4.8
Construction	4.1	6.6	12.6	8.1	0.4	13.3	7.3	0.5	4.4	4.7	18.1
Electricity, gas & utility	8.1	9.8	10.2	9.1	9.8	13.1	5.2	5.6	4.1	3.4	4.3
Transport, storage & communications	3.0	13.0	9.6	8.4	8.6	9.9	6.0	6.6	6.3	6.5	7.1
Wholesale & retail trade, hotels & restaurants	3.2	6.3	8.2	7.0	4.7	10.6	3.2	4.3	7.8	7.5	4.9
Finance, insurance, real estate & business services	5.4	7.2	8.0	7.2	8.4	10.7	6.7	8.1	8.3	6.3	7.6
Government services	5.2	10.1	9.0	9.8	4.0	6.7	4.6	6.7	6.7	12.3	9.5
Other services	4.7	9.3	6.6	5.1	4.9	7.7	3.2	4.8	1.0	4.8	3.8
GDP at purchasers' prices	5.5	7.1	8.6	5.8	6.7	8.7	4.0	4.5	3.8	5.1	5.6

Notes: GDP in 1965 prices for 1965–70; GDP in 1970 prices for 1971–80, in 1987 prices for 1981–95 and current prices for 1996–2000.

[a] GDP at factor cost for Peninsular Malaysia only.

Sources: 2MP, Table 2-5; 4MP, Table 2-1; 5MP, Table 2-1; 6MP, Table 1-2; 7MP, Table 2-5; 9MP, Table 2-2; Bank Negara Malaysia, *Monthly Statistical Bulletin*, various issues.

Table 1.5 Malaysia: Gross Domestic Product by Sector, 1970–2012 (%)

Industry	1970	1980	1990	2000	2010	2011	2012
Agriculture & forestry	29.0	22.9	18.7	8.6	10.4	11.8	10.1
Mining & quarrying	13.7	10.1	9.8	10.6	10.9	10.4	10.4
Manufacturing	13.9	19.6	26.9	30.9	24.5	24.3	24.2
Construction	3.8	4.6	3.6	3.9	3.4	3.4	3.9
Services	36.2	40.1	41.9	49.3	49.9	49.1	50.4
Less bank charges, add import duties	3.4	2.7	-1.4	-3.3	1.0	1.0	1.1
Total	100.0	100.0	100.0	100.0	100.0	100.0	100.0

Note: GDP for 1970–1990 in 1978 prices, for 2000–2011 in 2000 prices.
Sources: 5MP, Table 3–5; OPP2, Tables 2–3 and 3–2; OPP3, Table 2–5; 8MP Table 2-6 and 4-2; Bank Negara Malaysia, *Monthly Statistical Bulletin*, December 2011; Ministry of Finance, Malaysia, *Economic Report, 2011/2012*.

Table 1.6 Malaysia: Structure of Exports, 1970–2012 (%)

	1970	1975	1980	1985	1990	1995	2000	2005	2010	2011	2012
Agriculture & minerals	73.1	67.7	72.4	58.1	36.1	16.7	11.8	15.5	20.5	23.9	22.2
Manufactures	21.7	21.9	22.4	32.8	58.8	79.6	80.9	80.7	76.2	72.2	74.0
Others	5.2	10.4	5.2	9.1	5.1	3.7	7.3	3.8	3.3	3.9	3.8
Total	100.0	100.0	100.0	100.0	100.0	100.0	100.0	100.0	100.0	100.0	100.0

Sources: 4MP, Table 2–5; Rasiah, Osman and Alavi (2000); Bank Negara Malaysia, *Annual Report*, various issues.

Table 1.7 Malaysia: Structure of Imports, 1980–2012 (%)

	1980	1985	1990	1995	2000	2005	2010	2011	2012
Capital/investment goods	30.0	31.2	37.5	20.1	14.2	13.6	13.9	14.0	15.9
Intermediate goods	49.8	46.8	45.5	65.0	74.6	71.5	69.1	67.2	61.4
Consumption goods	18.4	21.0	16.4	6.2	5.5	5.6	6.5	7.2	7.5
Dual use	–	–	–	5.0	2.1	2.6	3.0	3.1	3.9
Others, transactions <RM5000	–	–	–	–	1.5	1.6	0.6	0.6	0.5
Import for re-export	1.7	1.0	0.7	3.7	2.1	5	6.7	7.9	10.8
Total	100	100	100	100	100	100	100	100	100

Sources: 5MP, Table 2-5; 6MP, Table 1-3; 7MP, Table 2-3; 8MP, Table 4-2; 9MP, Table 2-10; Bank Negara Malaysia, *Monthly Statistical Bulletin*, various issues.

Table 1.8 Malaysia: Employment Creation, 1970–2012 (% increase)

	1970–75	1976–80	1980–85	1985–90	1990–95	1996–2000	2001–05	2006	2007	2008	2009	2010	2011	2012[a]
Agriculture & forestry	7.4	0.2	2.2	4.4	-17.8	-5.7	-1.2	-0.6	-0.2	0.1	0.0	-0.1	-0.2	-0.1
Mining & quarrying	1.4	-9.5	-24.5	-11.9	10.0	1.7	2.4	-0.2	0.9	-0.2	-3.7	5.4	3.6	3.0
Manufacturing	107.0	21.2	9.7	50.8	53.9	26.2	22.1	3.0	2.2	1.3	0.6	0.5	0.4	0.5
Construction	126.4	31.2	40.2	-0.6	55.5	5.3	1.0	-0.6	0.3	0.1	3.0	2.3	2.7	2.2
Services	42.9	16.1	-19.9	-16.2	-15.6	-17.5	-19.1	3.3	3.0	2.1	0.6	2.7	2.5	2.0
Total	31.0	10.1	13.5	17.7	18.4	15.9	17.5	2.4	2.1	1.6	0.0	-0.1	-0.2	-0.1

Note: [a] Estimates.

Sources: Calculated with data from 5MP, Table 3-5; 6MP, Table 1-11; 7MP, Table 4-2; 8MP, Table 2-4; 9MP, Table 11-2; Ministry of Finance, Malaysia, *Economic Report*, various issues.

Table 1.9 Malaysia: Employment Increase by Sector, 1970–2012 (%)

Sector	1970	1980	1990	2000	2010	2011	2012[a]
Agriculture & forestry	53.5	39.7	26.0	20.0	-0.2	-0.5	-0.7
Mining & quarrying	2.6	1.7	0.5	0.5	0.0	-0.4	0.0
Manufacturing	8.7	15.7	19.9	23.9	54.1	41.3	42.0
Construction	2.7	5.6	6.3	7.4	1.2	1.1	1.6
Services	32.5	37.4	47.3	48.2	44.7	58.0	56.4
Total	100.0	100.0	100.0	100.0	100.0	100.0	100.0

Note: [a] Estimates.

Sources: 5MP, Table 3-5; OPP2, Tables 2-3 and 3-2; OPP3, Table 2-5; 8MP Tables 2-6 and 4-2; Bank Negara Malaysia, *Monthly Statistical Bulletin*, December 2011; Ministry of Finance, Malaysia, *Economic Report*, various issues.

Table 1.10 Malaysia: Distribution of Services Employment, 1965–2012 (%)

	P. Malaysia			Malaysia					
	1965	1970	1976	1985	1995	2005	2010	2011	2012[a]
Transport, storage & communications	11.6	10.5	10.9	9.3	9.7	9.6	10.3	10.7	10.8
Finance, insurance, real estate & business services	}	}	}	8.3	9.8	12.5	14.3	13.2	13.0
Wholesale & retail trade, restaurants & hotels	86.6	87.7	85.9	37.9	37.1	40.6	39.1	19.6	19.1
Other services				43.2	42.0	36.2	34.6	}	}
Utilities	1.8	1.8	3.2	1.2	1.3	1.0	1.7		
Total	100	100	100	100	100	100	100	100	100

Note: [a] Estimates.

Sources: *Labour Force Survey*, various issues; Ministry of Finance, Malaysia, *Economic Report*, various issues.

Table 1.11 Malaysia: Change in Real Wages, 1971–2012 (average % per annum)

Period	Growth rate
1971–79	1.58
1979–85	5.94
1985–90	1.17
1995	20.9
1996	4.4
1997	5.9
1998	-2.7
1999	-1.7
2000	12.9
2001	3.4
2002	11.0
2003	4.0
2004	4.1
2005	-9.1
2006	-11.1
2007	3.0
2008	-6.9
2009	13.3
2010	5.2
2011	-1.4
2012[a]	5.5

Note: [a] Estimates.
Sources: Rasiah (2002), Table 14; Appendix Table 4; Ministry of Finance, Malaysia, *Economic Report*, various issues.

Table 1.12 Malaysia: Gross Monthly Household Incomes, 1970–2009 (RM)

Year	Income
1970[a]	264
1974[a]	362
1976	505
1979	678
1984	1,098
1987	1,083
1989[b]	1,169
1992	1,563
1995	2,020
1997	2,606
1999	2,472
2002	3,011
2004	3,249
2007	3,686
2009	4,025

Notes: [a] Peninsular Malaysia only.
[b] Data from 1989 is for Malaysian citizens only.
Source: Economic Planning Unit (http://www.epu.gov.my/c/document_library/get_file?uuid=e2b128f0-c6fb-4980-8a17-3f708fc3d7a8&groupId=34492)

faire policies with minimal state interference and small budget deficits except in ensuring attractive conditions for new investments. The post-colonial government was committed to defending British business interests in Malaya, which also enabled the predominantly Chinese local businesses to consolidate and strengthen their position.

Development policy during this phase was therefore influenced by these compromises. The essentially laissez faire approach precluded direct government participation in profitable activities, such as commerce and industry, which were left exclusively to private business interests. Hence, a relatively low proportion of public development expenditure was allocated to commerce and industry. Within this overall strategy, the government made some highly publicized, but nonetheless feeble attempts to promote the interests of the nascent Malay business community, while also undertaking rural development programmes to secure predominantly Malay rural electoral support.

The increased allocations for social services (see Parts 2 and 3), particularly education, partly reflected the increased commitment to utilize educational expenditure to create a Malay middle class besides meeting the human resource requirements of the rapidly growing and modernizing Malaysian economy. The government increasingly regarded educational expenditure as an investment that would yield returns in the form of increased output from a more productive labour force, rather than merely as public consumption. Government agricultural development policies were essentially conservative. Rural development efforts were constrained by the government's reluctance to act against politically influential landed, commercial and financial interests. The main thrust of rural development efforts involved new land development by the Federal Land Development Authority (FELDA), other measures to increase agricultural productivity and rural incomes, as well as greater provision of rural facilities such as roads, schools, clinics, irrigation, etc.

During the early years after independence, the major physical development initiatives in the country were reflected in the annual budgets and the five-year Malaysia Plans. Almost all the infrastructure developments undertaken before the late 1980s were financed by the government, averaging about a third of overall public expenditure. Private sector involvement in infrastructure was largely as a service provider (e.g.

construction activities) and did not involve much financing or revenue collection from such developments.

Policy in the 1960s generally emphasized growth, assuming that its benefits would trickle down. Malaysia achieved impressive growth, with considerable infrastructure development, although economic diversification in both agriculture and industry was limited. The government pursued economic diversification efforts to reduce Malaya's over-reliance on tin and rubber on two main fronts. Firstly, plantations were encouraged to grow other crops, particularly oil palm, and an increasing number of FELDA-sponsored land development schemes were also planted with oil palm. Secondly, the state encouraged manufacturing by offering incentives, and providing infrastructure and other supportive economic measures, accelerating the growth of industry.

Over the 1960s, policy was increasingly made by Alliance ministers, senior Malayan civil servants and American advisers in the increasingly complex planning process, involving more bureaucratic organs. Policy in the 1960s also saw two other major changes from the 1950s. Firstly, the state was increasingly willing to incur budget deficits, especially for development expenditure. This involved increased borrowing from both domestic and foreign sources to finance rising public sector development expenditure. Secondly, more sophisticated planning techniques were adopted, e.g. the Harrod-Domar growth model was used to estimate the investment rate required to attain certain income and employment growth targets.

The government promoted moderate import-substituting industrialization, passing the Pioneer Industries Ordinance and creating institutions to facilitate this policy emphasis. However, due to the limited size of the domestic market, limited domestic linkages, growing unemployment and other problems, the government gradually shifted to export-oriented (EO) industrialization from the late 1960s. The Federal Industrial Development Authority (now the Malaysian Industrial Development Authority, or MIDA) was established to encourage industrial investment. The Industrial Incentives Act of 1968 was enacted, offering incentives to attract more labour-intensive EO industries.

Helped by favourable commodity prices and some early success in import-substituting industrialization, the economy sustained high growth with low inflation in the 1960s. Official statistics for 1957 and 1970

— though strictly non-comparable for methodological reasons — suggest a worsening income distribution over the 1960s, including a growing gap between town and country. Inequality within the Malay community increased most among all major ethnic groups — from least intra-ethnic inequality in 1957 to greatest inequality in 1970 (see Part 2).

However, this growing inequality did not only result in growing inter-class tensions. It was primarily perceived in racial terms, not least because of widespread political mobilization along ethnic lines. Hence, Malay resentment to domination by capital was primarily expressed against ethnic Chinese, who comprised the bulk of businessmen. Non-Malay frustrations were directed against the Malay-dominated state, widely identified with the United Malay National Organization (UMNO), the dominant partner in the ruling coalition. This led to racially-inspired opposition to the ruling coalition of ethnic parties in the Alliance in the 1960s, culminating in the 'race riots' of May 1969.

The Alliance in the 1960s had been marked by import-substituting industrialization and increased rural development efforts. Import-substituting industrialization through tariff protection generated relatively little employment and petered out by the mid-1960s, while rural development efforts that emphasized productivity avoided redistribution in favour of the poorly capitalized, land-hungry peasantry.

At the May 1969 general elections, the ruling coalition's grip on power was significantly challenged by non-Malay as well as Malay based opposition parties which secured over half the popular vote and deprived the ruling coalition of its target two-thirds majority. The poor electoral performance of the ruling coalition was probably the result of ethnic political mobilization, continued economic deprivation, growing unemployment, and persistent inter-ethnic disparities despite creditable economic growth (see Part 2). The general election results and 'race riots' of May 1969 thus reflected some ethnic dimensions of the new post-colonial socio-economic order. Meanwhile, the emerging Malay middle class, who had nominal political control, feared the gradual decline of British economic hegemony would lead to Chinese ascendance. This 'political-bureaucratic' faction, which had become more assertive from the mid-1960s, succeeded in establishing greater dominance after May 1969. The ethnic riots were probably initiated by the youth wing of the ruling party, led by a State Chief Minister whose own position was threatened by the election results. The riots probably facilitated the transition to a new regime based on a different 'political compact', including the redistributive NEP. The incumbent Prime Minister's position was undermined within the ruling party by those who supported his deputy in a 'palace coup', paving the way for a new regime.

The First Decade of the New Economic Policy (1970–1980)

The New Economic Policy (NEP) was announced in 1970 by Razak Hussein, then Deputy Prime Minister and Director of the National Operations Council set up during the state of Emergency after the events of May 1969. It sought to create the socio-economic conditions for 'national unity' through massive economic redistribution programmes to achieve its twin prongs of 'poverty eradication' and 'restructuring of society'. The NEP's first Outline Perspective Plan for 1971–1990 (OPP1) envisaged the incidence of poverty declining from 49 per cent in Peninsular Malaysia in 1970 to 16.7 per cent in 1990.

'Restructuring society' efforts sought to reduce inter-ethnic economic disparities, to 'eliminate the identification of race with economic function'. OPP1 envisaged raising the Bumiputera share of corporate equity from 2.4 per cent in 1970 to 30 per cent in 1990, ostensibly through growth rather than redistribution of existing wealth. Through ethnically differentiated financing of, and controlled access to tertiary level education, the NEP would reduce inter-ethnic disparities in the professions and other lucrative occupations.

Affirmative action programmes (for indigenes, especially Malays) from the early 1950s have increased after independence and especially from the mid-1960s. They included preferential access to educational opportunities, business licences, as well as employment and promotion, especially in the public sector with the 'Malayanization' of the civil service after independence. Greater Malay political hegemony after the events of May 1969 significantly enhanced such measures. Sanctioned by the NEP, government intervention in the economy grew. The number of state-owned enterprises (SOEs) increased during the 1970s, ostensibly for the primary purpose of NEP-type redistribution.

At the time of independence and even in the late sixties, the private sector was largely confined to local Chinese capitalists and the generally more powerful foreign investors. While the Chinese were mainly in retail and wholesale trade, rubber estates, tin mining, domestic transport, small-scale manufacturing and some banking, foreign interests dominated the formal economy, such as the large plantations, trading agencies, tin dredge mines, bigger banks and financial institutions (e.g. insurance), and manufacturing. Malay business interests were generally encouraged by the government through Bumiputera trust agencies and the state economic development corporations (SEDCs), with a few well-connected individuals spread over many boards desiring them for their political connections (Tan, 1982).

To raise the total Bumiputera share of corporate equity to 30 per cent by 1990 from 2.4 per cent in 1970, the government, especially the Ministry of Trade and Industry, began to find new ways and means to increase equity held by Bumiputera trust agencies as well as individuals. Educational spending significantly increased to finance Bumiputera secondary and tertiary education, especially with the preferential allocation of scholarships to attend universities in Malaysia and abroad. Bumiputera have also been favoured for employment and promotion opportunities, not only in the government and SOEs, but also in the private sector, especially enterprises requiring government approval of some kind or other.

The role of the state expanded in the 1970s. It involved greater political and bureaucratic control over planning as well as greater state intervention and a considerably larger public sector, particularly to promote the growth of the Malay capitalist and middle classes. As ethnic Malay demands for increased efforts to economically advance the indigenous Bumiputera community mounted from the mid-1960s, new legislation and institutions were set up. These were often in the form of public enterprises, such as statutory bodies enacted by legal statute. Examples of these include the Urban Development Authority, Perbadanan Nasional Berhad (Pernas) and the state economic development corporations (SEDCs). The other increasingly widespread form of public enterprise was government-owned, private or public limited companies (Jomo [ed.], 1995).

Development policy in the 1970s thus saw growing replacement of laissez faire policies by greater state intervention in public resource allocation as well as public sector ownership and control of business enterprises. Although such policies began to adversely affect private investments and cause capital flight, especially by ethnic Chinese, this was more than offset by growing public investments as well as foreign direct investment (FDI) in export-oriented (EO) industries.

Export-oriented manufacturing in Malaysia in the 1970s was largely limited to relatively low-skill, labour-intensive aspects of production, e.g. electronic component assembly. Although more skilled and complex production processes and training have emerged, Malaysia lagged behind neighbouring Singapore. Such progress has been shaped by the interests, preferences and influence of transnational corporations as well as by host government policies. EO industrialization has significant, but nonetheless limited potential for sustained and integrated industrial development, especially because of the technological and market dependence involved. Nevertheless, Malaysia registered impressive performance indicators, largely attributable to favourable resource endowments and external conditions, and exaggerated by the high import content of non-resource based manufactured exports. However, the sources of export-led growth are not sustainable indefinitely. In fact, the very success of export-led growth in the past has probably discouraged more serious efforts to develop a more balanced and integrated national economy.

Malaysia has seen a dramatic structural transformation of its economy in terms of the rapid growth of manufacturing and services as agriculture continued to expand. This structural change in output has been very much reflected in employment although the relationship between investment, output and employment is complex and has also varied over time. Manufacturing and services contributed 75 per cent of total output of the economy in 2012, compared to about half of total output in 1970. The significant transformation of employment has included significantly increased shares for manufacturing in the last three decades of the 20th century, and more steadily for services, especially modern services (Khong with Jomo, 2010).

In the early 1970s, the Free Trade Zones Act created new customs-free areas with facilities for the development of export-processing zones. The promotion of more labour-intensive, EO industries seeking cheap labour from the late 1960s and early 1970s succeeded in reducing unemployment.

Initially, the reduction in unemployment was achieved at the expense of real wages, until lower unemployment pushed wages up once again from the mid-1970s (see Part 2). After the 'tightening' of labour laws in 1980, the industrial relations machinery and labour policies also changed, largely at the expense of employees and unions. These were followed by amendments introduced to tighten up the already restrictive labour laws, further limiting union rights as well as encouraging 'in-house' or company unions and increasing government control over employees, who comprised an increasing majority of the labour force (see Part 2). Such policies were considered necessary to attract more private investments for rapid growth and industrialization.

Although there were government attempts to portray itself as a neutral arbiter mediating between capital and labour in the 1960s and 1970s, the state generally favoured investment promotion, as reflected in the various amendments to the labour laws. During the state of Emergency after May 1969, labour legislation had been amended to limit trade union organization and activity and to allow women to work around the clock as desired by some of the new (mainly electronic) industries. Labour legislation had been initially enacted to replace the special regulations introduced during the States of Emergency against the communist-led insurgency (1948–1960), but later reflected changing labour policies.

In the mid-1970s, petroleum production off the East Coast of Peninsular Malaysia began, and the government quickly pushed through the 1974 Petroleum Development Act to ensure that the federal government — instead of the states — would capture the lion's share of oil revenues. Petroleum revenue has played a crucial role in the country's development since; they have been used to salvage SOEs, e.g. the then largest bank, Bank Bumiputra Malaysia, thrice (first in the mid-1980s, after the Bumiputra Malaysia Finance scandal in Hong Kong, and then after the mid-1980s' recession, and again, after the 1997–1998 regional financial crisis), and prestige projects such as the Daya Bumi project in the mid-1980s and the world's tallest building, the Kuala Lumpur City Centre twin-towers project in the mid-1990s (now known as the Petronas Towers), the new Kuala Lumpur International Airport, the Formula One racetrack and the new capital city, Putrajaya.

Faster economic growth — with labour-intensive export-oriented industrialization and public sector expansion in the 1970s — greatly lowered unemployment over the decade (see Part 2). Also, emigration of Malaysian labour to Singapore and other countries increased in the mid and late 1970s. Real wages rose, and pockets of labour shortages emerged, usually in activities offering low wages and poor working conditions as well as future prospects. In order to offset the pressure on wages and overcome labour shortages, the government adopted several measures, most notably by tacitly and explicitly approving labour immigration. Immigration were primarily from Indonesia, Southern Thailand (especially to the northern States of Peninsular Malaysia), Southern Philippines (mainly to Sabah) and later, Bangladesh. While the magnitude of this immigration over the last two and a half decades is difficult to measure, current estimates vary from 1.5 to 4 million compared to a national population of 28 million and a labour force of almost 13 million.

Mahathir's Three Regimes

In mid-1981, Mahathir Mohamad took over as Prime Minister of Malaysia and as president of UMNO. Mahathir's ascension to national leadership coincided with declining primary commodity prices and accelerated foreign borrowings despite much higher real interest rates from 1980. The increase in public expenditure in the early 1980s until mid-1982 was originally counter-cyclical in intent, to augment declining private domestic and foreign investment. Such counter-cyclical spending was cut back from mid-1982. However, public sector spending rose sharply for the financing of non-financial public enterprises (NFPEs), or off-budget agencies in the first half of the 1980s. External debt more than tripled between 1980 and 1985, largely in the form of government-guaranteed external debt for the NFPEs.

More than any other prime minister of Malaysia, Mahathir wanted to transform Malaysia into a newly industrializing country (NIC) under indigenous Bumiputera entrepreneurial leadership. Mahathir's development strategy was not merely imitative. As contradictory and incoherent as his various economic development policies seemed, they represented efforts, in circumstances not of his own choosing, to transform Malaysia into a NIC. While Mahathir's policies eventually seemed to favour various well-connected business interests, he has to be credited with the major development policy innovations from 1981 until his retirement in late 2003. These include the 'Look East' policy, his labour policy, the 'Malaysia Incorporated' policy, the privatization policy, 'Vision 2020', and the policy responses to the 1997–1998 crisis, among others. The next three sections of this Part review his key policy initiatives in the context of three distinguishable economic policy regimes characterizing the Mahathir administration, which lasted more than two decades from mid-1981.

Mahathir Regime 1: New Roles for the State (1981–1985)

After Mahathir took over as Prime Minister, he introduced a second round of import-substitution to promote various heavy industries, similar to the heavy and chemicals industrialization drive in South Korea under General Park Chung Hee in the 1970s. For a year, until the April 1982 general elections, he continued to increase public sector employment in the face of the global recession from the early 1980s, induced by the deflationary interventions of US Federal Reserve chairman Paul Volcker. As the world economic slowdown dragged on, and commodity prices continued to decline, continued economic growth became more dependent on public — rather than private — investment. Soon, it was no longer possible to fend off the inevitable, and the economy contracted in 1985–1986.

There had been a rapid increase in the domestic public debt from the early 1970s, followed by a rise in sovereign foreign borrowings from late in the decade. In the early 1980s, the growing current account deficit became more pressing because of declining commodity export prices and weak demand for manufactured exports (especially electronics), as private investments outside of the oil and gas sector dropped sharply (World Bank, 1983). Domestic private investments also declined, largely due to ethnic discriminatory policies against Chinese business interests.

During the 1980–1982 international recession, the government adopted counter-cyclical fiscal policies with increased public sector con-sumption, investment and employment. While the government may have underestimated the causes and gravity of the recession, and presumed it could spend its way out of it, the new Mahathir administration from mid-

1981 probably also hoped to secure a strong electoral mandate through such deficit spending. Soon after winning the April 1982 general elections, the government announced an austerity drive, cutting back public spending and reducing earlier job creation commitments.

Mahathir was personally involved in drafting the first (1984) National Agricultural Policy (NAP), which sought to promote more commercially viable smallholder agriculture. However, careful consideration of the NAP, revised in 1993 and 1998, is of limited value for understanding Malaysia's success in agriculture and agricultural processing. Increased output of commercial crops was largely achieved using low-waged foreign labour. Domestic rural-urban migration continued in response to spatial inequalities, with agricultural expansion lacking behind manufacturing growth. In the early and mid-1980s, official attention was given to the promotion of commercial peasant agriculture — involving larger farms ostensibly using more profitable, productivity-raising and cost-saving modern management methods — for export markets. Land and regional development authorities continued to clear forested areas for plantation agriculture, increasingly in Sabah and Sarawak. Meanwhile, agricultural diversification continued, with cocoa promising to be the new hope in Sabah in the 1980s. Oil palm's success from the 1970s continued in most other parts of the country.

Malaysia's mild economic recession during the mid-1980s was due to a combination of factors: global recession, lower primary commodity prices, reduced demand for manufactured exports, reduced foreign private investment inflows, declining domestic private investments, deflationary fiscal and monetary policies (except for certain spending priorities such as heavy industries), concentration of public investments in import-substituting heavy industries characterized by low capital productivity, tighter international liquidity and higher real interest rates. Immediately, the government responded to the recession with various measures, such as deregulation as well as incentives to further encourage private investment.

Spending, especially by the government, was constrained by the sharp drop in oil prices in early 1986 to under US$10 per barrel. The poor price outlook for petroleum forced a drastic downward revision of growth and public sector investment targets (later revised upwards with higher petroleum and rubber prices in 1987 and increased logging). The major primary commodity price collapses — involving palm oil, tin and petroleum — and the electronics business cycle's low point occurred in 1985. It was only after petroleum price fell to its lowest in January 1986, that external demand for Malaysian exports — especially commodity prices — began to recover.

'Look East' Policy

In mid-1981, Mahathir announced his 'Look East' policy. Initially, this policy was widely believed to refer to changing foreign economic orientation and reference points in a wide variety of economic development matters. 'Looking East' seemed to refer not only to efforts to emulate specific aspects of Japanese and South Korean success in terms of economic development such as state intervention to develop heavy industries. The policy rubric also involved state encouragement of Japanese-style *sogoshosha* trading agencies, efforts to get the government bureaucracy to better serve private sector interests ('Malaysia Incorporated'), and even privatization. For a time, 'Looking East' was also believed to mean favouring Japanese and South Korean investors and companies bidding for Malaysian government tenders; e.g. an estimated six billion ringgit worth of construction projects were given to such companies in the early 1980s (Jomo [ed.], 1994).

Mahathir's exhortation to 'Look East' explicitly referred to Japan and South Korea (Jomo, 2004). Of the four East Asian NICs, Hong Kong and Singapore were disqualified because of the distinctly different features of their economies. Hence, the only real East Asian choices as models for emulation were Taiwan and South Korea. The choice of Taiwan was, of course, complicated by diplomatic considerations, besides the ethnic factor. Nevertheless, by early 1988, Mahathir and some of his ministers also began explicitly touting Taiwan for emulation. In the early 1990s, Malaysia successfully attracted considerable Taiwanese investments when the island's authorities' official 'southward' policy encouraged investing in Southeast Asia, instead of China.

The Singaporean option of espousing Confucian values — supposedly common to Japanese and Chinese cultures — was obviously not open to Mahathir, given Malaysia's dominant Malay-Muslim culture. Hence, Mahathir was obliged to emphasize that Japanese work ethics were not contradictory, but instead consistent with Islam. This, of course, begged the question of why 'Look East' if these values were all already embedded in Islam. He also launched a simultaneous campaign for the 'assimilation of Islamic values'; this policy was then often associated with the recruitment of erstwhile Islamic youth leader Anwar Ibrahim into the government, and the establishment of an Islamic bank and the International Islamic University.

'Looking East' involved more than abstract exhortations to work harder. If the 'work ethic' were to be considered in the abstract, the industriousness of the Kelantanese or Javanese would have been less controversial and better known, especially to Malays. But their essentially peasant cultures were, of course, quite irrelevant to the official desire to induce greater productivity by wage labour in an industrial capitalist context. The real thrust of the campaign appeared to be the promotion of labour discipline through organizing industrial relations to promote company loyalty (e.g. propaganda campaigns, company welfarism and in-house unions), increase productivity (e.g. work ethics and more 'incentive payments') and reduce losses (e.g. QCCs and 'zero defect' groups).

Although Mahathir later went to great pains to define the 'Look East' policy more narrowly in terms of new work ethics, labour discipline and greater productivity from the mid-1980s, the 'Look East' policy was nonetheless seen as a fairly wide-ranging series of initiatives to become a NIC by emulating the Japanese and South Korean 'economic miracles'. Before the 1986 general elections, many people presumed that Mahathir had abandoned the policy, given the little headway actually made, the seemingly diffident official Japanese response and the political liability the policy had become. After the elections, however, Mahathir reiterated his commitment to the policy, even claiming that the ruling coalition's electoral victory had proven popular support for it.

A host of Mahathir policy initiatives perceived to be linked to 'Looking East' include heavy industrialization, the preference for 'turnkey project' arrangements, the Proton (Malaysian car) project, the encouragement of more co-operative and complementary government-private sector relations associated with the 'Malaysia Incorporated' slogan, and the 'privatization' or 'denationalization' of potentially profitable economic activities previously undertaken by government. However, most such policy initiatives have had less to do with 'Looking East' than other influences on policymaking. For instance, while the Japanese developed viable SOEs in the nineteenth century only to pass them over to the private sector, the more immediate inspiration for 'privatization' in Malaysia was the dismantling of the public sector in the West identified with 'Thatcherism'.

The impact of the 'Look East' policy on the Malaysian economy has been considerable, though often either exaggerated or underestimated. Some still insist that it was anti-Western, or even 'anti-imperialist'. This, of course, ignores the fact that modern imperialism is hardly a Western monopoly. Undoubtedly, the Mahathir administration was more consistent in supporting demands associated with the South, e.g. higher and more stable commodity prices, better aid terms, greater technology transfer and reduced market restrictions in the 'North' on manufactured exports from the 'South' — though all this was not inconsistent with pro-active integration into the changing pattern of international economic specialization soon termed 'globalization'.

Heavy Industrialization

Before the 1980s, there was little deepening of import-substituting (IS) manufacturing into higher value-added import-substitution for several reasons: the domestic market was relatively small, the level of local technological capabilities low, levels of protection moderate by developing country standards (the average effective rate of protection for industry was 31 per cent in the late 1970s and declined to 17 per cent by 1987) and little pressure or encouragement from the government to deepen industrial linkages or to become internationally competitive. Tensions between the ethnic Malay-dominated government and ethnic Chinese business have also limited and biased official efforts to promote the Malaysian private sector, with much of the government effort limited to encouraging the growth of Malay business from the 1970s.

By the beginning of the 1980s, a substantial EO manufacturing sector had developed in Malaysia, superimposed on the IS manufacturing sector, promoted through the 1960s. This was the context for the new Mahathir government launching a heavy industrialization program in the early 1980s. The unacknowledged model for this attempted second stage of import-substituting industrialization was South Korea, which had vigorously promoted heavy industries from 1972 to 1979.

The government's objectives, *inter alia*, included the development of a capital goods sector and greater linkages with the domestic economy, especially with Bumiputera enterprises. The government increased domestic value addition and Bumiputera participation in Proton's development through an 'umbrella' approach to 'vendor' development. In Malaysia, 'heavy industrialization' meant setting up a hot briquetted iron and steel billets plant, two more cement plants, the Proton national car project, three motorcycle engine plants, a petroleum refining and petrochemical project, and a pulp and paper mill.

The heavy industrialization program was to be carried out through a new public sector agency, Heavy Industries Corporation of Malaysia (HICOM), set up in 1980. The government set up HICOM to further diversify manufacturing activity, develop more local linkages (which both IS and EO industries failed to do), promote small and medium Malay enterprises and lead technological development by collaborating with foreign firms and investing in local R&D. Mainly involving joint-ventures with Japanese firms, ownership of these industries was dominated by the government before the sale of shares to the public from the mid-1990s. The investment costs of these plants and of an industrial estate in Selangor for the HICOM totalled RM3.8 billion (Khor 1987: 147); a number of other HICOM projects were also approved in the early 1980s (see Jomo [ed.] 1985: 377; Chee 1994). With these investments in heavy industries, annual public sector investment in commerce and industry rose from RM0.3 billion in 1978–1980 to RM0.9 billion in 1982 and RM1.5 billion in 1984.

Being capital-intensive, the heavy industries were expected to require long gestation and pay-back periods, but even then, their performances are now generally acknowledged to have been disappointing. Unfortunately, most Malaysian government heavy industries faced stiff international competition from the outset, and have required heavy protection since. Competition has been very challenging in some cases, due to excessive global production capacity and major gluts on the world market. Hence, even if much better run, there was little likelihood of viability in the case of steel, cement, petrochemicals, shipbuilding and repairs (see Jomo [ed.], 1985; 1995; 2003; 2007).

The *Mid-Term Review of the Fifth Malaysia Plan* (Malaysia 1989: 196) stated that 'the public sector continued to play the leading role in the development of heavy industries', but complained that: 'In general, the performance of heavy industry projects sponsored by the public sector was far from satisfactory. A number of these projects suffered from heavy financial losses due to the sluggish domestic market and the inability of the industries concerned to compete in international markets'. The official document acknowledged that the costs of production and management were high by international standards, and that the situation had been exacerbated by low capacity utilization in the plants. The new heavy industries were not strategically linked with the rest of the economy, and hence, did not have much potential for significantly advancing Malaysia's industrialization.

The effective protection rates (ERPs) for the industries earmarked by the government for promotion rose in the early 1980s, e.g. the ERP for basic iron and steel rose from 28 per cent in 1969 to 131 per cent in 1987. In addition to special protection, the government also subsidized capital, imposed stringent controls on competition in the domestic market, and introduced other promotional measures to encourage the manufacture of cement (Kedah Cement and Perak Hanjoong), steel (Perwaja Steel) and motorcars (Proton). With the export push from the late 1980s, Proton's 'monopoly rents' from the heavily protected domestic market have been used to subsidize exports. By 1993, Proton domestically sourced 80 per cent of car components, and had forced firms supplying Proton to raise Bumiputera equity participation.

The government also revamped the managements of Perwaja Steel and Proton following severe losses in the early years, suggesting some disciplining by the state. Financial returns to Malaysian state-owned industries were poor or negative, but improved with better management, macroeconomic recovery and entry into export markets. The government heavy industries may also have experienced significant productivity improvements. Output-capital and output-labour ratios of non-metal mineral products, iron and steel, and transport equipment — activities dominated by the government's heavy industries — improved in the 1985–1990 period, for example, although data on these sub-sectors are aggregated and include privately owned enterprises. Improved financial performance may have been partly due to the government writing off debts as well as to accelerated depreciation allowances, reflected in declining capital-intensities in iron and steel, as well as transport equipment.

Services

Prior to the 1960s, the services sector was small, mostly comprising petty commerce and the export-import trade of the 'agency houses', the public sector, as well as transport and communications services. There have been important changes in services employment with a significant shift from traditional to modern services (Table 1.10). However, the significant increase in service employment has been partly demand-driven, e.g. with greatly expanded state employment in the 1970s, as well as due to changes in labour supply, owing to the significant expansion of non-vocational and non-technical schooling.

Demand factors — including increases in per capita income, urbanization and industrialization — have been important sources of growth in the service sector. A developing country must necessarily invest in infrastructural services, including transportation and utilities. Rapid urbanization was encouraged by the transformation of the agricultural and mining economy after independence, the encouragement of industrialization and public sector growth in the 1970s. Except for government services, the fastest growth in output during the 1970s and for a decade from the late 1980s was recorded by the manufacturing sector, resulting in greater demand for services through linkages. A UNIDO study (1985: 68) found that while the manufacturing sector was more dependent on its own intra-industry transactions for its output growth, services were more dependent on manufacturing than on intra-industry activities for its growth. Murthi (1988: 186) found that 43.1 per cent of total domestic intermediate service inputs went into manufacturing, and 40.5 per cent into the service sector itself.

Producer and distributive services posted high growth rates. The exception was social and personal services, possibly because the demands of a growing urban population are met not only by an expanding government sector, but also by informal sector services, which go largely under-enumerated. While all sectors experienced deteriorating growth rates during the mid-1980s' recession, the services sector experienced the highest growth rate of 3.9 per cent in output, suggesting that the sector was generally more insulated from the vicissitudes affecting tradeables. This was sustained by the government's early 1980s' counter-cyclical policy of expanding public services before growing budget deficits led to an austerity drive from mid-1982, freezing public sector employment. With public sector services employment largely frozen since then, the subsequent growth of services employment has largely involved the private sector, including the privatization of previously public sector services. Despite some recent trends involving casualization of employment relations, it is unlikely that much of this service sector growth is accounted for by the informal sector. However, much of the significantly increased demand for services has been met from abroad, resulting in a significant rise in the invisibles or services deficit in the trade balance, especially since the late 1970s.

Although per capita income in Malaysia increased from $1,934 in 1955 (in 1986 prices) to $4,098 in 1986, an increase of 112 per cent, the services share of national output increased by only 0.5 per cent, while services employment increased by 73.8 per cent. Like the banking and finance industries in the US, labour productivity grew slowly in the modern financial and business services. This was because of rapid recruitment from the late 1970s — particularly in the then relatively labour-intensive banking sector — when banks expanded their branch networks all over the country, even when business was not expanding as quickly in these areas. As these services started off at high productivity levels, opportunities for improvement were less.

The commerce sector experienced low productivity growth due to the combined effects of over-expansion of labour-intensive hotel business and the generally sluggish productivity of wholesale/retail businesses. Labour productivity grows slowly in private sector personal services, comprising small-scale, family-organized and labour-intensive services, because of the nature of labour organization and the modest investments in productivity-enhancing techniques. Government services are generally deemed the least productive of all modern sector services, probably because government employment is usually not governed by profitability or productivity considerations [see Heller and Tait (1984) and Bacon and Eltis (1979)].

The widespread wage and status bias against blue-collar work has resulted in an under-supply of basic technical skills among school-leavers, exacerbated by the official neglect of vocational education. Only 7.3 per cent of all secondary school enrolments in 1980 and 6.2 per cent in 1985 were in the vocational/technical stream. Of the 808,200 new entrants in the labour force during 1981–1985, approximately 79,640 (9.9 per cent) had some kind of technical training, while 123,000 had university/college education from local and foreign universities. Official reluctance to increase the number of vocational and technical schools, despite persistent complaints of shortages of skilled manual and technical workers, could also be due to the relatively greater cost of vocational schools *vis-à-vis* ordinary schools (ILO, 1988: 17–20, 107).

Bearing in mind the complexities and limitations of conventional measurement of productivity in the service sector however, available evidence (Khong, 1991: Chap. 1) suggests that the growth rate of labour productivity in all services (except commerce, finance and other personal services) has consistently exceeded that of manufacturing. Average productivity as measured by gross domestic product GDP per head and share of GDP divided by the share of total employment for the service sector is higher than for the extractive sector.

Furthermore, the Malaysian data support the argument that service sector employment is, in general, more insulated from business cycles than the tradeables sector, especially the manufacturing and primary commodities sectors. Khong (1991: Table 2.5) found that the shares of redundancies in services were much lower than their share of overall employment in the 1980s. Within the service sector, the highest redundancies are found in commerce, comprising wholesale/retail trade and hotels and restaurants, which are vulnerable to business cycles. In addition, these services are largely without effective workers' organizations, and utilize a greater proportion of secondary and marginal workers who incur low labour-turnover costs for employers.

In Malaysia, trade unions have never been particularly strong, with their powers limited by the state through labour legislation and the encouragement of collaborating and in-house (company's) unions. The small trade union membership in Malaysia has been a limitation. Only 11.1 per cent of the 4.7 million workers in the peninsula and 18.4 per cent of the 3.1 million wage employees were unionized in 1986 (calculated from the *Labour and Manpower Report, 1985/86*: Tables 4.18 and 9.14; the *Labour Force Survey, 1986*, unpublished statistics), with unionization rates declining despite the absolute and relative growth of wage employment. Within the service sector, the largest union membership is in the public sector (45.4 per cent unionized) and financial services (70.0 per cent unionized).

Although workers' organizations are fairly limited in Malaysia, they have had some influence. Modern services, such as finance and government services, provide greater security of employment. The higher degree of unionization in these services and collective agreements between employers and workers generally result in negotiations for wage freezes or recruitment freezes, rather than lay-offs, to avoid high labour-turnover costs associated with these services' utilization of a large proportion of elite-primary and secondary-primary workers. The service sector's role as an unemployment sponge during economic downturns generally only applies to the non-enumerated informal sector, poorly reflected in official statistics, and the self-employed.

The rising wages amidst increasing unemployment during the mid-1980s' recession triggered claims of wage rigidity and demands by employers for wage flexibility reforms. Wages in the unionized sector are generally determined by three-yearly collective agreements which are legally binding. These collective agreements are based on several practices not very conducive to wage flexibility in the short to medium term, e.g. predetermined annual increments with no explicit link to performance. Secondly, disputes are settled by the Industrial Court, which recommends that salary adjustments should not exceed two-thirds of the growth rate of the consumer price index over the previous three years. Thirdly, the collective agreement provides for the payment of annual bonuses equivalent to one or two months of the basic salary. The bonus is also contractual, and therefore, firms are legally bound to pay regardless of their financial position.

It has been argued that though only one-tenth of wage employees are unionized, their fate tends to influence wage trends in the non-unionized sector. However, the World Bank has suggested that present wage practices in Malaysia incorporate beneficial elements of the flexi-wage system. Malaysian employers use bonuses, overtime payments and other non-wage incentives to retain flexibility in wages and employment, and to lower labour turnover. While bonuses have a component that is collectively bargained, more than half of the bonuses paid in manufacturing in 1992 were incentive bonuses, while the ratio in services was even higher.

Mahathir's Labour Policies

The increasingly widespread use of less well paid immigrant labour — especially in plantation agriculture, land development schemes and construction — as well as Mahathir's enthusiasm for more easily controlled in-house or company unions further weakened the bargaining position of labour in the 1980s. In the meantime, the government's emphasis on work ethics and related innovations (such as quality control circles or QCCs) were intended to boost labour productivity at minimal cost to management.

The government imposed more severe penalties for those who stepped out of line to discourage labour militancy. The government also successfully took advantage of rivalries and corruption in the trade union movement to 'divide and rule' union officials, thus undermining their capacity to effectively serve their unions and the interests of labour more generally. Beginning in the mid-1980s, it patronized the leadership of civil service unions (though not unions of employees in the statutory bodies) as well as some smaller unions temporarily affiliated with the now-defunct Malaysian Labour Organization (MLO). MLO was a government-encouraged rival trade union centre to the Malaysian Trades Union Congress (MTUC), which the government had previously failed to bring under its total control.

Previous labour policy was more tolerant of a greater variety of trade unions as long as they did not align with the political opposition or promote labour militancy. In-house unions have existed for some time, mainly in statutory bodies. Blatant government promotion of in-house unions represented a departure from the previous policy. However, despite ostensible government support for in-house unions, very few new in-house unions were registered where no unions existed before. Instead, in-house unions seemed to be encouraged to replace 'troublesome' unions already in existence. Thus, government encouragement of in-house unions for the private sector further weakened the already weak trade union movement in the country.

During the 1960s and 1970s, there were several government attempts to portray itself as a neutral arbiter standing above and mediating between capital or management and labour. However, the state generally favoured capital over labour, as reflected in various amendments to the labour laws and the government's role in industrial relations. In the aftermath of the 1978/79 MAS industrial action, authoritarian and anti-labour policies, considered necessary for rapid growth and industrialization, became more pronounced. In the 1980s, the government introduced amendments to tighten up the already restrictive labour laws, further limiting union rights and increasing government control over them. At the same time, it increased overtime and some other benefits for workers as the sugar coating for the otherwise bitter pill. Although wage employment continued to grow, membership of trade unions declined in the early 1980s, and has continued to decline as a proportion of the wage labour force since.

In traditional services, unionization is extremely low in small firms with paternalistic employment relations. Although the minimum wages of workers in some of the 'lower' services — specifically shop assistants, employees in the hotel and catering trade, cinema workers, and cargo handlers — are governed by the National Wage Council Act of 1947, enforcement is low. Random inspections are conducted, but in most cases, inspections cover less than 5 per cent of all firms. The onus is on the employee to report any abuses. Employers' non-compliance is usually attributed to illiteracy or misinformation on the part of both employers and employees since these are low-skilled sectors. Also, the presence of unpaid family workers suggests that, sometimes, low money wages may be compensated for by other benefits. Even union members do not all enjoy the same benefits since collective agreements are negotiated between the unions and individual employers. In such cases, firm size and locality are important determinants of negotiated benefits.

During the mid-1980s, recession, deflationary policies and govern-ment expenditure cuts resulted in increased unemployment as well as pressures for greater labour flexibility. The increased use of immigrant labour and contract labour further weakened labour and depressed real wages, especially for the predominantly Malay and Indian unskilled and poorly skilled workers. Sometimes justified in terms of the desire for the Malay-dominated government to strengthen itself by increasing the number and proportion of ethnic Malays through immigration from neighbouring Indonesia, the tacit approval of massive, often illegal labour immigration adversely affected wages and working conditions. With close to full employment in the early and mid-1990s, real wages rose once again, though skilled workers gained more than immigrant labour and Malaysian unskilled workers. While the 1997–1998 ringgit devaluation lowered labour costs to foreigners, the expulsions of immigrant workers have sustained upward wage pressures.

Mahathir Regime 2: Inducing Private Investments (1986–1997)

The key turning point for government policy, in terms of economic liberalization, occurred around 1985.This followed Daim Zainuddin's appointment as Finance Minister in 1984, after then Finance Minister Tengku Razaleigh Hamzah's failed second challenge for the deputy leadership of the ruling party. The difficulties of introducing potentially unpopular economic measures were eased by Daim's appointment. As he had limited political ambitions, he was quite willing to take responsibility for measures that a politically more ambitious appointee might have preferred to avoid. Without any personal political base in the party, he owed his position to Mahathir, and was hence politically insulated from the party and others critical of or opposed to the economic reform measures.

By the mid-1980s, there was growing dissatisfaction with the government among many, including Bumiputeras, both in the public and private sectors, with some criticizing what they considered unfair government interference in the business world. Large Malay-controlled business groups had emerged on the corporate scene, and were calling for a less regulated economy. Indeed, some of them blamed excessive state intervention for slowing economic growth and undermining private business interests. Partial liberalization of the economy in response was probably a boon to the corporate sector, with most businesses benefiting, and hence supportive of further liberalization.

The government introduced some economic liberalization measures. This coincided with the contraction of loss-making SOEs, which had grown in the 1960s and expanded rapidly in the 1970s (after the implementation of the NEP), with new ones which grew in the early 1980s as others began contracting. SOE losses wasted precious investment resources, increased the government's financial burden and allegedly slowed economic growth. Privatization, which had been officially announced in 1983, gained vigour, and the government actively privatized its assets until there were some 200 privatization projects in the pipeline by the mid-1990s.

The government also sought to attract new, especially foreign investments, with the 1986 Promotion of Investments Act. The timing was perfect, as manufacturers from Northeast Asia (especially Japan and later, Taiwan) relocated their industries to take advantage of the enhanced incentives, relatively good infrastructure and more lax environmental and other regulations, as well as comparatively lower production costs due to the lower wages and devalued exchange rates. The mid-1980s' depreciation of the Malaysian ringgit against the US dollar (Table 1.2) enhanced Malaysia's attractiveness, especially to East Asian investors.

The debt crisis of the early 1980s provided the OECD economies, especially the US, with an unprecedented opportunity to impose policy reforms over the largely indebted South after the heady 1970s' attempts to establish a New International Economic Order. However, Malaysia did not experience many of the painful economic problems other less fortunate economies of the South experienced in the 1980s. For instance, Malaysia never really suffered from capital shortages, and never really borrowed heavily from abroad until the early 1980s — ironically, when liquidity was tighter and real interest rates higher. However, its borrowing binge soon came to an end from the mid-1980s.

Labour shortages and the 1988 withdrawal of privileges under the General System of Preferences from the first-tier East Asian new industrializing economies encouraged relocation of production facilities abroad. Meanwhile, reforms, selective deregulation as well as new rules and incentives made relocation in Southeast Asia as well as China more attractive. The Southeast Asian boom from the late 1980s greatly benefited from investments from these first-generation newly industrialized East

Asian economies experiencing rising production costs (due to tighter labour markets), strengthened intellectual property rights as well as stricter environmental regulations. From late 1985, the Japanese yen and then the Korean won, the new Taiwanese dollar and the Singapore dollar appreciated against the US dollar, and hence, even more against the ringgit, enhancing Malaysia's attractiveness to foreign investors, particularly those from East Asia (Table 1.2).

Thus, the policy changes of the mid and late 1980s appeared successful in reviving growth and industrialization (Table 1.4). Confirmation of the new change in policy direction since the mid-1980s came with the 1991 enunciation of Vision 2020, seen to favour growth, modernization and industrialization. Although FDI began levelling off in the mid-1990s, increased domestic investments — inspired by greater domestic investor confidence — sustained the momentum of rapid economic growth until the 1997–1998 regional crisis. The gravity of the crisis and the difficulties of recovery were exacerbated by injudicious policy responses, compromised by cronyism, though there is little persuasive evidence that cronyism itself precipitated the crisis.

Transition from the NEP

After the government introduced new liberalising economic policy reforms, business sentiment improved. In addition, new investments poured in from more developed countries in East Asia, notably Japan, Singapore and later, Taiwan. As the government policy reform efforts not only benefited foreign investors, but were also seen as encouraging non-Malay investors, domestic firms became more supportive of policy reforms. Politically influential corporate groups developed various means to better advance their interests, while appreciating the greater freedom, flexibility as well as reduced tax burdens and regulations.

Initially driven by East Asian EO manufacturing investments, the Malaysian economy recovered significantly from 1987, and maintained growth rates of over eight per cent per annum for a decade from 1988. Thus, the policy changes of the mid-1980s appeared successful in reviving growth and industrialization. The sequence has encouraged the attribution of the economic boom to the policy changes. However, as the preceding account suggests, several developments were occurring at the same time, and while all may well have contributed to the recovery, it is difficult to disaggregate their respective contributions. Growth in other economies of Southeast Asia (Singapore, Thailand and Indonesia) seems to have accelerated at around the same time, i.e. from the late 1980s. Though most also introduced some economic liberalization measures around the same time, there is no evidence that the most successful or fastest growing have been the most liberalized economies, or that such measures contributed crucially to the boom.

In 1990, the twenty-year period of OPP1 for Malaysia's NEP came to an end. The ambitious NEP redistribution targets had been largely achieved by then, with most progress made before the mid-1980s. Despite some controversy over the reliability and comparability of official data, the reduction in official poverty incidence was impressive.

With the 1991 enunciation of Vision 2020 to achieve growth, modernization and industrialization, instead of the NEP's emphasis on inter-ethnic redistribution, foreign investors continued to be courted. The government also further reduced restrictions on ethnic Chinese capital, which had been encouraged by various other reforms, e.g. easier access to listing on the stock market, greater official encouragement of small and medium industries, other official efforts mitigating the continued impact of the 1975 Industrial Co-ordination Act (ICA) as well as greater overall emphasis on the market, rather than regulatory measures. Hence, domestic investments were encouraged by the partial liberalization from the mid-1980s. With such liberalization, many Chinese-owned firms were able to obtain stock market listing, and could thus tap into the domestic capital market for funds for development. With listing, they have had to comply with more stringent reporting requirements and have had to modernize management and operations. However, it remains unclear whether public listing has been primarily intended to raise capital or to enable the beneficial owners to 'cash out'.

In the early and mid-1990s, official policy encouraged Malaysian firms (especially large corporations) to invest in other developing countries in Southeast Asia, as well as Africa, South Pacific, the central Asian former Soviet republics, and even Europe and the US (Jomo [ed.], 2002). The Malaysian South-South Corporation Berhad was formed to help large

Malaysian firms invest elsewhere in the 'South'. The government helped such firms by setting up agencies to facilitate trade, export credit and insurance, signing double taxation agreements with various countries, and organizing numerous trade and investment missions led by government ministers. At the same time, it also favoured multilateral and regional trade liberalization with some exceptions. However, this policy was suspended following the 1997–1998 crisis in an attempt to revive domestic investments until Mahathir's retirement in 2003 led to bilateral trade and investment liberalization.

Over the years, the government has changed its industrialization strategy. In response to problems and new priorities in December 1996, the government announced the Second Industrial Master Plan (IMP2) for 1996–2005 to replace the (first) Industrial Master Plan (IMP) for 1986–1995. In September 1996, the government also set up the Multimedia Super Corridor to promote certain information technology investments in the country. The government committed over RM50 billion for the development of infrastructure to support this initiative. At the same time, the government strengthened intellectual property laws to reassure investors and provided more generous incentives for new investments in this area.

There were also some interesting developments in the property sector before the 1997–1998 crisis. Following the 1980s' recession, the government had allowed foreign purchases in the property market. The massive influx of Singaporean buyers — especially in the state of Johor — sent property prices soaring in the 1990s. In response, the government imposed a tariff on foreigners buying residential properties, dampening the property markets. Meanwhile, state governments have posed bureaucratic obstacles to registering land transfers and dealings, thus raising transactions costs.

Unemployment rates fell sharply from the late 1980s (Tables 1.2, 1.8), and labour shortages grew, especially in the early and mid-1990s. With the growing sophistication of the economy, shortages have also emerged in urban, white-collar service occupations. Wage rates rose sharply by well over 50 per cent on average during 1990–1997. Rapid economic growth has pushed up wages across all skill categories, but wages for the very skilled and the unskilled have risen more rapidly, implying greater shortages for these occupational categories. Malaysia has also taken in professionals, e.g. in medicine, engineering and architecture, from other countries. Leading professionals in some sectors are significantly foreign, especially when professional restrictions have been easily circumvented through various regulatory loopholes. Rising wages have also narrowed the gap between labour productivity and wages, thus exerting upward pressure on unit labour costs. Labour productivity, measured as value added per worker, rose by 5.2 per cent per annum, whereas wages grew by 4.1 per cent.

'Malaysia Incorporated': State-Business Corporatism

The expanded role of the Malaysian state with the NEP and other developments since the 1970s came under critical scrutiny early in the Mahathir administration. Regulation had grown in the 1970s and early 1980s together with the public sector. Instead, Mahathir advanced the 'Malaysia Incorporated' slogan to improve relations between the government and the private sector, and to try to get the previously ascendant government to its ostensibly 'traditional' role of serving private business. The term 'Malaysia Incorporated' was adapted from the originally pejorative term, 'Japan Incorporated', which had emerged in the West in the late 1960s as it faced what it considered 'unfair' competition from more strongly state-backed Japanese business interests.

With the Malaysia Incorporated policy enunciated in 1983, government officers were encouraged to find ways to better serve the private sector instead of treating it as an adversary. Many government agencies improved counter services, and some established high-level government-private sector committees to involve the latter in dialogues to listen to their views. Though welcomed by the private sector, these efforts were not sustained, except with the more powerful business interests on a personal basis.

While the 'Malaysia Incorporated' slogan provided a useful reminder of the role of government desired by much of the private sector, it addressed rather different problems in quite a different context than what the slogan 'Japan Incorporated' or actual Japanese experience suggested. In Malaysia, the slogan referred to efforts to curb and rectify 'excesses' associated with overzealous implementation of the NEP — mainly by ethnic Malay officials, and resented by ethnic Chinese business interests.

Privatization

SOEs in Malaysia were first set up during the colonial period, with some created for the purpose of social policy and ethnic affirmative action from the early 1950s. In the 1960s, and especially in the 1970s, the state established a large number of public enterprises in all sectors, sometimes in collaboration with private capital. Thus, SOEs grew modestly from the mid-1960s and much faster in the 1970s, following the first announcement of the NEP in 1970. State intervention grew more generally, with the Government participating directly in the economy through establishment of a large number of public enterprises and state agencies. In the early 1980s, new SOEs spearheaded the economy's diversification into heavy industries.

From 10 in 1957 and 22 in 1960, public enterprises grew to 109 in 1970, 656 in 1980 and 1,014 in 1985, before almost ceasing to grow, except for a few projects favoured by the executive (Khalid, 1987). The two main types of SOEs were statutory bodies established by special legislation, and those operating as private companies registered under the Companies Act. Major public enterprises owned by the federal, state and regional authorities have many subsidiaries and joint-ventures.

SOEs in Malaysia were held almost equally in number by federal and state governments, with only four per cent owned by the regional development agencies (Jomo [ed.] 1995: Table 1.4). State SOEs predominated in the primary sectors — agriculture, extractive industry, plantation agriculture, and logging — while the transport and finance sectors were dominated by federal SOEs. There were a large number of state manufacturing and service SOEs, mostly created to promote regional growth. Federal SOEs were much more highly capitalized, but had relatively smaller shares of the total capital of SOEs. Federal SOEs tended to be significantly larger than those held by state or regional agencies in terms of equity, accounting for 78 per cent of total equity and 79 per cent of debt. State and regional SOEs were significantly smaller, and much less likely to raise capital from sources other than the government (Jomo [ed.] 1995: Table 1.5).

Interestingly, the level of debt as a share of total capital did not decline very much, as federal SOEs became slightly less dependent on federal government loans, but more dependent on both private domestic and foreign loans. Average debt (from all sources) was RM61 million for federal SOEs, RM15 million for state SOEs and less than RM5 million for regional SOEs. Federal SOEs also had, on average, much larger exposure to domestic and foreign financial markets (accounting for 51 per cent and 27 per cent of total debt respectively), while debt for state and regional SOEs was principally from the federal government. The overall SOE debt-equity ratio of 180 per cent was significantly higher than the average private-sector ratio, estimated then to be approximately 100 per cent. While the government extended cheap credit to SOEs, it was also a less demanding shareholder in terms of requiring dividends, i.e. it was associated with exercising 'soft budget constraints'.

Aggregate performance of the SOE sector has been overwhelmingly determined by the performance of PETRONAS and its subsidiaries. Ministry of Finance data show that despite its relatively poor operating performance, the SOE sector had very high levels of development expenditure (Jomo [ed.] 1995: Table 1.8). However, the generally weak SOE performance was obscured by high profits for PETRONAS and its subsidiaries (whose surplus reached 5 per cent of GDP in 1982). The counter-cyclical fiscal strategy of the early 1980s saw a huge expansion of development expenditure from 1981 to 1984. This was accompanied by rapid expansion in SOE development expenditure — mainly to promote heavy industrialization — which rose from 4.2 per cent of GDP in 1981 to almost 10 per cent in 1984 (Jomo, 1990). This surge in public-sector capital expenditure was — for the three years 1981–1983 — consistently in excess of 25 per cent of GDP.

Poor SOE co-ordination and accountability became more evident in the 1980s. For instance, of the more than 900 identified SOEs in 1984, the Ministry of Public Enterprises could only report annual returns for 269, which recorded accumulated losses of RM137.3 million (Supian, 1988). The rapid growth of public enterprises in the 1970s generally involved limited efforts to ensure accountability and efficiency. State intervention seemed almost singularly committed to inter-ethnic wealth redistribution, ostensibly favouring the indigenous Malay community.

Such interventions primarily favoured politically influential rentiers, rather than genuine entrepreneurs.

The growth and proliferation of public enterprises came to an end in the mid-1980s as the government reduced financial support for most of them, except for the politically favoured heavy industries. The NEP public enterprises supposed to serve as vehicles for creating a Bumiputera entrepreneurial community came to be portrayed as institutions draining state resources with little social benefit except to a few direct beneficiaries. The growth of public enterprises from the 1970s, especially the heavy industries in the early 1980s, was accompanied by declining capital productivity in the economy.

The average incremental capital-output ratio (ICOR) rose from 2–3 in the 1970s to 5–6 in the first half of the 1980s, while the public sector ICOR rose from 6–7 in the 1970s to 15–16, suggesting declining returns to investments, especially by the public sector in the latter period. By the mid-1980s, public sector spending was also constrained by reduced and more expensive resource availability. Public sector spending was sustained at high levels in the early 1980s by incurring massive external debt. The profligacy and higher interest rates of the early 1980s, and the ringgit and US dollar depreciation from 1985 reduced resource availability. Mahathir's privatization policy was actually western in inspiration, following Thatcher in Britain. However, the generally lacklustre performance of the Malaysian public sector, including most SOEs, could hardly be denied.

The privatization policy in Malaysia was officially announced in 1983. The Malaysian government summed up the official arguments for privatization as follows (EPU 1985): 'Privatization has a number of major objectives. First, it is aimed at relieving the financial and administrative burden of the Government in undertaking and maintaining a vast and constantly expanding network of services and investments in infrastructure. Second, privatization is expected to promote competition, improve efficiency and increase the productivity of the services. Third, privatization, by stimulating private entrepreneurship and investment, is expected to accelerate the rate of growth of the economy. Fourth, privatization is expected to assist in reducing the size and presence of the public sector with its monopolistic tendencies and bureaucratic support, in the economy. Fifth, privatization is also expected to contribute towards meeting the objectives of the NEP especially as Bumiputera entrepreneurship and presence have improved greatly since the early days of the NEP and they are therefore capable of taking up their share of the privatized services.'

However, this official rationale for privatization in Malaysia has been refuted on the following grounds. The public sector need not be badly run, as has been demonstrated by some other public sectors. Privatization does not provide a miracle cure for all problems (especially inefficiencies) associated with the public sector, nor can private enterprises guarantee that the public interest is most effectively served by private interests taking over public sector activities. Unlike the 'Look East' policy, which faded in significance by the mid-1980s, privatization achieved greater vigour from the late 1980s. Undermining the public sector, especially public services, through privatization has important welfare implications, including for public sector employees, consumers and the poor. While most potentially affected public sector employees initially felt threatened by privatization (in the sense that job security could no longer be taken for granted), many other Malaysians — fed up with the waste, inefficiency and corruption usually associated with the public sector — were indifferent, if not supportive of the policy.

Many Malaysians also associated the growth of the public sector with increased state intervention and the ascendance of Malay political and economic hegemony under the NEP. They saw privatization as a desirable policy change that would check, if not reverse these trends, which were believed to have discouraged productive private sector investments and thus slowed down growth. Unlike elsewhere, few in Malaysia identified state intervention with socialism, but many viewed privatization as a measure to restore a more laissez faire capitalism.

Privatization involves changing the status of a business, service or industry from state, government or public to private ownership or control. The term often also refers to the use of private contractors to provide services previously supplied by the public sector. In practice, privatization in Malaysia also referred to the following:

1. the sale or divestment of state concerns;
2. public issue of shares in a state-owned public company;
3. placement of such shares with institutional investors;

4. sale or lease of physical assets;
5. public-private sector joint ventures;
6. schemes to attract private financing into previously state financed projects;
7. 'contracting out' public services by enabling private contractors to provide services previously provided by the public sector; and
8. allowing private competition where the public sector previously enjoyed a monopoly.

The adoption of the Privatization Master Plan (PMP) in 1991 marked a new stage of the private sector moving into activities mainly involving the public sector previously. Privatization gathered momentum with the PMP. Private sector participation in various activities increased significantly, including large infrastructure projects (which involve long gestation periods and high investment costs), manufacturing, and services, especially education and health. After the end of the NEP's first Outline Perspective Plan (OPP1) for 1971–1990, the National Development Policy (1991–2000) emphasized the promotion of a strong private sector to lead the next phase of growth and development.

Mahathir consolidated his position in the late 1980s, after fending off political challenges from ruling party colleagues following economic difficulties from the mid-1980s. Privatization became an increasingly important means for sponsoring, supporting and subsidizing the emergence and consolidation of new, politically well-connected, predominantly, but not exclusively, Malay rentiers. Many Malaysians associated public sector growth with increased state intervention following the ascendance of Malay political and economic hegemony under the NEP. Although some SOEs continued to perform well, the public sector had come to be associated with inter-ethnic redistribution. It also became increasingly associated in the public mind with abuses such as corruption and waste, besides exacerbating the impression of public sector inefficiency. They saw privatization as a desirable policy change that would check, if not reverse these trends, which were believed to have discouraged productive private sector investments, and thus slowed growth.

The key policy question is whether inefficiencies are inherent characteristics of the public sector, and cannot be overcome except through privatization. If the poor record of Malaysian public enterprises was primarily due to the nature, interests and abilities of those in charge rather than solely due to the fact of state or public ownership, then privatization could not and will not overcome the root problems involved. Though privatization may increase enterprise efficiency to increase profits for the private owners concerned, such changes will not necessarily benefit the public or consumers as a whole. Also, by diverting private capital from productive new investments to buying over existing public sector assets, investment and economic growth rates can be retarded rather than augmented. Greater accountability and transparency as well as more effective popular control would advance the public and national interest, while also limiting public sector waste and borrowing.

Privatization exercises in Malaysia often did not even pretend to achieve supposed efficiency gains, especially when NEP restructuring considerations were invoked, ostensibly to increase Bumiputera wealth ownership and business opportunities. With increased Bumiputera competition, where collusion was not easily arranged, political influence and connections became increasingly decisive. In many cases, effective lobbying by private interests determined what was privatized, in what manner, and to whom. Often, privatization in Malaysia did not involve the formalities of an open tender system. Many beneficiaries were chosen on the basis of political and personal connections. This was legitimized by the authorities, who claimed to have a 'first come, first serve' policy to reward those who first made 'viable' privatization proposals to the government. Such formal and informal collusion in bidding for contracts has caused widespread concern over the years.

The government was only able to privatize profitable or potentially profitable enterprises and activities because the private sector was only interested in these. Privatization did not resolve the fiscal problem in the medium term, as the government lost income from profitable public sector activities and was stuck with financing unprofitable ones. The government rationalized subsidizing private sector beneficiaries of privatization by arguing that the privatized firms would pay taxes on their profits to the government, although this claim obviously was contradicted by the generous tax breaks and revenue guarantees provided by the government.

The privatization policy also put increasing pressure on public sector employees and those dependent on public services. The burden of privatization proved to be harsher because it began during the mid-1980s' recession, e.g. the government's austerity drive for mid-1982 and the privatization policy were invoked to justify the reduction of government health expenditure, when the recession forced more people to turn to public health services. Privatization gave priority to profit maximization, at the expense of social welfare and the public interest, except on the rare occasions when the former and the latter coincided; hence, for example, only profitable new services were introduced rather than services needed by the people, especially the poor, unless required by the terms of privatization.

In the area of infrastructure development, such as power supply, telecommunications, water supply, sanitation ports, and highways, as well as in natural monopolies, such as municipal services, the government actively privatized its assets. By the mid-1990s, the government had some 200 privatization projects in the pipeline. The government has long been talking about setting up a mega regulatory agency to achieve economies of scale in regulation (*New Straits Times*, 18 October 1996), and to redress existing problems in regulating the many privatized firms.

Although privatization was generally well-managed by the government to ensure popular participation and enthusiasm (mainly through discounted share issues), popular outrage against privatization grew with the high charges following the amalgamation of municipal sewerage systems under a 'crony' firm, Indah Water Konsortium (IWK) in 1993. The 1997–1998 crisis led to suspension of the privatization program as well as bail-outs, including re-nationalization of some major privatized entities at great public cost. In recent years, Khazanah has emerged as the principal government holding company for previously privatized enterprises. Although public sector inefficiencies and other problems needed to be overcome, privatization in Malaysia primarily enriched a few with strong political connections. They secured some of the most profitable opportunities, as public welfare became increasingly subject to the power and interests of private business.

Mahathir Regime 3: Crisis Management, 1997–2003

There is now little serious disagreement that the East Asian economic crises since mid-1997 began as currency crises. It has become increasingly clear that the crises were due to the undermining of previous arrangements for international and national economic governance due to deregulation and other developments associated with financial liberalization and globalization. The subversion of effective financial governance at both international and national levels created conditions that led to the crises.

This does not mean that all was well from a macroeconomic perspective. Large current account deficits in Malaysia and some other countries had been financed by short-term capital inflows into the stock market and loans from abroad. Crony capitalism and rent-seeking had also been thriving, but cannot, by themselves, explain the crisis. However, cronyism, nepotism and new crisis-induced political developments did compromise official policy responses as the crisis unfolded. More importantly, they exacerbated the crisis and undermined confidence, and thus delayed recovery. The currency and financial crises became a crisis of the 'real economy' in Malaysia mainly due to poor government policy responses.

Despite official claims that the ringgit was pegged to a 'basket of the currencies of Malaysia's main trading partners', it was virtually pegged to the US dollar for decades from the mid-1970s, albeit at different rates. This offered certain advantages, including the semblance of exchange rate and even currency stability — especially low inflation. These advantages were desired by the politically influential financial sector, dominated by foreign multinationals and ethnic Chinese. The state of affairs also reflected the political weakness — in influencing economic policy-making — of exporting manufacturer interests in Malaysia, compared to the financial community. However, much of the industrial capability of the Malaysian exporting manufacturing interests outside of ethnic Chinese dominated resource-based manufacturing is foreign-owned — the same ethnicities as for the financial community.

Equity finance, involving financial dis-intermediation, grew in significance from the 1980s in Malaysia. The establishment of the Labuan International Offshore Financial Centre in Malaysia in 1993 eased access to foreign funds while reducing transparency in related banking practices. These and other reforms — as well as the growth of 'private banking' and 'relationship banking' in the region and increased competition among 'debt-pushing' competitors — weakened the scope and efficacy of national prudential regulation. Other domestic financial sector reforms had also reduced the powers and jurisdiction of Bank Negara Malaysia, the central bank. Not surprisingly, bank intermediation declined in overall importance and contributed proportionately less to financing productive investments.

Capital inflows — into the stock market as well as through bank borrowings — helped bridge current account deficits due to the growing proportion of 'non-tradeables' produced in Malaysia, much related to construction. These flows were ostensibly 'sterilized' to minimize consumer price inflation as desired by the financial community, but instead fuelled asset price inflation, mainly involving real estate and share prices.

Malaysia's resource wealth and relatively cheap labour have sustained production enclaves for the export of agricultural, forest, mineral and manufactured products (Tables 1.6, 1.7). Much of the retained wealth generated has been captured by the business cronies of those in power, who have contributed to growth by re-investing the captured rents, mainly in the 'protected' domestic economy, e.g. in import-substituting industries, commerce, services and privatized utilities and infrastructure. Despite various weaknesses, this Malaysian brand of ersatz capitalism — involving changing forms of crony rentierism — sustained rapid growth for four decades (Tables 1.1, 1.4). These arrangements came unstuck due to 'irrational' herd behaviour greatly exaggerating the impact of 'rational' (rent seeking) speculative market behaviour to gain advantage from the region's currency appreciations (Jomo, 2001) (see Figure 1.2).

The over-valued ringgit and other regional currencies following the mid-1995 reversal of the decade long yen appreciation, plus the new investment opportunities following partial financial liberalization created the conditions for the asset price inflationary bubbles. The bubbles burst with devastating consequences for the region, exacerbated by injudicious policy responses. Failure to recognize the nature of the processes of accumulation and growth has generally prevented the design and implementation of an adequate more pro-active developmental strategy. It is not clear if Malaysian central bank-guided consolidation of the banking sector has helped ensure its greater robustness and readiness for further financial liberalization, as the bank restructuring in the wake of the crisis does not seem well conceived.

In spite of deregulation measures, Malaysian government controls on the economy have not disappeared. For instance, the central bank still sets the pace and parameters for liberalization of the banking industry.

Figure 1.2 Malaysia: Portfolio Investment, 1991–2012

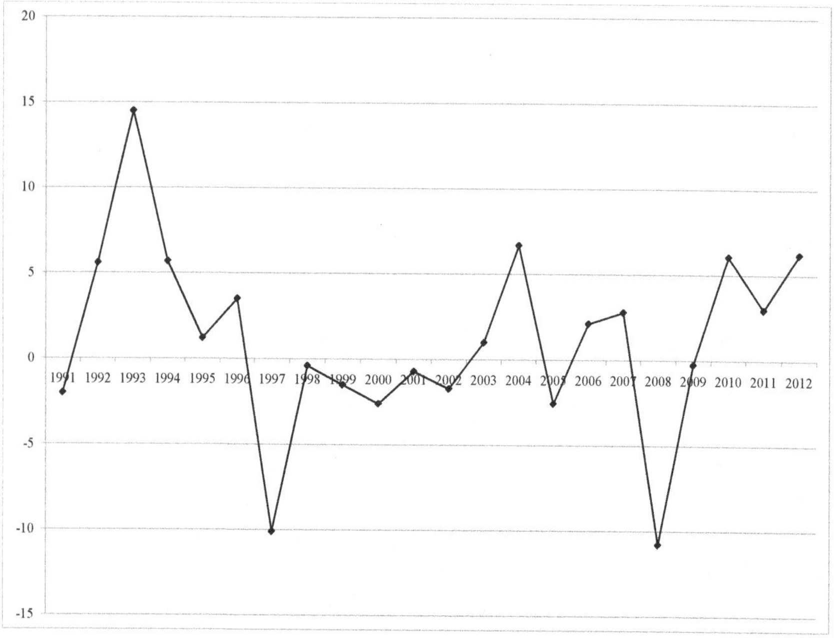

Sources: Calculated with data from Bank Negara Malaysia, *Monthly Bulletin of Statistics*, various issues.

It has forced local banks to merge, ostensibly to give them a better chance of survival as the industry opens up to international participation.[1] Meanwhile, the foreign banks already in Malaysia have been repositioning themselves to take advantage of the new opportunities with the changing policy and regulatory environment as the government prepares to open up the country's banking system to other foreign banks. The Securities Commission, set up to regulate the equities market, has put new regulation in place, in the face of market developments and political pressures. Unfortunately, few such reforms have prioritized the governance requirements of new development challenges, but have instead been principally concerned with financial liberalization and deepening.

The currency and financial crises suggest that Malaysia's decade-long economic boom until 1997 was built on some shaky and unsustainable foundations. Limited and inappropriate public investments in human resources have held back the development of greater industrial and technological capabilities (see Part 2). Malaysia has been reliant on foreign resources, especially immigrant labour. Future economic progress cannot be secured by relying on cheap labour alone. With full employment (Tables 1.8, 1.11) and slower investment and productivity growth, private investment as a share of gross national product (GNP) has been lower since the 1997–1998 crisis (Table 1.3). Employment creation has not recovered to the pre-crisis level (Table 1.8) in spite of continued labour force growth, with the share of employees still rising (see Part 2).

Despite slower growth, unemployment has remained low since 1997, hovering at around 3.5 per cent. Nonetheless, graduate unemployment has been on the rise. The poor quality of unemployed graduates, mostly from local public institutions of high learning, as well as inappropriate choices of courses are blamed for their failure to gain employment. State support for these graduates includes free or subsidized retraining, job search and temporary job creation.

After 1997

Although Malaysian economic growth was strong for about a decade before the 1997–1998 East Asian crisis, it has never really fully recovered since the crisis. Compared to an average of 9.2 per cent, or about six per cent per capita after considering labour immigration, during 1991–1997, Malaysian economic growth has averaged five per cent, or about three per cent on a per capita basis during 1998–2012. Hence, growth in the decade and a half since the 1997–1998 crisis has been about half the average for almost a decade before the crisis.

This can be attributed to the decline in private investment which went down dramatically with the 1997–1998 crisis, as reflected in Figure 1.3. Total investment growth per annum fell from 15.3 per cent during 1991–1997 to decline by an average of -0.6 per cent over 1998–2012. While private consumption grew by an average of 7.5 per cent during 1991–1997, it grew by 3.2 per cent during 1998–2012, i.e. by less than half the earlier rate.

Thus, the collapse in private investment has been partially compensated for by increased government spending, both for consumption as well as investment (Figure 1.4). Higher government expenditure has

Figure 1.3 Malaysia: Private and Public Investment, 1990–2012 (RM thousands)

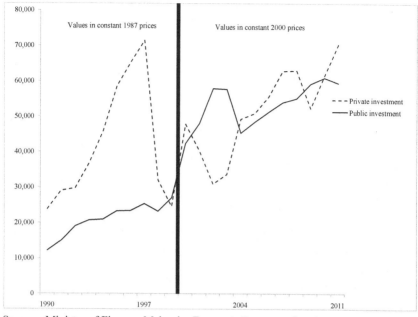

Sources: Ministry of Finance, Malaysia, *Economic Report*, various issues.

Figure 1.4 Malaysia: Government Spending on Investment and Consumption, 1991–2012

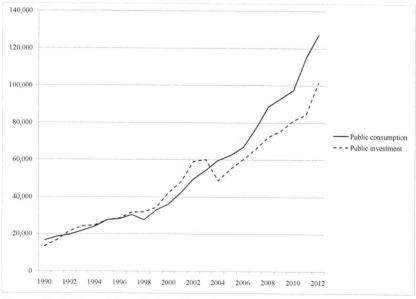

Sources: Bank Negara Malaysia, *Monthly Bulletin of Statistics*, various issues.

involved a significant fiscal deficit since 1998, which has been propping up economic growth. Clearly, the 5+ per cent average post-crisis growth rate — in contrast to the 8+ per cent earlier — has been largely due to greater government spending.

A temporary increase in government spending during a downturn is desirable from a counter-cyclical point of view, but this stance since 1998 for a decade and a half cannot be reasonably characterized as counter-cyclical, having been sustained through the global economic boom during the middle of the last decade. Of course, deficit funded development expenditure can also be justified, but government consumption expenditure has increasingly outstripped government investment spending since 2004, i.e. after Mahathir's exit (Figure 1.4). This consistent government support for growth through fiscal deficits for a decade and a half has only been possible because of revenue streams associated with oil wealth.

Clearly, domestic investor confidence fell significantly after the 1997–1998 crisis. Many observers attribute the decline of private investment to the collapse of FDI, believing that foreign investment leads, and domestic investment follows. On the contrary, the evidence generally supports the converse proposition, namely that domestic investment leads and foreign investment follows. But FDI was never really all that high, and has remained more or less at the same level since the mid-1990s, i.e. before and after the 1997–1998 crisis (Figure 1.5). This is an important reversal of conventional economic wisdom about the ostensibly leading role of FDI.

After Mahathir

The preceding discussion ends with the Mahathir era, more specifically with the major policy changes following the 1997–1998 Asian financial crisis. With the benefit of hindsight, this has been the defining watershed for the economic policy context since. In some crucial respects, there have not been major fundamental policy changes since then. Undoubtedly, the next Prime Minister, Abdullah Ahmad Badawi was expected by his supporters to return to the NEP's emphasis on economic redistribution, especially in favour of ethnic Malays. However, he disappointed many

Figure 1.5 Malaysia: Gross Domestic Investment and Net FDI Inflows as Share of GDP, 1987–2012

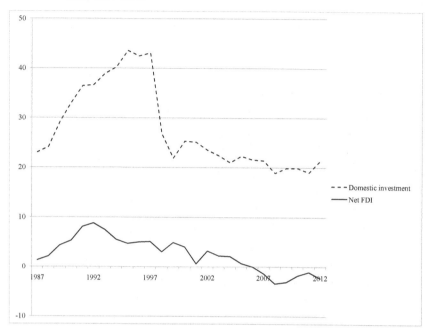

Sources: Calculated with data from Bank Negara Malaysia, *Monthly Bulletin of Statistics*, various issues.

such supporters. Along similar lines, Abdullah also emphasized greater attention to agriculture, which most observers acknowledge was largely neglected by Mahathir despite its continued importance and growth during his long tenure. But despite some real attempts to give greater attention to agricultural development, Abdullah's five year tenure is now seen as having achieved little beyond a rhetorical return to agriculture.

Although he began by securing the biggest parliamentary majority ever for the ruling coalition in the first post-Mahathir general elections in 2004, the ruling coalition performed poorly against the Anwar Ibrahim-led opposition coalition in the 2008 general elections. This led to Abdullah's early ouster in favour of his party and government deputy, Najib Abdul Razak. Besides the opposition coalition, Abdullah had come under intense pressure from his own party, with the internal party opposition believed to have been led by Mahathir.

Since taking over as Prime Minister in 2009, Najib has cast himself in the image of a modernizing economic and political liberal of sorts while remaining mindful of the potential dangers posed by such internal opposition. Failing to create the conditions for a renewed manufacturing boom, he has instead emphasized modern, high value-added services. Meanwhile, he has sought to justify his liberalizing economic measures as necessary to restore Malaysian economic competitiveness, not only to attract new investments, especially from abroad, but also to overcome an ostensible economic growth *cul de sac* faced by middle income countries. However, average growth rates have remained largely the same in the last post-Mahathir decade, mainly supported by government spending.

Examining the sources of Malaysian economic growth leads to counter-intuitive findings from the perspective of conventional economic wisdom. Why are there serious problems in sustaining growth in Malaysia? One problem has been its weak industrialist class, allowing finance to become more dominant and influential. This is true in several neighbouring Southeast Asian countries as well, and is not a peculiarly Malaysian phenomenon. Nevertheless, the consequences have been quite important, especially in contributing to the 1997–1998 financial crisis (Jomo 1998, 2001).

Over the last decade, the middle income country 'cul-de-sac' argument — arguing that there is a limit to how much manufacturing growth can sustain rising incomes — has gained popularity. As Figure 1.6 suggests, Malaysia's fastest manufacturing growth was probably achieved just before the 1997–1998 Asian crisis. Ever since then, manufacturing expansion has been less impressive and significant for Malaysian economic growth.

One important measure to break out of the 'middle income trap' would be the formulation and implementation of effective and sustained industrial policy. Industrial policy — or more accurately, investment and technology policy — is not only relevant for the manufacturing sector. Such policy, for example, could be used to promote the development of high-end services as well.

But all this is not going to happen spontaneously. Such new activities would need to be deliberately induced and developed through a variety of interventions — not 'one-shot' interventions, but rather, well-designed, coherent and sustained interventions. But such sustained interventions are often associated with protracted, dirigiste government rule. In Malaysia,

Figure 1.6 Malaysia: Structural Change, 1970–2012

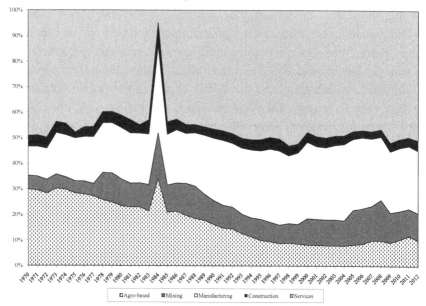

Note: 1970–77 GDP in constant 1970 prices, 1978–1999 GDP in constant 1978 prices; 2000–
          2004 GDP in constant 2000 prices and 2005–2012 GDP in constant 2005 prices.
Sources: Calculated with data from Ministry of Finance, Malaysia, *Economic Report*, various
          issues.

the ruling coalition has remained the same since independence, but there have been considerable changes in policy emphasis, especially during the Mahathir era (1981–2003). More importantly, there have not been sustained policy priorities or implementation.

A quick comparison between Southeast and Northeast Asia reveals that the main difference between Southeast and Northeast Asia is how the two sub-regions have developed. From the outset, Southeast Asia's recent economic development has been inferior to Northeast Asia's. Comparing growth rates before the Asian crisis, Southeast Asia was averaging about 6 per cent while Northeast Asia was averaging about 8 per cent on a per capita basis. Another difference is that Southeast Asia's population was growing at a much faster rate than Northeast Asia's. As a consequence, the two per cent became almost three per cent on a per capita basis. The two per cent difference extended about over a quarter of a century has had a very significant impact for their economic development.

Also, there has been less policy space and initiative in Southeast Asia. While the Southeast Asian region has privileged FDI, Northeast Asia has gone out of its way to support an autochthonous industrial community. For political reasons, Malaysia and Singapore have been the most FDI oriented. Southeast Asia has been much more reliant than Northeast Asia on FDI. In Northeast Asia, before the end of the 20th century, FDI accounted for less than 2 per cent of gross domestic capital formation. In Southeast Asia, FDI generally averaged more than the developing country average of about 5 to 6 per cent. In Malaysia, the FDI share of gross domestic capital formation was long in double digits. In Singapore, the FDI share has been even higher than in Malaysia, but it has been able to successfully pursue FDI-led industrialization with a clearer and more elaborate strategy on leveraging FDI strengths.

Malaysia's poor emulation of Singapore in this regard has become quite problematic as high levels of FDI have basically meant limited manufacturing capabilities and capacities, with the process of industrialization heavily reliant on foreign capital, markets, technology and management, and hence, less sustainable. Not surprisingly then, Malaysia has a weak industrialist class. In the absence of a strong industrial class, financial rentiers — as Keynes put it, often influential with the state — have become more dominant in influencing policy making and priorities.

There is a critical need to re-examine the claim that the country has a 'middle-income country trap' problem, as suggested in the last decade by the World Bank for Malaysia and elsewhere. One has instead to look at what underlies the economic phenomena associated with the alleged 'middle-income country trap'[2]. Following the 2008–2009 crisis, rich countries have become more protectionist, while developing countries can no longer rely on export-oriented growth, but have limited domestic markets which they cannot easily turn back to. It is not easy to just switch policies at will, e.g. WTO trade commitments cannot be reversed. Capacities have already been developed in many developing economies for export orientation, but many parts of the world, including Southeast Asia, are now being told to rely less on export-led growth and to focus instead on domestic markets.

In Southeast Asia, there is little strong empirical basis for the common claim that productivity trends have not kept up with wage trends.

Productivity and wage rates are not directly related, as suggested by neoclassical economic theory[3]. In the post-war industrialized economies, workers were able to capture part of their productivity gains in the form of higher wages or remuneration, at least until recently. But in most developing countries, until mass unemployment and underemployment is eliminated, there is less pressure to push up wages due to weak unions, etc. So, for example, China is just beginning to see real wage increases, partly due to deliberate government policy, including the renminbi or yuan appreciation of recent years, but also because labour supplies have been exhausted and skill requirements are going up as China moves rapidly into higher value-added production. However, in recent decades, Malaysia and Thailand have seen increases in wage rates after 'full employment' was achieved in the 1990s. Yet, Malaysia is not considered a high-cost destination for investment. In the last decade, Kuala Lumpur has come to be considered a lower cost investment location than Bangkok.

One big problem in Southeast Asia generally (with Singapore a very important exception in this regard) is the lack of explicit industrial policy. And where it exists in the region, industrial policy has been weak, compromised or inconsistent. It is not that there have been no efforts at formulating industrial policy. There have been several such efforts in Malaysia, but they have not been sustained or well implemented. As a consequence, a strong industrial capitalist class is absent as FDI has been favoured instead.

During the 1970s, per capita growth was actually higher than in the 1960s for a variety of reasons. Besides a successful adoption of export-oriented industrialization, much of the growth was sustained by the government's enhanced fiscal means. Public investments continued to sustain rapid growth in the first half of the 1980s, although they were more narrowly focused on heavy industries.

Before the 1980s, the fiscal deficits were financed by government borrowings from forced savings in the Employees Provident Fund (EPF). The advent of significant oil revenues from the mid-1970s gave much more fiscal space to the authorities. For a variety of reasons — including the change in tax structure after 1984, justified as inducing more private investment — much less fiscal space has been available since the 1980s. The government began borrowing heavily from abroad, ironically as real interest rates rose sharply from 1981, due to US Fed actions. Soon after Malaysia began borrowing heavily from Japan, which continued to offer relatively lower interest rates, the yen almost doubled in value against the ringgit between 1984 and, say, 1987. As a consequence, the government authorities have not been able to do as much as they were able to in the past.

As with Indonesia, and Thailand, the high growth experienced by Malaysia after the mid-1980s can be attributed to the deliberately depreciated exchange rates in the mid-1980s. Over this period, the Malaysian ringgit depreciated slightly against the US dollar during 1984-1987, from RM2.4 to RM2.7 against the US dollar. Indonesia had long depreciated its exchange rate, and had three devaluations in the mid-1980s, from 1984 to 1987 while Thailand had a major depreciation in 1985. But the strength of the yen grew in the period of the 'high yen' (*endaka*) from 1985 to 1995, especially after the Plaza II agreement of September 1985. Thus, the modest depreciation of the ringgit against the US dollar meant an even greater depreciation against the yen, but also the Korean won, the new Taiwan dollar, the Singapore dollar, the Deutschemark and others. The ringgit depreciation thus lowered production costs in Malaysia for prospective foreign investors.

The country was thus able to attract investment, not only from Japan, but also from the other first generation East Asian newly industrialized economies. Although not all that successful operationally, the SIJORI (Singapore–Johor–Riau) 'growth triangle' was a very important co-operative arrangement committing to the transfer of economic activities, particularly in manufacturing and related service activities, from Singapore into its immediate Southeast Asian periphery, particularly into the southern Peninsular Malaysian state of Johor.

Another popular argument is that Malaysia's preoccupation with redistribution since the 1970s has been the problem. But economic redistribution initiatives during the 1970s were associated with and contributed to rapid economic growth. Hence, it is difficult to sustain the argument that redistribution inherently subverts growth. In fact, recent analyses of the factors impeding economic recovery have come to consider growing inequality to be an obstacle to sustaining growth. Nevertheless, it is quite possible that certain redistributive measures in particular contexts may well impede growth. Hence, it is important to look at specific redistribution measures in order to ascertain if and how they may have subverted growth, rather than just making the blanket assertion that redistribution is either good or bad for growth.

In Malaysia, it is now widely believed that ostensible economic recovery efforts since 1997 have often been 'compromised' by giving 'jobs to the boys' with political connections. Government contracts and privatization projects have often been suspected of going to the politically well-connected, rather than on the basis of best bids or demonstrated capacities and capabilities. This is the reason why government investments have not been as effective in contributing to sustained growth as they had been. Government investments can undoubtedly induce or 'crowd in' — rather than 'crowd out' — private investments, but this is not ensured and has to be well managed to ensure desired outcomes.

Policy Lessons

Malaysia has gone through several different development strategies in the half century since Malaysia's formation in 1963. Its economic development policy has been primarily shaped by the nature of the regimes, the dominant interests represented, and their respective views of what would be desirable to advance their own interests and to secure legitimacy in order to remain in power. The second and third premiers, covering the first half of OPP1 for the NEP in the 1970s, are considered together in this review. Three distinct phases are identified with Mahathir's 22 year tenure.

In the face of a communist-led insurgency during the late colonial period of the early and mid-1950s, the British government initiated social reforms. The social reforms included rural development efforts to consolidate a Malay yeoman peasantry, protect labour and allow limited popular political participation through elections. In the first dozen or so years after independence in August 1957, largely laissez faire policies were pursued by the first Prime Minister, Tunku Abdul Rahman. These were complemented by 'mild' IS industrialization, some agricultural diversification, greater rural development efforts and modest, but increasing ethnic affirmative action policies.

The next dozen years saw growing state intervention under the second and third relation Prime Ministers, Razak Hussein (1970–1976) and Hussein Onn (1976–1981). The NEP provided the legitimization for increasing state intervention and public sector expansion, especially for inter-ethnic redistribution. Meanwhile, EO industrialization from the late 1960s succeeded in reducing unemployment, while increased petroleum revenues financed rapidly growing public expenditure.

The heavy industrialization push began under the leadership of Malaysia's fourth Prime Minister, Mahathir Mohamad, during the early and mid-1980s. Counter-cyclical expansionary public expenditure expansion from 1980 was followed by cuts from mid-1982. However, government-sponsored joint ventures with Japanese firms to develop heavy industries — constituting a second round of import-substitution — grew in the face of declining foreign investments. The economic slowdown and other difficulties of the mid-1980s led to some economic and cultural liberalization. Massive ringgit depreciation from the mid-1980s was accompanied by privatization, greater official support for the private sector, increased investment incentives and regressive 'supply side oriented' tax reforms.

Significant relocation of manufacturing investments from Japan and the other first-generation newly industrialized East Asian economies resulted in a decade of sustained growth and rapid industrialization in Malaysia and its immediate neighbours. These policies were reversed by the regional economic crisis in 1997–1998, which led to increased government intervention, especially to protect politically influential Malaysian business interests.

Malaysia's development experiences since independence for Malaya in 1957 suggests at least five distinct periods of development policy. Policy changes were generally preceded by political changes, such as the political crisis culminating in the events of May 1969. During Mahathir's long tenure from 1981, policy changes were driven by economic crises — in 1981–1982, 1985–1986 and 1997–1998. With the benefit of hindsight, it is clear that new policies responded to seeming problems and failures of earlier policies.

However, it is difficult to evaluate the successes or failures simply in terms of subsequent economic performance. Malaysia's very open economy has meant that it has often been subject to circumstances not of its own choosing or making. The decline of rubber prices in the 1960s must surely have affected economic performance and policy. Malaysia's experiment with import-substituting industrialization under foreign (principally British) auspices was quite different from most other developing countries. SOEs in the other countries played leading roles, and effective protection was conditional on export promotion in Northeast Asia. Malaysia's transformation from net oil importer to exporter in the mid-1970s, when petroleum prices rose sharply, allowed the government to spend much more and to borrow from abroad at low cost. This went on until the Volcker intervention of the early 1980s precipitated a global recession, bringing commodity prices down. The Plaza Accord of September 1985 led to the strong yen just as Malaysia's sovereign foreign debt became yen-denominated. Limits on private foreign borrowings from abroad were imposed, limiting vulnerability on that front.

The 1980s' recession precipitated a banking crisis, which led to banking reform. But the reforms from the mid-1980s also involved significant economic deregulation, including financial liberalization, which eventually culminated in the 1997–1998 crisis. The impact of Mahathir's controversial measures of early September as he moved to politically eliminate his deputy cannot be properly evaluated as the East Asian economic recovery from the last quarter of 1998 followed after the Russian and Long-Term Capital Management (LTCM) crises.

The very different economic policies pursued over the last half century as well as the often crucial role of exogenous circumstances makes evaluation of Malaysian economic development strategy very complicated. Malaysia is considered successful because of its generally rapid rates of economic growth and structural transformation over this period. These achievements are often attributed by the Washington-based Bretton Woods institutions to its exceptionally open economy, in terms of trade and reliance on FDI, relatively low inflation, management of resource wealth and the political stability of its multi-ethnic society.

In such approving accounts, two periods tend to be emphasized — the 1970s, which is associated with EO industrialization, and the second Mahathir period, i.e. the decade from 1988 to 1997, when there was a return to such EO industrialization. Other aspects of these periods are less mentioned, e.g. the huge growth of state intervention and the public sector in the 1970s or Mahathir's other more heterodox policies. The IS industrialization of the 1960s and early 1980s are seen as mistakes overcome by subsequent policies, while most government roles beyond macroeconomic management, infrastructure as well as basic social provisioning and maintaining law and order are considered to be undermining good governance.

The growing dominance of UMNO in the ruling coalition has meant that inter-ethnic redistribution, particularly to benefit politically connected business interests, has been the major underlying theme of much policy reform over the years. The regime's electoral longevity has not only relied on the advantages of long-term incumbency, superior financial resources, a virtual media monopoly as well as an effectively controlled electoral system, but has also depended on its ability to deliver sustained economic growth, 'law and order' as well as some basic infrastructure and social provisioning.

Malaysia has also been successful in leading in the production and even the processing of several primary commodities such as tin, rubber, palm oil, timber and cocoa, while its state-owned petroleum company has been better managed than most. It was also a leader in producing several electronics components and other manufactured products such as air-conditioners, airplane tyres and rubber gloves. However, it now appears to have lost its lead in many of these, particularly with the rise of China as the manufacturing workshop for the world. Further, its car, steel and multimedia software initiatives under Mahathir appear less than successful.[4]

The preceding survey has highlighted how policies changed, why they changed as well as their outcomes or consequences. It has highlighted the domestic as well as international conditions prevailing. Some of the discussion has indicated the changing educational characteristics of the labour force with some mention of changing employment and income distribution along ethnic lines, as inter-ethnic disparities remain the major concern of public policy in Malaysia.

It is generally agreed that most of Peninsular Malaysia's arable land was under cultivation by the 1980s while the debate on the remaining scope for agricultural expansion in the Borneo states of Sabah and

Sarawak continue to be dated. Perhaps more importantly, it is now generally acknowledged that Malaysian agriculture only remains viable due to the continued availability of less well remunerated immigrant labour since the 1980s, especially from Indonesia and the Indian subcontinent. Owing to its economic significance for the British Empire, Peninsular Malaysia's infrastructure has been quite well developed since the colonial period, while post-colonial infrastructure developments have continued to support economic development with criticisms of wasteful state support for such construction in recent decades.

It is then suggested that trade liberalization and policies favouring FDI will lead to comparable growth and development as Malaysia, often been cited as an open economy which has successfully achieved economic development. A more nuanced understanding of what actually happened in Malaysia suggests a more complex experience with different policy lessons. During the colonial period, the British colonial power minimized export taxes on tin and rubber, dominated by British corporate interests. Instead, 'sin' taxes on opium, alcohol, gambling and prostitution figured much more prominently before the Second World War, especially in the Straits Settlements ports under direct British control. British Malaya's export earnings after the war were the main source of foreign exchange for the Empire and British reconstruction after the War. Imperial preference meant less taxes on imports from Britain compared to those from outside the empire and this continued for a time after independence as Commonwealth preference.

After independence, tariffs were imposed on some imports to favour the new import-substituting industries being promoted by the government in the early 1960s and early 1980s. Meanwhile, taxes on smallholders were reduced to secure their electoral support. From the early 1970s, the Free Trade Zones Act enabled the establishment of customs-exempt export processing zones as well as light manufacturing warehouses to promote EO industrialization. These were augmented by the provision of infrastructure and other indirect subsidies as well as labour and training policies.

The privileged role of foreign investments in post-colonial Malaysia can be traced to the bargain made with the Malayan elite before in-dependence in the face of a communist-led radical nationalist insurgency which threatened to nationalize British corporate interests. FDI was also encouraged to offset the ubiquitous Chinese business presence and its likely ascendance after independence and to secure advanced technology, access to foreign markets and foreign corporate expertise[5]. Some investment regulation (e.g. the 1975 ICA) and other constraints on ethnic Chinese capital accumulation may well have prevented a greater role for Malaysian entrepreneurship and corporate expansion comparable to Japan, Korea and Taiwan Province of China. Various investment promotion policies over the decades have sought to encourage investments in particular sectors and industries.

To equate such measures with an economy open to trade and FDI obfuscates the crucial role of selective interventions to promote certain investments and technology upgrading. Except for the government's agricultural promotion initiatives, such efforts have declined in the last half decade since Mahathir's retirement. The decline of the efforts have been associated with more modest growth at a time when many other developing countries have actually accelerated economic growth with higher primary commodity prices due to higher demand as well as low interest rates due to US Federal Reserve Bank interventions.

More of the same policies are probably inadequate in the face of the changed world economic situation. Rather, more sophisticated, consistent and pragmatic investment and technology policies will probably need to be sustained for some time to pave the conditions for a new phase of economic development cognizant of existing problems and weaknesses, as well as strengths and potential. Unfortunately, the conditions for an informed public debate in Malaysia over the basic contours of such policy have not existed because of the continuing preoccupation with inter-ethnic distributional issues and the continuing ideological denial of the role of industrial policy in Malaysian economic development.

In the 12th Malaysian general election on 8 March 2008, the ruling coalition lost its two-thirds parliamentary majority for the first time since 1969, with its simple majority crucially dependent on the less Malay and Muslim Borneo states of Sabah and Sarawak as well as the southern peninsular state of Johor. For the first time ever, five states in the peninsula — Selangor, Perak, Kedah and Penang besides Kelantan, which has been under PAS leadership since 1989 — are now under the governments led by the People's Alliance (Pakatan Rakyat). The gerrymandering and changing boundaries of constituencies in recent years have favoured multi-ethnic coalitions in the peninsula, which served the opposition this time as it forged a credible multi-ethnic coalition under the leadership of former Deputy Prime Minister Anwar Ibrahim.

Since the election, various opposition controlled state governments have started taking actions favouring the poor, though their fiscal means are very circumscribed. The impact of state government programmes will not be as great as those of the federal government, with its larger revenue base and fiscal capacity. Soon after the election, the federal government announced its withdrawal from earlier commitments to various programmes for these states. The federal government has also announced its intention to channel funds to the states through federal-controlled agencies such as MARA, rather than through the opposition-controlled SEDCs, adopting the *modus operandi* used for the lone opposition-controlled Kelantan state previously.

Most importantly, the election forced the early retirement of UMNO President and Prime Minister Abdullah Badawi in favour of his government and party deputy, Najib Abdul Razak. Najib introduced several economic and political modernization and liberalization measures, enhancing his personal political popularity with little advantage to his dominant UMNO party, or even the ruling Barisan Nasional coalition. He abandoned Abdullah's feeble attempts to revive agriculture, instead focusing on financial and other modern services, including a highly publicized government transformation program.

In the May 2013 13th general election, the ruling Barisan Nasional lost a plurality of the popular vote, but retained three-fifths of parliamentary seats. The BN also recaptured the Kedah State government, leaving three States in opposition hands: Kelantan had been held by the opposition PAS Islamic party since 1989 (and before that, from 1959 to 1978). The DAP led Penang government increased its State Assembly seats after capturing the State in 2008 while the PKR led Selangor government significantly increased its share of seats in the State Assembly after capturing the State at the same time. The BN's political success in retaining control of the Federal and most State governments continues to be largely due to its effective control of the electoral system (Elections

Commission and its effective gerrymandering of the electoral process), most of the broadcast and print media, other profitable businesses and various other Federal and State Government resources.

Nevertheless, it retains popular electoral support, especially in the countryside in much of the country, by presenting itself as the guardian of a particular, albeit evolving ethno-populist developmentalism. Hence, economic, including development policies cannot simply be reduced to and explained by rent-seeking, although there remains a great deal of it. Even corruption and abuses of power (involving rent appropriation) are presented to presumed clientelistic ethnic electorates as the unavoidably necessary costs of political arrangements and compromises to retain power in order to deliver development and thus enhance their economic welfare. Ironically then, the very market and rights ideologies associated with economic liberalism offer a powerful critique to such ethno-populist developmentalism as publics increasingly recognize alternative views of entitlements.

Notes

1. The then Finance Minister's original six bank proposal, widely suspected as intended to give him greater personal control of the banking sector, was revised. Some concessions were given to those with access to Prime Minister Mahathir, who intervened after some special pleading by those with access to him.

2. This hypothesis has its origins in Latin America which achieved higher incomes than Southeast Asia much earlier. As the limits of import substitution were achieved, economic growth often gave way to stagnation and high inflation by the early 1970s when higher oil prices became the explanation. However, higher commodity prices and the availability of cheap credit, thanks to recycled petrodollars, saw resumed growth until the US Fed raised interest rates from late 1980 precipitating fiscal and debt crises in Latin America and elsewhere. This gave rise to stabilization and structural adjustment programmes associated with the Washington Consensus, which resulted in a Latin American 'lost decade' that seemed to stretch beyond for many economies. Over the last three decades, Latin American countries have liberalized their economies, and not only in terms of trade. Their capital accounts have been opened, and foreign investment has been encouraged. In spite of these measures, there has not been significant progress in Latin America since the 1980s compared to East Asia. In fact, the limited industrial capacities developed in the earlier period were considered 'undesirable' and have often been lost with the reforms.

3. In fact, productivity itself has not been the issue. What has happened is that, in many developing countries, the subsistence wage is the prevailing wage rate floor or subsistence wage in the classical economic (Arthur Lewis) sense.

4.   In this connection, it is worth noting that despite the availability of natural rubber and petroleum (for synthetic rubber) in Malaysia, the Republic of Korea has been far more successful in producing and exporting rubber tyres. Also, Korea's Pohang Steel Corporation (Posco) worked successfully with Nippon Steel to become the world's most efficient steel producer in the 1980s and 1990s while Malaysia's Perwaja has been an expensive failure.

5.   FDI was promoted in Singapore to ensure a strong international commitment to the survival of the island republic after its 1965 secession from the Malaysian federation.

Part 2

Distribution

Economic distribution issues, especially inter-ethnic disparities, have long dominated social, economic and political discourses in Malaysia. Part Two summarizes available evidence on economic distribution in the country. After briefly reviewing poverty trends and household income distribution in the country since 1970, the discussion reviews the spatial distribution of the population, labour force participation and unemployment rates, education level, wage rates as well as industry, employment and occupational status. These are reviewed in terms of ethnicity (or race, the preferred term in Malaysia), gender and state or region in so far as information is available.

The major source of household income has been from employment, which this Part will focus on. It starts with labour force characteristics such as the participation rate, education level and employment status. It then relates these characteristics to race and gender. Unemployment by race and state, occupational status and mobility by race and gender, as well as wage rate by occupational status and industry all influence household income inequality. Industrial wage rates by state provide a picture of regional disparities, which may be traced to uneven structural changes, partly due to economic development strategies and performance, investment rates and labour migration.

Following the events of May 1969, the Malaysian government began to report on poverty on a regular basis. Economic growth since Malayan independence in 1957 and the formation of Malaysia in 1963 has lifted most boats, thus drastically decreasing the incidence of poverty (Table 2.1). However, such improvements have been uneven as this Part's focus on distribution matters will elaborate. The official poverty rate has fallen considerably, especially in the 1970s and early 1980s, although there is some debate on the measurement of poverty generally as well as in Malaysia. Nevertheless, official figures suggest significant improvements in general living standards in Malaysia, not only in urban areas, but also in the countryside. The incidence of poverty in rural areas has been higher, increasing from less than three times that for urban areas in 1970 to almost five times in 2009. There have also been major differences in poverty rates among the states in the federation (Table 2.2).

Income Distribution

Malaysian economic development over the decades has involved much structural change, with considerable changes in employment, occupation, income and poverty. As household incomes have increased (Table 2.3),

Table 2.1 Malaysia: Incidence of Poverty, 1970–2009[a] (%)

Year	Rural	Urban	Total
1970[b]	58.7	21.3	49.3
1976	45.7	15.4	37.7
1979	45.8	17.5	37.4
1984	27.3	8.5	20.7
1987	24.8	8.5	19.4
1989	21.1	7.1	17.1
1992	18.2	4.7	12.4
1995	14.9	3.6	8.7
1997	10.9	2.1	6.1
1999[c]	14.8	3.3	8.5
2002	13.5	2.3	6.0
2004	11.9	2.5	8.4
2007	7.1	2.0	3.6
2009	8.4	1.7	3.8

Notes: [a] Data from 1989 is for Malaysian citizens only.
         [b] Peninsular Malaysia only.
         [c] Data from 1999 is based on 2005 methodology.
Source: Economic Planning Unit (http://www.epu.gov.my/c/document_library/get_file?uuid=5bf3a7ca-37a7-4ebb-96c6-634ce17141dc&groupId=34492).

Table 2.2 Malaysia: Incidence of Poverty by State, 1970–2009 (%)

	1970	1976	1979	1984	1987	1989[a]	1992	1995	1997	1999[b]	2002	2004	2007	2009
More developed states														
Johor	45.7	29.0	18.2	12.2	11.1	9.8	5.6	3.1	1.6	3.2	2.5	2.0	1.5	1.3
Melaka	44.9	32.4	20.4	15.8	11.7	12.4	8.5	5.3	3.5	2.9	1.8	1.8	1.8	0.5
Negri Sembilan	44.8	33.0	26.3	13.0	21.5	9.1	8.1	4.9	4.7	4.1	2.6	1.4	1.3	0.7
Perak	48.6	43.0	30.5	20.3	19.9	19.2	10.2	9.1	4.5	6.9	6.2	4.9	3.4	3.5
Pulau Pinang	43.7	32.4	19.7	13.4	12.9	8.7	4.0	4.0	1.7	0.7	1.2	0.3	1.4	1.2
Selangor	29.2	22.9	14.5	8.6	8.9	7.6	4.3	2.2	1.3	1.9	1.1	1.0	0.7	0.7
Less developed states														
Kedah	63.2	61.1	53.8	36.6	31.3	29.9	21.1	12.2	11.5	14.2	9.7	7.0	3.1	5.3
Kelantan	76.1	67.1	55.0	39.2	31.6	29.6	25.9	22.9	19.2	15.2	17.8	10.6	7.2	4.8
Perlis	43.2	38.9	26.9	15.7	12.3	10.0	6.9	6.8	4.4	9.8	9.4	4.0	1.7	2.1
Pahang	73.9	59.8	63.1	33.7	29.1	17.4	19.8	11.8	10.7	13.6	8.9	6.3	7.0	6.0
Sabah	n.a.	58.3	40.7	33.1	35.3	27.9	27.8	22.6	16.5	23.4	16.0	23.0	16.0	19.2
Sarawak	n.a.	56.5	47.8	31.9	24.7	21.0	19.2	10.0	7.3	10.9	11.3	7.5	4.2	5.3
Terengganu	68.9	60.3	53.3	28.9	36.1	31.3	25.6	23.4	17.3	22.7	14.9	15.4	6.5	4.0
Malaysia	49.3	37.7	37.4	20.7	19.4	16.5	12.4	8.7	6.1	8.5	6.0	5.7	3.6	3.8

Notes: n.a. – not available.
  [a] Data from 1989 is for Malaysian citizens only.
  [b] Data from 1999 is based on 2005 methodology.

Source: Economic Planning Unit (http://www.epu.gov.my/c/document_library/get_file?uuid=5bf3a7ca-37a7-4ebb-96c6-634ce17141dc&groupId=34492).

Table 2.3 Malaysia: Gross Monthly Household Income, 1970–2009 (RM)

Year	Income
1970[a]	264
1974	362
1976	505
1979	678
1984	1,098
1987	1,083
1989[b]	1,169
1992	1,563
1995	2,020
1997	2,606
1999	2,472
2002	3,011
2004	3,249
2007	3,686
2009	4,025

Notes: [a] Peninsular Malaysia only.
         [b] Data from 1989 is for Malaysian citizens only.
Source: Economic Planning Unit (http://www.epu.gov.my/c/document_library/get_
         file?uuid=e2b128f0-c6fb-4980-8a17-3f708fc3d7a8&groupId=34492).

gains from this growth and related wealth accumulation have been unevenly distributed. Malaysia is said to have one of the highest Gini coefficients, the most commonly used measure of inequality, in East Asia for household income. However, Table 2.4 suggests that Malaysia's Gini coefficient has continued to decline, albeit unevenly, since 1970, from 0.513 in 1970 to 0.441 in 2009. Household income surveys in Malaysia only began in 1984, with the Gini coefficient initially declining from 0.483 in 1984 before the Gini for citizens only rose from 0.422 in 1989 to 0.441 in 2009. The Gini index fell following the 1997-1998 crisis, and has declined slightly since 2004, but has remained higher than in 1989.

Unlike many other countries, official Malaysian data for the last two decades suggest a decline in overall household income inequality, not just of inter-ethnic disparities. In contrast, most other countries in the West, the former Soviet Union, China and most developing countries experienced rising inequality over the same period. Only Northern Europe

Table 2.4 Malaysia: Gini Coefficients, 1970–2009

	1970[a]	1974[a]	1976[b]	1979	1984	1987[a]	1989[b]	1992	1995	1997	1999	2002	2004	2007	2009
Stratum															
Urban	n.a.	0.541	0.531	0.491	0.468	0.449	0.444	0.439	0.431	0.427	0.432	0.439	0.444	0.427	0.423
Rural	n.a.	0.473	0.540	0.471	0.450	0.427	0.416	0.401	0.410	0.424	0.421	0.405	0.397	0.388	0.407
Ethnicity															
Bumiputera	0.466	0.476	0.506	0.468	0.464	0.447	0.429	0.442	0.441	0.448	0.433	0.435	0.452	0.430	0.440
Chinese	0.466	0.520	0.541	0.474	0.452	0.428	0.419	0.420	0.428	0.416	0.434	0.455	0.446	0.432	0.425
Indian	0.472	0.451	0.509	0.460	0.419	0.402	0.390	0.402	0.404	0.409	0.411	0.399	0.425	0.414	0.424
Malaysia	0.513	0.530	0.577	0.505	0.483	0.456	0.422	0.459	0.456	0.459	0.443	0.461	0.462	0.441	0.441

Notes: n.a. – not available

[a] For Peninsular Malaysia only.

[b] Data from 1989 is for Malaysian citizens only.

Source: Economic Planning Unit (http://www.epu.gov.my/c/document_library/get_file?uuid=bc7f0f87-72d4-48d8-8c8f-65920e480738&groupid=34492).

Table 2.5 Malaysia: Monthly Household Income by Stratum and Ethnicity, 1970–2009 (RM)

	1970[a]	1974[a]	1976	1979	1984	1987	1989[b]	1992	1995	1997	1999	2002	2004	2007	2009
Stratum															
Urban (U)	428	570	843	1045	1573	1488	1606	2050	2589	3357	3103	3652	3956	4356	4705
Rural (R)	200	269	385	523	842	881	957	1009	1326	1704	1718	1729	1875	2283	2545
U/R	2.14	2.12	2.19	2.00	1.87	1.69	1.68	2.03	1.95	1.97	1.81	2.11	2.11	1.91	1.85
Urban															
Top 20%	–	1798	2384	2827	4114	2968	4068	5133	6474	8470	7580	9085	9863	10567	11348
Middle 40%	–	441	663	869	1355	1244	1426	1812	2323	3000	2844	3265	3524	3947	4296
Bottom 40%	–	172	255	331	521	549	583	748	942	1193	1155	1344	1450	1655	1794
Top/Bottom	–	10.45	9.35	8.54	7.90	5.41	6.98	6.86	6.87	7.10	6.56	6.76	6.80	6.38	6.33
Rural															
Top 20%	–	735	1051	1365	2110	1756	2270	2332	3153	4130	4124	4057	4330	5220	6033
Middle 40%	–	240	328	457	756	764	871	946	1235	1564	1577	1612	1762	2104	2313
Bottom 40%	–	92	109	169	292	333	371	410	515	649	670	699	783	994	1033
Top/Bottom	–	7.99	9.64	8.08	7.23	5.27	6.12	5.69	6.12	6.36	6.16	5.80	5.53	5.25	5.84
Ethnicity															
Bumiputera (B)	172	242	345[a]	492	844	868	940	1237	1604	2038	1984	2376	2711	3156	3624
Chinese (C)	394	534	787[a]	1002	1552	1488	1631	2196	2890	3738	3456	4279	4437	4853	5011
Indian (I)	304	408	518[a]	756	1107	1105	1209	1597	2140	2896	2702	3044	3456	3799	3999
C/B	2.29	2.21	2.28[a]	2.04	1.84	1.71	1.74	1.78	1.80	1.83	1.74	1.80	1.64	1.54	1.38
I/B	1.77	1.69	1.50[a]	1.54	1.31	1.27	1.29	1.29	1.33	1.42	1.36	1.28	1.27	1.20	1.10
C/I	1.30	1.31	1.52[a]	1.33	1.40	1.35	1.35	1.38	1.35	1.29	1.28	1.41	1.28	1.28	1.25

Table 2.5 (continued)

	1970[a]	1974[a]	1976	1979	1984	1987	1989[b]	1992	1995	1997	1999	2002	2004	2007	2009
Bumiputera															
Top 20%	444	669	849[a]	1274	2176	1726	2264	3100	3986	5195	4855	5849	6877	7666	8976
Middle 40%	151	209	264[a]	429	738	740	832	1093	1461	1795	1810	2167	2408	2863	3272
Bottom 40%	57	84	84[a]	164	285	322	356	449	572	724	742	868	952	1194	1300
Top/Bottom	7.79	7.96	10.10[a]	7.77	7.64	5.36	6.36	6.90	6.97	7.18	6.54	6.74	7.22	6.42	6.90
Chinese															
Top 20%	1036	1644	2085[a]	2630	3953	2959	3925	5348	7270	9246	8470	10914	11131	11878	12152
Middle 40%	331	424	509[a]	859	1363	1289	1482	1973	2560	3405	3168	3780	3951	4389	4560
Bottom 40%	136	180	202[a]	331	541	581	633	842	1062	1356	1271	1485	1597	1805	1897
Top/Bottom	7.62	9.13	10.32[a]	7.95	7.31	5.09	6.20	6.35	6.85	6.82	6.66	7.35	6.97	6.58	6.41
Indian															
Top 20%	821	1071	1585[a]	1966	2694	2127	2844	3743	5100	7038	6456	7055	8405	9119	9774
Middle 40%	237	337	419[a]	636	974	946	1093	1458	1954	2606	2460	2860	3116	3393	3569
Bottom 40%	112	159	177[a]	272	447	476	523	662	868	1149	1092	1249	1339	1545	1547
Top/Bottom	7.33	6.74	8.95[a]	7.23	6.03	4.47	5.44	5.65	5.88	6.13	5.91	5.65	6.28	5.90	6.32

Notes: [a] For Peninsular Malaysia only.

[b] Data from 1989 is for Malaysian citizens only.

Source: Economic Planning Unit (http://www.epu.gov.my/c/document_library/get_file?uuid=e2b128f0-c6fb-4890-8a17-3f708fc3d7a8&groupId=34492; http://www.epu.gov.my/c/document_library/get_file?uuid=5b461e12-9843-47d4-b54f-4c50e258c540&&groupId=10124).

and Northeast Asia (Korea and Japan) have maintained low inequality, while some countries in South America have seen declines in inequality in the last decade after decades of rising inequality.

The ratio of urban to rural household incomes among citizens increased from 1.68 in 1989 to 1.85 in 2009, with peaks of 2.11 in 2002 and 2004 (Table 2.5). Disparities within urban areas have also been higher than in rural areas. The Gini coefficient for urban citizens fell from 0.444 in 1989 to 0.423 in 2009, with a corresponding decline for rural citizens from 0.416 to 0.407. Comparison of the richest 20 per cent of households with the poorest 40 per cent also reflects the gravity of the inequality for both. The incomes of the former were 6.33 to 7.10 times those of the latter in urban areas during 1989–2009, while the rural ratio rose from 5.25 to 6.36. The Bumiputeras have had the lowest average household incomes, followed by Indians and then Chinese.

There has been a very significant reduction in inter-ethnic income disparities over the last four decades, especially during the 1970s and 1980s. The ratio of average incomes for the Chinese to the Malays has declined over the last four decades, from 2.29 in 1970 to 1.38 in 2009. The ratio for Chinese to Indians improved from 1.30 to 1.25 while that for Indians to Malays improved from 1.77 to 1.10 over the period. Higher disparity ratios involving Bumiputeras were found with data including non-Malay Bumiputeras (mainly in Sabah and Sarawak) for 1990–2004, but these declined over time.

Table 2.5 suggests similar trends for ethnic household incomes as well as decreased overall income disparities. Average gross household incomes have significantly increased for all ethnic groups, including the bottom 40 per cent of the population. The increase in average incomes has been disproportionately greater for the top quintile or upper fifth of households.

While official policy has been primarily concerned with inter-ethnic or 'racial' disparities, intra-ethnic or 'within race' disparities have been and become more serious. The average household income for the richest 20 per cent to that for the poorest 40 per cent increased from 6.39 in 1989 to 7.18 in 1997 for Bumiputera citizens, before declining to 6.90 in 2009. This ratio for Chinese also grew from 6.20 to 6.41, as did the ratio for Indians, from 5.44 to 6.31.

The Bumiputeras have had the lowest average household incomes, followed by Indians and then Chinese. The ratio of average incomes for the Chinese to the Malays has declined over the last four decades, from 2.29 in 1970 to 1.38 in 2009. The ratio for Chinese to Indians improved from 1.30 to 1.25 while that for Indians to Malays improved from 1.77 to 1.10 over the period. Higher disparity ratios were found with data including non-Malay Bumiputeras for 1990-2004, but these declined over time.

Although official policy has been primarily concerned with inter-ethnic or 'racial' disparities, intra-ethnic or 'within race' disparities have been and become more serious. The average household income for the richest 20 per cent to that for the poorest 40 per cent increased from 6.39 in 1989 to 7.18 in 1997 for Bumiputera citizens, before declining to 6.90 in 2009. The ratio for Chinese also grew from 6.20 to 6.41, as did the ratio for Indians, from 5.44 to 6.31.

Population and Labour

The Malaysian population increased from about 10.44 million in 1970 to an estimated 28.33 million in 2010 (Table 2.6). The transformation of Malaysian society has been noteworthy, with a great shift of its population from rural to urban areas over the past half century. Urbanization has progressed over the years, with the urban population increasing from 19.0 per cent in 1957 to 71.0 per cent in 2010 (Table 2.7). In 1957, over 90 per cent of Malaya's population lived in rural areas. By 2010, only

Table 2.6 Malaysia: Population and Labour Force Participation, 1970–2010

	1970	*1980*	*1990*	*2000*	*2005*	*2010*
Population (million)	10.44	13.76	17.76	23.3	26.13	28.33
Labour force (thousand)	3.61	5,109	7,893	9,556	10,413	11,517
Labour force participation rate (%)	65.3	64.9	66.5	65.4	63.3	62.7
Male	87.6	85.9	85.3	83.0	80.0	78.7
Female	43.1	44.0	47.8	47.2	45.9	46.1

Sources: Department of Statistics, *Labour Force Survey*, various issues.

Table 2.7 Malaysia: Population by Location, 1957–2010 (%)

	1957	1970	1980	1991	2000	2010
Rural	91.0	73.2	65.8	49.3	38.0	29.0
Urban	19.0	26.8	34.2	50.7	62.0	71.0

Sources: Department of Statistics, Malaysia, *Population Census*, 1957, 1970; Malaysia Plan documents, various years; Department of Statistics, Malaysia, *Yearbook of Statistics, 2005.*

Table 2.8 Malaysia: Urbanization Rate by State, 1970–2010 (%)

	1970	1980	1991	2000	2010
More developed states					
Johor	26.3	35.2	48.0	63.9	71.9
Melaka	25.1	23.4	39.4	67.3	86.5
Negri Sembilan	21.6	32.6	42.5	55.0	66.5
Perak	27.5	32.2	54.3	59.3	69.7
Pulau Pinang	51.0	47.5	75.3	79.5	90.8
Selangor	9.5	34.2	75.0	88.3	91.4
Less developed states					
Kedah	12.6	14.4	33.1	38.7	64.6
Kelantan	15.1	28.1	33.7	33.5	42.4
Pahang	19.0	26.1	30.6	42.1	50.5
Perlis	12.6	8.9	26.7	33.8	51.4
Sabah	16.9	19.9	32.8	49.1	54.0
Sarawak	15.5	18.0	38.0	47.9	53.8
Terengganu	27.0	42.9	44.6	49.4	59.1
Malaysia	28.3	34.2	51.1	61.8	71.0

Sources: Calculated with data from various Malaysia Plan documents; Department of Statistics, Malaysia, *General Report of the Population and Housing Census of Malaysia*, various issues.

about 29 per cent of the Malaysian population lived in the countryside. Not surprisingly, urbanization has proceeded faster in the more developed states (Table 2.8).

The Malaysian labour force grew from 3,619,000 in 1970 to 11,517,000 in 2010, with labour force participation rates of 65.3 per cent and 62.7 per cent respectively. Male labour force participation has exceeded 75 per cent, while female participation has never exceeded half.

Employment Status

Economic development in the post-colonial Malaysian economy has been uneven in many respects. Employment statistics suggest dramatic changes since Malayan independence in 1957, pointing to a major increase in wage employment among Malays and other Bumiputeras as well as Chinese, with a corresponding decline of unpaid family workers as well as own account workers, i.e. the self-employed. Ethnic proportions in economic activities and occupations increasingly reflect demographic shares except in agriculture and government services (which remain predominantly Bumiputera), and in wholesale and retail trade (which remain Chinese-dominated) (Table 2.9). The number of wage earners among working Malaysians significantly increased from over half in Peninsular Malaysia alone in 1957 to almost three-quarters in the entire country, as shown in Table 2.9.

Non-wage employment — such as self-employment and unpaid family workers[1] — was significant in 1957, accounting for 43.3 per cent of the total labour force, with wage employment constituting the remaining 56.7 per cent. The majority of workers, with limited access to land and capital, have sought wage employment, which has soared with industrialization and urbanization. Since 1957, wage employment has increased greatly among Malays, although the shares have declined slightly for Chinese and Indians, more of whom have become self-employed (Table 2.9). Throughout, Indians have remained predominantly working class in character, with the greatest proportion of wage employees (over four fifths) among those employed.

Historically, the self-employed Chinese include many petty employers, whereas Malay peasant self-employment generally involves own account work; both often involved unpaid family members, but only the former were likely to employ others. More Chinese have been employers compared to their share of those in employment. Besides Malay peasant farms, Chinese employers have run most small-scale enterprises using a high, albeit gradually declining proportion of unpaid family workers. Such Chinese hiring practices in small-scale enterprises help account for the relatively lower unemployment rates among Chinese. In the 1967/1968 Socio-Economic Survey and subsequent labour force surveys, the Chinese consistently had lower open unemployment rates than either the Malays or

Table 2.9 Malaysia: Employment Status by Ethnicity and Gender, 1957, 1980, 1990, 2010 (%)

P. Malaysia, 1957	Malay	Chinese	Indian	Others	Total	Male	Female
Employer and own account worker	49.0 (66.1)	28.3 (28.8)	9.8 (4.1)	14.5 (1.1)	35.0 (100.0)	38.4 (82.7)	24.6 (17.3)
Unpaid family worker	14.1 (80.0)	4.2 (17.8)	0.5 (0.9)	4.1 (1.3)	8.3 (100.0)	4.8 (43.7)	18.7 (56.3)
Employee	37.0 (30.8)	67.6 (42.5)	89.6 (22.9)	81.4 (3.7)	56.7 (100.0)	56.8 (75.5)	56.7 (24.5)
In employment	100.0 (47.3)	100.0 (35.7)	100.0 (14.5)	100.0 (2.6)	100.0 (100.0)	100.0 (75.4)	100.0 (24.6)

P. Malaysia, 1980	Malay	Chinese	Indian	Others	Total	Male	Female
Employer	2.6 (35.5)	5.8 (51.5)	4.6 (12.3)	4.1 (0.7)	4.0 (100.0)	4.4 (75.5)	3.0 (24.5)
Own account worker	32.9 (64.5)	24.7 (31.5)	8.3 (3.2)	32.1 (0.8)	27.4 (100.0)	28.9 (71.2)	24.4 (28.8)
Unpaid family worker	9.2 (67.9)	5.4 (26.2)	3.3 (4.9)	10.1 (1.0)	7.3 (100.0)	4.9 (45.8)	12.1 (54.2)
Employee	55.2 (48.3)	64.1 (36.5)	83.8 (14.6)	53.8 (0.6)	61.4 (100.0)	61.8 (68.1)	60.5 (31.9)
In employment	100.0 (53.6)	100.0 (35.0)	100.0 (10.7)	100.0 (0.7)	100.0 (100.0)	100.0 (67.6)	100.0 (32.4)

Malaysia, 1990	Bumiputera	Chinese	Indian	Others	Total	Male	Female
Employer	1.4 (27.5)	6.0 (67.0)	1.6 (5.0)	2.3 (0.5)	2.9 (100.0)	4.1 (91.4)	0.7 (8.6)
Own account worker	24.4 (68.3)	17.6 (27.8)	7.5 (3.2)	22.0 (0.7)	20.7 (100.0)	23.5 (73.2)	15.6 (26.8)
Unpaid family worker	12.0 (66.7)	9.4 (29.4)	3.7 (3.2)	10.9 (0.7)	10.4 (100.0)	5.7 (35.2)	18.9 (64.8)
Employee	62.2 (54.6)	67.1 (33.2)	87.2 (11.6)	64.6 (0.6)	66.0 (100.0)	66.7 (65.2)	64.7 (34.8)
In employment	100.0 (57.9)	100.0 (32.7)	100.0 (8.8)	100.0 (0.7)	100.0 (100.0)	100.0 (65.5)	100.0 (34.5)

Table 2.9 (continued)

Malaysia, 2010	Bumiputera	Chinese	Indian	Others	Total	Male	Female
Employer	2.7	8.1	4.0	2.8	3.9	5.2	1.7
	n.a.	n.a.	n.a.	n.a.	(100.0)	(84.7)	(15.3)
Own account	19.2	16.6	10.0	20.9	17.2	20.1	12.1
worker	n.a.	n.a.	n.a.	n.a.	(100.0)	(74.7)	(25.3)
Unpaid family	5.2	4.7	1.5	7.2	4.5	2.6	7.9
worker	n.a.	n.a.	n.a.	n.a.	(100.0)	(37.0)	(63.0)
Employee	73.0	70.6	84.5	69.2	74.4	72.1	78.4
	n.a.	n.a.	n.a.	n.a.	(100.0)	(69.9)	(38.1)
In employment	100.0	100.0	100.0	100.0	100.0	100.0	100.0
	n.a.	n.a.	n.a.	n.a.	(100.0)	(63.9)	(36.1)

Note: Figures in brackets indicate the proportion of each employment category by ethnicity and gender. These figures are not available for 2010.

Sources: Data for 1957 and 1980 are from Khong (1985); Department of Statistics, Malaysia, *Labour Force Survey*, various issues.

the Indians, due to their generally higher education level and fewer barriers to employment for them in the private sector where there was much more significant Chinese ownership and control (Table 2.9).

Initially, ethnic hiring biases were justified by ethnic preferences in service and product markets and other social and cultural preferences such as language and customs. However, ethnic hiring practices have persisted over time such that ethnic occupational or industrial identification seems self-perpetuating even when the original entry barriers no longer exist (see Waldinger, 1985).

Education and Employment

The overall unemployment rate in Malaysia (Table 2.10) has been comparatively low by developing country standards. It was lowest in the early and mid-1990s, when high economic, especially manufacturing growth rates were accompanied by increases in foreign labour immigration. Following the increase in such immigration, Malaysia 'limited' the likely increase in unemployment by repatriating foreign workers during the 1997–1998 financial crisis.

Table 2.10 Malaysia[a]: Unemployment Rates by Ethnicity, 1967–2010 (%)

Year	Malay	Chinese	Indian	Others	Total
1967/68	5.7	5.1	8.4	4.9	5.8
1970	8.1	7.0	11.0	3.1	8.0
1975	6.1	6.3	10.5	9.2	6.7
1980	6.5	3.9	6.3	3.3	5.6
1983	7.0	4.0	6.4	3.8	5.8
1985	8.7[b]	5.5	8.4	5.0	7.6
1990	5.8[b]	4.5	4.9	1.7	5.1
1993	3.3[b]	2.5	2.7	2.3	3.0
1995	4.6[b]	1.5	2.6	0.4	3.1
2000	4.6[b]	1.5	2.7	0.8	3.1
2003	4.9[b]	1.9	3.0	2.4	3.8
2005	5.3[b]	2.4	3.1	4.1	4.2
2010	3.9[b]	2.5	4.3	2.0	3.4

Notes: [a] 1985–2005 figures are for Malaysia; the earlier ones are for Peninsular Malaysia only.
        [b] For all Bumiputeras from 1985.
Sources: 5MP, Table 3.5; 7MP, Table 3.2; 8MP, Table 3.7; MTR8MP, Table 3.7; 9MP, Table 16.4; 10MP, 2011–2015; Department of Statistics, Malaysia, *Labour Force Survey*, various issues; Ministry of Finance, Malaysia, *Economic Report*, various issues.

Inter-ethnic sectoral (Table 2.11) and occupational (Table 2.12) disparities have greatly declined. One exception is agriculture, where Bumiputeras are more dominant than ever. The proportion of ethnic Indians in agriculture, even plantations, has also declined greatly. Constraints on inter-sectoral (Table 2.11) and inter-occupational (Table 2.12) mobility have often been due to internalized customary rules effecting labour demand and supply. While educational expansion facilitated upward mobility, the education system itself has tended to perpetuate socio-economic inequalities inherited from the past. Access to modern wage employment in Malaysia depends largely on educational credentials, used as a proxy for skills and other attributes desired by employers, such as acceptance of discipline and subordination, and to legitimize the differentiation of functional roles and positions of authority within the hierarchy.

Public education has raised the educational level of the labour force; the proportion with tertiary education increased from less than 2 per cent in 1974 to 24.2 per cent in 2010, while that with primary education only dropped from over half to 16.5 per cent over the period (Table 2.13). Barriers to entry unrelated to qualifications have also structured labour supply in terms of training or educational choices.

While educational expansion has facilitated upward mobility, the education system itself has tended to perpetuate socio-economic inequalities inherited from the past. Initial access to modern wage employment in Malaysia often depends on educational credentials. Schooling qualifications serve as a proxy for skills and other attributes desired by employers, such as acceptance of discipline and subordination. Differential qualifications also serve to legitimize the differentiation of functional roles and positions of authority within organizational hierarchies. At higher levels, this is especially true for professional qualifications, but vocational and skills training is also increasingly appreciated by employers. Historically, this has been more true of the public sector and the modern corporate sector, especially those owned by foreign, especially Western corporations.

The stratification of access to wage employment by educational attainment may be best understood with reference to the employment and remuneration policies of the public sector since colonial times. Among local employees, strict rules of access to the occupational and wage structure were imposed. Over time, the meritocratic idea that those with higher educational qualifications should occupy positions of greater authority and income became entrenched. Malays, who were overwhelmingly rural during the colonial era, were clearly at a historical disadvantage since virtually all English medium schools were in large towns until the 1960s. Hence, English-medium education, offering greater upward mobility, was more readily available to the more urbanized non-Malays and to privileged Malays, thus perpetuating some degree of occupational inheritance (see Table 2.12).

Educational attainment is heavily influenced by parental means and culture. Despite the introduction of free schooling since 1970, the costs of schooling are still high, especially for the poor. This is because of out-of-pocket expenditure for school transport, books, school uniforms and stationery. Hoerr (1975) showed that substantial out-of-pocket expenditure

Table 2.11 Peninsular Malaysia: Employment by Sector and Ethnicity, 1957, 1970, 1986, 2003, 2010

Economic Activity	1957				1970			
	M	C	I	T	M	C	I	T
Extractive	75.6	46.2	59.0	61.3	65.2	33.5	47.6	51.6
	(58.3)	(26.9)	(13.9)	(100.0)	(67.6)	(23.0)	(9.4)	(100.0)
Agriculture	74.6	40.9	56.8	58.5	64.3	29.7	46.0	49.6
	(60.3)	(24.9)	(14.0)	(100.0)	(69.3)	(21.2)	(9.5)	(100.0)
Mining & quarrying	1.0	5.3	2.2	2.8	0.9	3.8	1.6	2.0
	(16.9)	(67.5)	(11.4)	(100.0)	(24.1)	(67.2)	(8.2)	(100.0)
Industry	4.8	17.1	7.3	9.6	6.0	21.0	5.9	11.4
	(23.6)	(63.6)	(11.0)	(100.0)	(28.2)	(65.2)	(5.3)	(100.0)
Manufacturing	2.6	12.8	3.3	6.4	5.1	16.6	4.6	9.2
	(19.2)	(71.3)	(7.5)	(100.0)	(29.7)	(63.8)	(5.1)	(100.0)
Construction	2.2	4.3	4.0	3.2	0.9	4.4	1.3	2.2
	(32.5)	(47.9)	(18.1)	(100.0)	(21.9)	(70.8)	(6.0)	(100.0)
Services	19.0	35.4	33.0	28.3	23.7	40.0	40.9	31.6
	(31.7)	(44.6)	(16.9)	(100.0)	(40.1)	(44.8)	(13.2)	(100.0)
Finance, insurance, real estate & business[c]	3.2	16.7	10.7	9.2	4.5	18.2	10.2	10.0
	(16.4)	(64.7)	(16.8)	(100.0)	(24.1)	(64.4)	(10.4)	(100.0)
Transport, storage & communications	2.7	3.8	5.2	3.5	2.9	3.9	5.3	3.6
	(36.5)	(38.7)	(21.5)	(100.0)	(43.1)	(38.4)	(15.0)	(100.0)
Wholesale & retail; hotels & restaurants[c]								
Utilities	0.4	0.4	1.4	0.5	0.7	0.4	2.2	0.7
	(37.8)	(28.5)	(40.5)	(100.0)	(53.5)	(20.2)	(32.1)	(100.0)
Community, social & personal services	12.7	14.5	15.7	15.0	15.6	17.5	23.2	17.3
	(40.0)	(34.5)	(15.1)	(100.0)	(48.2)	(47.5)	(13.7)	(100.0)
All Sectors	100.0	100.0	100.0	100.0	100.0	100.0	100.0	100.0
	(47.3)	(35.7)	(14.5)	(100.0)	(53.5)	(35.4)	(10.2)	(100.0)

Key: M: Malay, C: Chinese, I: Indian, B: Bumiputera, T: Total

Notes: [a] For Malaysia. [b] No data on ethnicity by industry.

       [c] For 1957 and 1970, these were jointly categorized as the 'commerce' sector.

Table 2.11 (continued)

1986				2003				2010[ab]			
M	C	I	T	M	C	I	T	B	C	I	T
35.1	14.7	30.1	27.4	10.8	5.1	7.8	11.9	15.1	5.0	5.4	12.0
(68.6)	(18.8)	(11.7)	(100.0)	(72.7)	(18.9)	(8.4)	(100.0)				
34.4	14.0	29.1	26.7	10.5	4.9	7.4	11.6	14.5	4.6	5.1	11.6
(69.1)	(18.4)	(11.6)	(100.0)	(73.0)	(18.8)	(8.2)	(100.0)				
0.7	0.7	1.0	0.7	0.3	0.2	0.4	0.3	0.6	0.4	0.3	0.4
(48.9)	(34.6)	(14.7)	(100.0)	(63.3)	(23.2)	(13.5)	(100.0)				
18.5	30.9	23.4	23.4	30.5	32.6	36.8	30.4	23.2	29.1	32.0	34.7
(42.5)	(46.3)	(10.6)	(100.0)	(56.2)	(33.0)	(10.8)	(100.0)				
13.9	20.9	19.1	16.9	22.8	20.2	30.9	21.3	15.4	17.6	26.5	28.3
(44.1)	(43.4)	(12.0)	(100.0)	(58.7)	(28.6)	(12.7)	(100.0)				
4.6	10.0	4.3	6.5	7.7	12.4	5.9	9.1	7.8	11.5	5.5	6.4
(38.2)	(53.8)	(7.0)	(100.0)	(49.8)	(44.1)	(6.1)	(100.0)				
46.4	54.4	46.6	49.2	58.7	62.3	55.4	57.7	54.5	71.2	67.0	53.3
(50.6)	(38.7)	(10.0)	(100.0)	(57.6)	(33.7)	(8.7)	(100.0)				
3.6	5.9	4.5	4.5	6.3	9.1	8.3	6.9	2.8	5.3	4.4	7.0
(42.6)	(46.0)	(10.6)	(100.0)	(49.9)	(39.6)	(10.5)	(100.0)				
4.0	4.2	6.5	4.3	5.6	4.3	8.6	5.3	6.2	5.8	13.3	5.7
(49.7)	(34.1)	(15.8)	(100.0)	(60.0)	(25.3)	(14.7)	(100.0)				
12.7	30.0	14.4	19.0	19.0	37.5	19.4	23.8	19.5	37.6	18.8	}
(36.0)	(55.3)	(8.1)	(100.0)	(44.5)	(48.3)	(7.2)	(100.0)				} 30.0
0.7	0.1	1.0	0.9	0.2	0.6	0.6	0.8	1.2	0.5	1.6	}
(71.4)	(8.8)	(19.6)	(100.0)	(81.4)	(10.0)	(8.7)	(100.0)				
25.4	14.2	20.2	20.9	26.9	11.2	18.5	21.1	24.8	22.0	28.9	10.4
(65.3)	(23.8)	(10.3)	(100.0)	(74.7)	(17.1)	(8.2)	(100.0)				
100.0	100.0	100.0	100.0	100.0	100.0	100.0	100.0	100	100	100	100
(53.6)	(35.0)	(10.6)	(100.0)	(58.5)	(32.2)	(9.3)	(100.0)				

Sources: Department of Statistics, Malaysia, *Population Census*, 1957, 1970; Department of Statistics, Malaysia, *Labour Force Survey, 1986*; *Labour Force Survey Report, 2003*: Table A 3.10.

Table 2.12 Malaysia: Occupation by Ethnicity, 1970–2010 (%)

	1970			1975			1985			1995			2005			2010		
	B	C	I	B	C	I	B	C	I	B	C	I	B	C	I	B	C	I
Senior officers & managers	24.1	62.9	7.8	28.1	38.7	7.3	34.8	57.5	5.1	36.8	52.4	4.8	37.1	55.1	7.1	42.7	45.7	7.3
Professionals	47.0	39.5	10.8	48.0	58.8	11.0	58.8	30.9	8.7	64.4	25.7	7.0	58.5	31.7	8.2	60.0	27.9	8.3
Technicians & associates	–	–	–	–	–	–	–	–	–	–	–	–	–	29.7	59.5	65.3	24.8	7.2
Clerical workers	35.4	45.9	17.2	46.0	40.8	12.0	54.1	37.8	7.6	57.5	33.8	7.4	56.7	34.3	8.4	60.5	30.5	6.8
Service workers	44.3	39.6	14.6	46.8	39.6	12.6	61.6	27.8	10.1	57.3	21.6	8.2	51.5	39.6	8.0	58.2	29.4	4.9
Sales workers	26.7	61.7	11.1	24.8	65.7	9.1	33.2	59.2	6.8	36.4	50.2	6.2						
Agriculture workers	72.0	17.3	9.7	70.5	18.2	10.4	75.9	15.2	8.2	61.3	11.9	6.9	80.8	11.3	4.3	66.4	7.7	1.9
Craft & related trade workers	–	–	–	–	–	–	–	–	–	–	–	–	46.0	44.6	8.2	51.5	31.9	4.7
Production workers	34.2	55.9	9.6	40.6	48.4	10.5	47.3	41.8	10.5	44.2	33.7	9.6	60.4	24.8	12.9	58.2	14.9	14.4
Elementary occupations	–	–	–	–	–	–	–	–	–	–	–	–	54.4	25.2	14.7	53.8	11.5	7.2
Total	51.8	36.6	10.6	52.0	36.5	10.6	57.3	33.2	8.8	51.4	29.6	7.9	56.4	32.5	9.1	58.2	24.1	6.8

Key: B: Bumiputera, C: Chinese, I: Indian.
Source: NECC Report, Table 28; 6MP, Table 1-9; MTR7MP, Table 3.6; 9MP, Table 16-4.

Table 2.13 Malaysia: Educational Level of Labour Force, 1974–2010 (%)

	1974[a]	1980	1990	2000	2010
No formal education	20.6	18.8	9.8	6.2	3.6
Primary	51.5	43.6	34.5	26.4	16.5
Secondary	25.8	34.0	48.6	53.5	55.7
Tertiary	1.8	3.6	8.8	13.9	24.2
Total	100.0	100.0	100.0	100.0	100.0

Note: [a] Peninsular Malaysia only
Sources: Department of Statistics, Malaysia, *Labour Force Survey, April/May 1974*;
         Department of Statistics, Malaysia, *Yearbook of Statistics, Malaysia*, various
         issues.

was incurred. Meerman (1979) estimated that out-of-pocket expenditure for schooling came to about 13.0 per cent of average household income in the lowest income decile; clearly, the relative burdens of these costs are higher for lower income groups.

Moreover, the opportunity cost of schooling was high, particularly where employment opportunities for children abound, although this has declined over time. Even if a poor child manages to continue in school, the home environment tends to undermine the child's academic performance. As income and occupation depend on educational attainment, in turn influenced by parental means, the education system tends to reproduce inequality over generations.

As part of the Malaysian government's policies, education was vastly expanded, especially in rural areas, and Malay replaced English as the medium of instruction over the 1970s. In the 1970s, English, Chinese and Tamil essentially became second languages, with Malay becoming the official language of instruction. Communal hiring preferences and practices continued, especially among smaller businesses, later legitimized as responses to the NEP's pro-Malay affirmative action stance.

Education enrolment, particularly at the secondary level, expanded rapidly, improving the educational level of the workforce (Table 2.13). However, rapid expansion of secondary education resulted in an excess of secondary-school graduates compared to the number of lower level white-collar occupations created. This mismatch resulted in a decline in relative wages as well as credential bumping and upgrading by employers.

Khong (1991: Statistical Annex 4) showed a significant fall in real wage differentials between clerical workers and general and factory workers between 1971 and 1986. Middle and lower secondary school-leavers have since adjusted their expectations. This process also shifted unemployment from those with basic education to those with secondary education, and eventually to those with higher education.

Numerous government scholarships were granted to Malay students to pursue higher studies, both locally and abroad, with the aim of creating a Malay middle class. For example, a survey covering half the graduates of each of the five local universities in 1982/83 found two-thirds on government scholarships, of which four-fifths had been awarded to Malays (Mehmet, 1988: 118–119). Four-fifths wound up in government employment because of the standard practice of government 'scholarship bonding'. During 1980–1984, more than 90 per cent of government-sponsored students overseas were Malays.

Historically, especially in the 1960s and the 1970s, Malay students tended to choose liberal arts or social science courses (in anticipation of public sector administrative jobs), while non-Malays sought professional or scientific courses, but this has changed in recent decades with special programmes and differential entry requirements. Private investments in university education have also escalated since the mid-1980s because of the historically high private returns to tertiary education, offering upward social and economic mobility.

In many professional occupations, entry has been restricted by institutional rules requiring certain educational or professional credentials, ostensibly to ensure professional standards. But this requirement also serves to protect the interests and privileges of the educated or qualified through control over supply, and hence access to professional advancement.

For eight well remunerated professions, the Bumiputera share rose from 4.9 per cent in 1970 to 38.8 per cent in 2005, the Chinese share declined from 51.0 to 48.7 per cent and the Indian share fell from 23.3 to 10.6 per cent over the same period (Table 2.14). Although there has been a substantial increase in Malay shares in all professions since 1970, Malays are still under-represented in the medical, legal, engineering, accountancy and technical professions. In contrast, Indians are significantly over-

Table 2.14 Malaysia: Registered Professionals by Ethnicity, 1970–2008 (% of total)

	1970			1975			1980			1985			1995			2008		
	B	*C*	*I*	*B*	*C*	*I*	*B*	*C*	*I*	*B*	*C*	*I*	*B*	*C*	*I*	*B*	*C*	*I*
Accountants	6.8	65.4	7.9	7.7	73.8	8.2	7.6	77.3	7.3	11.2	81.2	6.2	16.1	75.2	7.9	25.0	n.a.	n.a.
Architects	4.3	80.9	1.4	6.7	87.7	0.7	11.0	85.2	1.2	23.6	74.4	1.2	27.6	70.7	1.5	60.0	n.a.	n.a.
Doctors	3.7	44.8	40.2	4.4	48.7	38.7	8.6	44.2	42.2	27.8	34.7	34.4	33.4	32.1	32.0	53.0	n.a.	n.a.
Dentists	3.1	89.1	5.1	2.6	75.8	12.5	9.2	65.9	19.7	24.3	50.7	23.7	30.9	45.7	21.9	49.0	n.a.	n.a.
Veterinary surgeons	40.0	30.0	15.0	38.6	36.4	13.6	52.0	30.7	10.7	35.9	23.7	37.0	40.2	23.7	33.5	43.0	n.a.	n.a.
Engineers	7.3	71.0	13.5	7.5	76.1	10.5	11.6	77.4	7.4	34.8	58.2	5.3	21.6	71.8	6.6	53.0	n.a.	n.a.
Surveyors	–	–	–	–	–	–	29.9	59.6	7.5	44.7	49.6	3.7	48.3	45.6	3.2	55.0	n.a.	n.a.
Lawyers	–	–	–	12.8	50.7	35.2	13.0	50.0	35.8	22.4	50.0	26.5	29.0	43.3	26.6	39.0	n.a.	n.a.
Total	4.9	51.0	23.3	6.7	64.1	22.0	11.0	63.5	21.1	29.0	55.9	13.2	27.3	54.4	17.0	n.a.	n.a.	n.a.

Key: B: Bumiputera, C: Chinese, I: Indian.
Source: NECC Report Table 29; 6MP, Table 1-10; 8MP, Table 3-9; 9MP, Table 16-5; 10MP, Box 4-1.

represented in the legal and medical professions, while Chinese are over-represented in all but the veterinary profession.

After 1970, the levels and growth rates of real earnings in lower white-collar occupations — such as clerical and technical/supervisory occupations — declined relative to skilled and unskilled manual jobs (see Khong, 1991: Statistical Annex 4). Workers with higher levels of education displaced workers with less education from lower-level occupations, even for jobs where formal qualifications beyond a certain level were not associated with improved labour productivity [See Khong (1991: Appendix 3.1) for an explanation of the Malaysian educational system.] With the rapid expansion of secondary and then university/college education, the advantage of having a basic university degree has gradually eroded, as witnessed by the upsurge in graduate unemployment and the decline in real wages for new university graduates.

Wealth Ownership Disparities

The main bone of contention in Malaysian political economy discourse is over corporate share ownership. There was a very significant increase in the Bumiputera owned proportion of corporate stocks from 1969 until the early 1980s. Through government regulation of business opportunities and investments as well as preferential policies for Bumiputera business interests, the Bumiputera share of equity in public listed companies rose from 1.5 per cent in 1969 to 19.1 per cent in 1985. It has, however, risen only modestly since then to about 23 per cent. The share of foreigners went down very dramatically in the 1970s, but has recently gone up almost as dramatically from a quarter in 1990 to almost two fifths in 2008 (Table 2.15). Meanwhile, various observers have claimed considerable underestimation of the actual Bumiputera share of corporate wealth by calculating at par value rather than at market value.

There has been a rise in the private individual share of overall Bumiputera wealth since the early 1980s. During the 1970s, Bumiputera wealth was largely held through certain state owned enterprises known as Bumiputera trust agencies. Since then, however, there has been a large increase in individual Bumiputera wealth ownership facilitated by privatization as well as significant increases in Bumiputera incomes,

Table 2.15 Malaysia: Ownership of Share Capital (at par value) in Limited Companies, 1970–2008 (% of total)

	1970[a]	*1985*	*1990*	*2000*	*2004*	*2008*
Bumiputera	2.4	19.1	19.3	18.9	18.9	21.9
Individuals	1.6	11.7	14.2	14.2	15.0	18.9
Institutions	0.8	7.4	5.1	3.0	2.2	1.9
Trust agencies				1.7	1.7	1.1
Non-Bumiputera	28.3	35.8	46.8	41.3	40.6	36.7
Chinese	27.2	33.4	45.5	38.9	39.0	34.9
Indians	1.0	1.2	1.0	1.5	1.2	1.6
Others	0.0	1.3	0.3	0.9	0.4	0.1
Nominee Companies	6.0	19.0	8.5	8.5	8.0	3.5
Foreigners	63.4	26.0	25.4	31.3	32.5	37.9
Total	100.0	100.0	100.0	100.0	100.0	100.0

Note: [a] Peninsular Malaysia only.
Sources: NECC Report, Table 16; 7MP, Table 3-7; 9MP, Table 16-6; 10MP, Appendix 2.

particularly among those best placed to take advantage of the new opportunities due to the NEP and related affirmative action policies, 'Ali Baba' partnerships and other measures. Hence, there is now a significant class of Bumiputera stock or wealth owners, but it is unclear to what extent they are entrepreneurial.

The government's concern over ethnic socio-economic inequalities as well as disproportionate wealth ownership is supposed to be the basis of ethnic affirmative action policies, including the NEP and related policies. Yet, despite considerable achievement of the OPP1 targets, it is far from clear how much progress had been made in achieving 'national unity', the NEP's ostensible purpose, i.e. achieving 'national unity' by improving inter-ethnic relations through reducing inter-ethnic resentment. However, with some economic, cultural and educational deregulation from the mid-1980s and the economic boom of the early and mid-1990s, ethnic tensions seemed to have receded somewhat. Political developments since the 1997–1998 financial crisis have significantly reconfigured Malaysian politics, resulting in the emergence of two rival multi-ethnic populist political blocs, vaguely but increasingly distinguished along some political, ideological and policy lines.

Table 2.16 Malaysia: Employed Workforce by Industry and Gender, 1957–2010 (%)

Economic Activities	P. Malaysia, 1957			P. Malaysia, 1975			P. Malaysia, 1986			Malaysia, 1995			Malaysia, 2010		
	Total	Male	Female	Total	Male	Female	Total	Male	Female	Total	Male	Female	Total	Male	Female
Extractive	61.3 (100.0)	55.7 (68.5)	78.5 (31.5)	43.3 (100.0)	39.6 (59.8)	50.7 (40.2)	27.4 (100.0)	27.2 (64.7)	27.8 (35.3)	20.4 (100.0)	22.1 (71.6)	17.1 (28.4)	13.8 (100.0)	16.6 (77.2)	8.7 (22.8)
Agriculture, forestry, fishery	58.5 (100.0)	52.7 (67.8)	76.7 (32.2)	42.3 (100.0)	38.2 (59.1)	50.3 (40.9)	26.7 (100.0)	26.2 (64.1)	27.5 (35.9)	20.0 (100.0)	21.6 (74.1)	16.9 (25.9)	13.3 (100.0)	16.0 (76.9)	8.5 (23.1)
Mining and quarrying	2.8 (100.0)	3.1 (83.8)	1.8 (16.2)	1.0 (100.0)	1.4 (87.7)	0.4 (12.3)	0.7 (100.0)	1.0 (84.6)	0.3 (15.4)	0.4 (100.0)	0.5 (93.4)	0.2 (6.6)	0.5 (100.0)	0.6 (83.3)	0.2 (16.7)
Industry	9.6 (100.0)	10.9 (86.3)	5.3 (13.7)	19.6 (100.0)	20.5 (68.5)	17.9 (31.5)	23.4 (100.0)	23.3 (65.1)	23.5 (34.9)	31.3 (100.0)	31.5 (66.5)	30.9 (33.5)	26.0 (100.0)	29.3 (72.0)	20.2 (28.0)
Manufacturing	6.4 (100.0)	7.0 (83.4)	4.3 (16.6)	15.0 (100.0)	13.9 (60.7)	17.0 (39.3)	16.9 (100.0)	13.9 (53.7)	22.5 (46.3)	23.3 (100.0)	20.2 (57.2)	29.4 (42.8)	16.9 (100.0)	16.3 (61.6)	17.9 (38.4)
Construction	3.2 (100.0)	3.9 (92.1)	1.0 (7.9)	4.6 (100.0)	6.6 (93.6)	0.9 (0.9)	6.5 (6.5)	9.4 (9.4)	1.0 (1.0)	8.0 (100.0)	11.3 (93.5)	1.5 (6.5)	9.1 (100.0)	13.0 (91.1)	2.3 (18.1)
Services	28.3 (100.0)	32.4 (86.5)	15.6 (13.5)	36.9 (100.0)	39.9 (70.7)	31.4 (29.3)	49.2 (100.0)	49.4 (65.6)	48.8 (34.4)	48.3 (100.0)	46.4 (63.4)	52.0 (36.6)	60.2 (100.0)	54.1 (57.4)	71.1 (42.6)
Utilities	0.5 (100.0)	0.7 (96.6)	0.1 (3.4)	1.0 (100.0)	1.5 (96.8)	0.1 (3.2)	0.5 (100.0)	0.8 (97.1)	0.0 (2.9)	0.6 (100.0)	0.9 (90.4)	0.2 (9.6)	1.1 (100.0)	1.3 (79.9)	0.6 (20.1)
Transport, storage and communications	3.5 (100.0)	4.6 (98.8)	0.3 (2.0)	4.1 (100.0)	5.9 (93.7)	0.7 (6.3)	4.3 (100.0)	6 (90.7)	1.2 (9.3)	4.7 (100.0)	6.2 (87.9)	1.7 (12.1)	6.2 (100.0)	8.0 (81.7)	3.2 (18.3)

Table 2.16 (continued)

Economic Activities	P. Malaysia, 1957			P. Malaysia, 1975			P. Malaysia, 1986			Malaysia, 1995			Malaysia, 2010		
	Total	Male	Female	Total	Male	Female	Total	Male	Female	Total	Male	Female	Total	Male	Female
Wholesale and retail, restaurants and hotel							19.0 (100.0)	18.4 (63.3)	20.1 (36.7)	17.9 (100.0)	16.6 (61.3)	25.5 (38.7)	18.9 (100.0)	22.2 (60.6)	25.7 (39.4)
Finance, insurance, real estate and business services	9.2 (100.0)	11.0 (90.4)	3.6 (9.6)	13.8 (100.0)	15.4 (73.1)	10.8 (26.9)	4.5 (100.0)	4.4 (64.5)	4.6 (35.5)	4.8 (100.0)	4.3 (60.1)	5.6 (39.9)	3.3 (100.0)	2.5 (49.4)	4.6 (50.6)
Community, social and personal services	15.0 (100.0)	16.1 (79.2)	11.7 (20.8)	18.0 (100.0)	17.1 (62.1)	19.8 (37.9)	20.9 (100.0)	19.9 (62.0)	22.9 (38.0)	20.3 (100.0)	18.4 (60.0)	24.0 (40.0)	30.7 (100.0)	20.1 (48.8)	37.0 (51.2)
Total	100.0 (100.0)	100.0 (75.4)	100.0 (24.6)	100.0 (100.0)	100.0 (65.5)	100.0 (34.5)	100.0 (100.0)	100.0 (65.2)	100.0 (34.8)	100.0 (100.0)	100.0 (66.1)	100.0 (33.9)	100.0 (100.0)	100.0 (63.9)	100.0 (39.1)

Sources: Department of Statistics, Malaysia, *Population Census, 1957*; Department of Statistics, Malaysia, *Labour Force Survey*, various issues; 8MP, Table 20-1.

Gender Disparities

Discourses on Malaysia tend to focus on inter-ethnic disparities while neglecting other inequalities, including class and gender differences. The female labour force participation rate rapidly increased from 30.8 per cent in 1957 to 45.1 per cent in 1986, owing to increased education and employment opportunities and household needs for additional income. Historically, women have been significantly over-represented in unpaid family work and under-represented as employers in most societies, and Malaysia is no exception. The pattern of female employment in Malaysia is different from that in most industrialized market economies where women are concentrated in services (see also Khong, 1991: Statistical Annex 6). Although working women were traditionally concentrated in agriculture (Table 2.16) (see also Khong, 1985: Chapters 3 and 7), women have been increasingly found in wage employment in selected manufacturing industries (Table 2.17), retail trade and services.

In 1983, women formed between around 70 per cent of the workforce in the textiles and garments industry, and some 90 per cent of the workforce in electronics factories. The skills required for these assembly operations are ostensibly related to having more nimble and quick fingers; from a young age, women have been socialized into domestic roles and skills, which have related attributes (Khong, 1986). Women were over-represented as maids, cooks and housekeepers (95.0 per cent), in beauty/cosmetic services (75.3 per cent), in laundry and cleaning services (63.7 per cent), in medical and dental services as nurses and medical assistants (64.1 per cent); in educational services, they comprised 47.4 per cent by 1986. They were also commonly found in un-enumerated informal employment as street vendors, petty traders or other gender-typed occupations, e.g. as child-minders or seamstresses.

One reason why women have been traditionally confined to bad jobs was poorer access to education (Table 2.18). For some families in Malaysia, parents are more reluctant to invest their limited incomes in daughters' education because: (i) they may still earn less because of job and wage discrimination, (ii) it is presumed that the gains from education will accrue to the son-in-law's family after the daughter marries, (iii) daughters are needed to help with housework, (iv) other beliefs and ideologies favour boy children over their sisters. As a result, rural illiteracy is considerably higher for women than for men; women formed 54.8 per cent of the 1985 workforce without any formal education. Although illiteracy has fallen significantly since 1970, 33.9 per cent of the 1980 rural female population were illiterate compared to 16.2 per cent of rural men; 29.2 per cent of the total female population were illiterate compared to 13.2 per cent of men (Khong, 1986: 13).

Table 2.17 Malaysia: Manufacturing Workers by Gender, Occupation and Skill, 1983–2009 (%)

	1983	*1985*	*1990*	*1995*	*1999*	*2011*
Female share	44.62	45.51	50.79	45.61	46.81	36.46
Full-time employees:						
Professional	1.90	2.16	2.03	2.43	3.22	8.6
Non-professional managerial workers	2.27	2.43	1.75	2.26	2.78	
Technical & supervisory	8.46	9.08	8.60	9.60	10.57	11.28
Clerical & related	8.21	8.91	6.70	6.51	6.58	6.75
General	5.71	5.62	4.02	3.93	3.23	4.10
Production workers	73.46	71.80	76.9	75.29	73.62	68.60
Skilled & semi-skilled/ all production workers	56.11	58.67	54.75	45.30	62.56	n.a.
Female skilled/ all production workers	39.70	43.79	35.65	36.54	34.53	n.a.
Male skilled/ all production workers	40.39	38.12	32.53	33.69	35.08	n.a.
Female share of production workers:						
Skilled	50.52	54.79	59.11	51.92	52.00	n.a.
Semi-skilled	43.79	36.68	50.62	45.58	51.96	n.a.
Unskilled	53.96	54.18	58.01	50.81	52.70	n.a.
Ratio of average wages:						
Skilled: unskilled	1.61	1.70	1.64	1.66	1.70	n.a.
Semi-skilled: unskilled	1.20	1.27	1.25	1.22	1.23	n.a.

Note: n.a. – not available
Sources: Department of Statistics, Malaysia, *Labour Force Survey*, various issues; Department of Statistics, *Report on the Annual Survey of Manufacturing Industries, 2008*, Table 10.

Table 2.18 Malaysia: Employment by Ethnicity, Gender, Education Level, 1985,
2010 (%)

1985	*Bumiputera*	*Chinese*	*Indian*	*Total*	*Male*	*Female*
Total	100.0	100.0	100.0	100.0	100.0	100.0
	(57.2)	(33.1)	(9.0)	(100.0)	(65.5)	(34.5)
No formal education	18.9	6.9	9.3	14.1	8.9	23.8
	(76.6)	(16.3)	(5.9)	(100.0)	(41.6)	(58.4)
Primary	38.9	41.0	41.6	39.7	42.9	33.6
	(56.0)	(34.2)	(9.4)	(100.0)	(70.7)	(29.3)
Secondary	37.8	47.1	45.3	42.2	43.4	40.1
	(51.3)	(37.0)	(9.6)	(100)	(67.2)	(32.8)
Tertiary	4.4	5.9	3.8	4.7	4.8	4.5
	(54.0)	(35.0)	(7.3)	(100.0)	(67.0)	(33.0)
2010	*Bumiputera*	*Chinese*	*Indian*	*Total*	*Male*	*Female*
Total	100.0	100.0	100.0	100.0	100.0	100.0
	(65.4)	(27.0)	(7.6)	(100.0)	(63.9)	(36.1)
No formal education	3.1	1.3	2.5	3.6	3.1	4.3
	(78.9)	(13.7)	(7.4)	(100.0)	(56.8)	(43.2)
Primary	13.0	13.7	13.0	16.7	18.2	14.1
	(64.4)	(28.1)	(7.5)	(100.0)	(69.5)	(31.5)
Secondary	56.9	59.8	61.1	55.5	58.3	50.6
	(64.1)	(27.9)	(8.0)	(100.0)	(67.1)	(32.9)
Tertiary	27.1	25.1	23.4	24.2	20.3	31.0
	(67.4)	(25.8)	(6.8)	(100.0)	(53.7)	(46.3)

Note: Shares in brackets show percentage distributions by ethnicity, gender and
educational status.
Sources: Department of Statistics, Malaysia, *Labour Force Survey Report*, Malaysia,
various issues.

Although female access to secondary and higher education has
improved tremendously over time, sexual stereotyping in the education
system persists. From school to vocational training courses, the system
encourages gender specialization of young women and men in subjects for
jobs stereotyped as feminine or masculine, contributing to segmentation
along gender lines (see Shamsulbahriah, 1988). Socialization, schooling
and training thus reinforce the sexual division of labour; segmentation, in
turn, is reflected and reinforced by job and wage discrimination.

Despite the Equal Pay for Equal Work Act of 1969, substantial female/male wage differentials persist. There are wider differentials higher in the occupational pyramid, where employment opportunities for women are fewer than for men of equal qualification. There is greater likelihood of wage discrimination higher in the occupational pyramid since standardized union-negotiated wages are rare at higher occupational levels.

Anand (1983) found female mean incomes lower than average male incomes in every occupation. Even if wage rates were similar for men and women for the same job, actual wage incomes may be considerably different since women tend to work fewer hours due to family and housekeeping commitments. If and when they leave the labour force for such reasons, such breaks in their employment history further lower their seniority-related wage rates and wage earnings. Even in the more regulated government sector, the Equal Opportunities Act of 1967 has not been sufficient to abolish job and wage discrimination.

Such discrimination is clearly rooted in the low labour market status of women, which lowers the minimum 'supply price' that women can demand for their labour. Hiring, promotion and pay policies further influence future female labour supply. The male-female wage gap is fairly large in Malaysia. On average, men's wages are nearly twice as high as women's wages. The gap is increasing at higher occupational categories, and the trend has worsened in recent decades. The outlook for a more equitable access and reward system for female labour is not good, as Malaysian women remain politically divided and weak.

Women have increasingly accounted for a substantial proportion of professional/technical, clerical and service-related occupations. Compared with their 24.5 per cent share of the employed population in 1957, women had only 2.0 per cent of administrative/managerial positions and 7.9 per cent of clerical positions (Table 2.19); by 2010, these female shares were 24.0 per cent and 69.9 per cent respectively. Although women's shares of higher-level occupations — such as doctors, lawyers, engineers and middle and senior management — have been gradually increasing, these trends obscure the tendency for women to occupy secondary and subordinate positions within the same industry, occupation or profession. Often, as jobs become 'feminized', their prestige, skill grading and remuneration decline.[2]

Table **2.19**   Peninsular Malaysia: Employment Distribution by Occupation and Gender, 1957, 1975, 2010

Occupation	1957			1975			2010		
	Male	Female	Total	Male	Female	Total	Male	Female	Total
Professional or technical	2.9 (71.8)	3.5 (28.2)	3.0 (100.0)	5.5 (65.1)	5.6 (34.9)	5.5 (100.0)	20.3 (58.3)	25.7 (41.7)	22.3 (100.0)
Administrative or managerial	1.5 (98.0)	0.1 (2.0)	1.1 (100.0)	1.9 (96.3)	0.1 (3.7)	1.3 (100.0)	8.8 (76.0)	4.9 (24.0)	7.4 (100.0)
Clerical and related	3.5 (92.1)	0.9 (7.9)	2.8 (100.0)	6.9 (64.0)	7.4 (36.0)	7.1 (100.0)	4.9 (30.1)	20.1 (69.9)	10.4 (100.0)
Sales and related	10.0 (90.1)	3.4 (9.9)	8.4 (100.0)	11.6 (73.3)	8.0 (26.7)	10.4 (100.0)	15.6 (57.2)	20.6 (42.3)	10.4 (100.0)
Services and related	12.9 (84.3)	7.4 (15.7)	11.6 (100.0)	6.8 (54.8)	10.7 (45.2)	8.2 (100.0)			
Agriculture and related	49.1 (66.9)	(74.9 (33.1)	55.4 (100.0)	37.6 (58.8)	50.0 (41.2)	41.9 (100.0)	15.6 (82.2)	20.6 (17.8)	17.4 (100.0)
Production and related	17.8 (87.0)	8.2 (13.0)	15.4 (100.0)	29.6 (75.6)	18.1 (24.4)	25.7 (100.0)	10.5 (74.2)	4.0 (35.8)	8.2 (100.0)
Total	100.0 (75.5)	100.0 (24.5)	100.0 (100.0)	100.0 (65.5)	100.0 (34.5)	100.0 (100.0)	100.0 (63.9)	100.0 (39.1)	100.0 (100.0)
Number ('000)		2126.2			3567.2			8092.0	

Note: Values in brackets are for the shares of each gender and ethnic group for the occupational category. No strictly comparable data are available for recent years. Data on sales and related workers are estimated from the similar categories in *Labour Force Survey Report, 2004.*

Sources: Khong (1985: 36); Department of Statistics, Malaysia, *Labour Force Survey Report*, various issues.

Regional Disparities

Meanwhile, regional grievances, especially in Sabah and Sarawak, became more pronounced, especially in the 1980s and 1990s, with non Malay Bumiputeras, who form the majority in Sabah and Sarawak, reputedly more alienated. Average household incomes in Sabah have declined relative to other Malaysian states over the years. Although Sabah and Sarawak have not been among the states with the lowest household incomes, their real incomes have been lower because of their relatively

Table 2.20 Malaysia: Household Size by Region, 1970–2010

	1970	*1980*	*1991*	*2000*	*2010*
Sabah	5.26	5.37	5.10	5.16	5.88
Sarawak	5.98	5.45	4.70	4.76	4.47
Peninsular Malaysia	n.a.[a]	5.14	4.75	3.58	n.a.[a]
Malaysia	5.21	5.22	4.80	4.59	4.31

Notes: n.a. – not available.
   [a] Since the national average is less than that for Sabah and Sarawak, the household size for Peninsular Malaysia should be smaller than the latter's.
Sources: Calculated with data from *Population and Housing Census of Malaysia, 1990* and *Population and Housing Census of Malaysia, 2000*; Department of Statistics, Malaysia (http://www.statistics.gov.my/portal/images/stories/files/LatestReleases/banci/jadual3.pdf).

Table 2.21 Malaysia: Household Food Expenditure by Region, 1973, 1980, 1982, 1993/94, 1998/99, 2004/05, 2009/10 (%)

	Sabah	*Sarawak*	*Peninsular Malaysia*
1973 (urban areas only)	29.4	33.7	30.1
1980	–	–	71.6
1982	31.3	39.0	–
1993/94	29.1	25.9	22.7
1998/99	28.7	25.3	21.8
2004/05	27.5	23.2	19.2
2009/10	25.9	26.3	19.2

Sources: Department of Statistics, Malaysia, *Household Expenditure Survey*, Malaysia, various issues.

higher costs of living, larger household sizes (Table 2.20) and relatively higher household food expenses (Table 2.21).

The uneven economic development of the country dating back to colonial times has been largely perpetuated in the post-colonial period with the western states of Peninsular Malaysia generally more developed than the less developed states of the East Coast and northern Peninsular Malaysia besides Sabah and Sarawak (Table 2.22). Kelantan has had the lowest household income by state, at least since 1984 (Table 2.23). The rate of employment creation has been uneven among and within the Malaysian States (Table 2.24). Where agriculture is still the mainstay of

Table 2.22 Malaysia: Economic, Social and Composite Development Indices by State, 1990, 2000, 2005

Indicators	Economic Development Index			Social Development Index			Development Composite Index		
	1990	2000 (1990=100)	2005 (2000=100)	1990	2000 (1990=100)	2005 (2000=100)	1990	2000 (1990=100)	2005 (2000=100)
More developed states									
Johor	102.9	131.6	102.9	101.6	134.3	98.1	102.2	132.9	100.5
Melaka	100.8	131.7	106.4	105.5	132.5	102.1	103.2	132.1	104.2
N. Sembilan	100.7	129.7	101.8	104.9	134.1	102.9	102.8	131.9	102.3
Perak	99.4	131.0	99.7	100.6	133.0	101.2	100.0	132.0	100.4
Pulau Pinang	110.6	142.1	109.0	108.3	136.3	102.4	109.5	139.2	105.7
Selangor	112.6	137.3	108.4	107.0	140.6	98.0	109.9	139.0	103.2
Less developed states									
Kedah	93.9	123.7	95.5	95.7	128.5	100.2	94.8	126.1	97.8
Kelantan	90.4	117.9	91.9	92.2	120.8	94.4	91.3	119.4	93.1
Pahang	96.7	123.2	96.3	100.9	128.2	99.0	98.8	125.7	97.6
Perlis	94.9	123.2	95.0	98.7	128.5	104.9	96.8	125.8	99.9
Sabah	89.9	117.1	82.9	83.6	110.4	100.8	86.8	113.8	96.2
Sarawak	92.6	122.1	94.8	89.0	126.2	97.2	90.8	124.2	90.0
Terengganu	95.2	125.0	91.5	96.1	124.7	98.4	95.7	124.8	96.6

Source: OPP3, Table 4-8; 9MP, Table 17-1.

Table 2.23 Malaysia: Household Income by State, 1970–2009 (RM per month)

	1970	1974	1976	1979	1984	1987	1989[a]	1992	1995	1997	1999	2002	2004	2007	2009
More developed states															
Johor	237	382	513	731	1065	1060	1220	1708	2138	2772	2646	2963	3076	3457	3835
Melaka	265	410	568	772	1040	1034	1190	1466	1843	2276	2260	2650	2791	3421	4184
N. Sembilan	286	386	505	629	1039	908	1162	1378	1767	2378	2335	2739	2886	3336	3540
Perak	254	305	436	559	883	863	1067	1276	1436	1940	1743	2153	2207	2545	2809
P. Pinang	292	471	589	840	1183	1130	1375	1845	2225	3130	3128	3496	3531	4004	4407
Selangor	421	598	735	1067	1590	1558	1790	2275	3162	4006	3702	4406	5175	5580	5962
Less developed states															
Kedah	189	256	306	382	690	718	860	1049	1295	1590	1612	1966	2126	2408	2667
Kelantan	151	231	269	341	625	667	726	901	1091	1249	1314	1674	1829	2143	2536
Perlis	140	206	338	316	692	711	852	1038	1158	1507	1431	2006	2046	2541	2617
Pahang	286	305	477	702	960	900	1092	1253	1436	1632	1482	1991	2410	2995	3279
Sabah	n.a.	n.a.	513	676	1212	1116	1358	1286	1647	2057	1905	2406	2487	2866	3144
Sarawak	n.a.	n.a.	426	582	1033	1141	1199	1524	1886	2242	2276	2515	2725	3349	3581
Terengganu	173	206	339	360	756	694	905	948	1117	1497	1600	1837	1984	2463	3017

Note: [a] Data from 1989 is for Malaysian citizens only.

Source: Economic Planning Unit (http://www.epu.gov.my/c/document_library/get_file?uuid=e2b128f0-c6fb-4890-8a17-3f708fc3d7a8&g roupId=34492)

Table 2.24 Malaysia: Unemployment by State, 1980–2011 (%)

	1980	1985	1990	1995	2000	2005	2011
More developed states							
Johor	5.3	6.9	3.3	2.5	2.3	5.8	2.5
Melaka	6.4	8.3	4.0	2.2	2.0	–	0.7
N. Sembilan	5.5	7.5	3.7	3.0	3.3	3.5	3.0
Perak	6.3	8.1	4.5	3.8	3.5	3.5	1.7
P. Pinang	5.1	6.4	3.4	1.3	1.7	2.0	1.8
Selangor	4.4	6.3	2.9	1.9	1.9	3.0	2.4
Less developed states							
Kedah	6.6	8.4	4.4	1.9	2.7	3.5	3.5
Kelantan	7.4	8.1	5.9	3.4	3.4	3.5	1.9
Pahang	4.7	7.2	4.0	3.5	2.8	3.5	2.6
Perlis	7.2	7.6	4.7	1.3	1.9	3.5	3.9
Sabah	5.3	6.9	9.1	5.4	5.6	6.1	5.6
Sarawak	8.3	9.3	8.9	4.7	4.6	3.5	4.6
Terengganu	5.1	8.7	7.4	5.9	3.3	3.5	3.2
Malaysia	5.7	7.6	5.1	3.1	3.1	3.8	3.1

Sources: Various Malaysia Plan documents; Calculated with data from Department of
Statistics, Malaysia, *Labour Force Survey Report*, various issues.

the economy, as in Sabah and Terengganu, unemployment has remained relatively higher. Sabah, Sarawak, Terengganu and Kelantan were among the states with the highest unemployment rates from the 1990s, with Sabah's position deteriorating in recent years. Due to locational factors and less attractive infrastructural facilities, these states have not been able to attract many industries, unlike more industrialized regions, such as Penang, Kuala Lumpur and Selangor.

Spatial differences in growth and industrialization as well as costs and standards of living have also affected remuneration expectations and practices as well as working conditions (Table 2.25). There are significant differences in conditions in the three industrial growth poles of Penang (and Province Wellesley), the Kelang Valley and Southern Johor, especially with the rest of the country. In Sabah and Sarawak, different

Table 2.25 Malaysia: Average Manufacturing Wage Rates by State, 1981–2008 (RM/month)

	1981	*1990*	*1995*	*2000*	*2008*
More developed states					
Johor	421	541	978	1,313	1,650
Melaka	330	470	894	1,259	1,741
N. Sembilan	444	730	971	1,475	2,078
Perak	333	542	839	1,109	1,492
P. Pinang	407	692	1,087	1,614	2,375
Selangor	516	828	1,269	1,712	2,166
Less developed states					
Kedah	286	453	817	1,038	1,602
Kelantan	182	369	420	601	825
Pahang	413	617	888	1,379	1,961
Perlis	417	636	668	1,037	1,571
Sabah	502	680	603	751	1,040
Sarawak	333	628	747	922	1,370
Terengganu	283	759	793	1,252	2,724
Average	413	661	1,008	1,382	1,896

Sources: Calculated with data from Department of Statistics, Malaysia, *State/District Data Bank, Malaysia*, various issues; *Yearbook of Statistics, Sabah*, various issues; *Yearbook of Statistics, Sarawak*, various issues.

labour laws, e.g. for workmen's compensation, were enforced until the late 1980s. Smallholder agriculture is still far more significant in the northern and eastern parts of Peninsular Malaysia as well as in Sabah and Sarawak, where some shifting cultivation persists. With the increasing use of immigrant labour, wage and working conditions in plantation agriculture are now even worse than in most other waged employment. Similarly, such conditions are generally better in larger, compared to smaller, enterprises in the same industry. Foreign employers are generally considered better than private sector Malaysians, though there is perceived to be considerable variation among foreigners.

Notes

1. An 'unpaid family worker' usually works as part of a family work group. While unpaid in the sense that they do not receive a formal wage, they receive a share of the output or proceeds of the output as part of family consumption. Social reciprocities — with respect to the family, households, kith and kin, and community — were important in pre-industrial production relations, usually motivated or sustained economic considerations. Today, these have often been replaced by modern industrial relations such as labour contracts.

2. For instance, in the colonial era, clerical occupations were the domain of men and were highly regarded, with white collar occupations generally dominated by men. Over time, as educated men moved into the higher white-collar occupations once held by British expatriates and the Malay aristocracy, and their places was increasingly taken over by women, the prestige and general skills associated with clerical work were eroded. Another example is the downgrading of some manufacturing jobs as these jobs become feminized, e.g. in the textile industry.

Part 3

Public Finance

This Part is primarily concerned with the distributional consequences of Malaysian public finances, principally taxation and expenditure. Taxation is the main source of government revenue although governments may also receive incomes from other sources, including the assets they own. While taxation finances government programmes (public investment and consumption), it reduces disposable household incomes that would affect aggregate private consumption and also investment. The welfare of poor households can be jeopardized by taxation if tax incidence and/or public spending are regressive. Taxation can also be progressive if those poorer are taxed proportionately less than the rich, or if revenue is used to finance programmes with a progressive impact.

Government expenditure includes what is called government consumption as well as investment. Public spending on services is generally referred to as consumption while its development or capital expenditure is presumed to be investment. It is often presumed that public social spending is progressive in impact, but greater subsidies for the better off can make such expenditure regressive. Such social spending can also be seen as providing public goods, e.g. through prevention of the spread of contagious diseases or by increasing labour productivity.

The largest Malaysian federal government allocations have gone to education services, public order and security as well as defence, administration, economic services and health services. Education facilitates entry into the job market while employment has been the major source of income for most. Health services are likely to be similar in impact. Conversely, public administration and economic services are less likely to be progressive in impact. Public administration is generally presumed to help maintain the status quo, thus offering more to those with more and less to those with less. Economic services are also expected to provide more opportunities for the more capable to increase their incomes more than for the less capable.

Examining the distributional aspects of federal government finance involves the incidence of taxation and government expenditure, including expenditures on social services such as health and education services. It discusses various types of taxes and the changes over the years. It reviews studies on the incidence of taxation and estimates differential tax burdens to assess whether they have been progressive, regressive or neutral. It also relates household income distribution to the use of government health and education services to assess their distributional impact.

The following Part 4 considers some implications of Malaysia's status as a federation, with the Federal Government taking a minimum 75 per cent of consolidated government revenue and incurring at least 80 per cent of consolidated government expenditure. The major source of federal government revenue has been from taxation while most state governments run by parties in the ruling coalition typically rely on federal government grants to supplement their own state government revenue. As the Malaysian federation has complex origins reflected in varying constitutional arrangements, the sources of state government revenues vary significantly, especially between Peninsular Malaysia and the Borneo States. Such variation also reflects their varied land and other natural resource revenue streams.

However, the focus in this Part will be on federal government finances, particularly on (direct and indirect) taxation as well as social (mainly health and education) expenditure. Hence, it largely ignores other roles of the federal government. The Malaysian public sector accounted for at least 10 per cent of GDP up to 1991, before decreasing to 8.5 per cent in 2012. Its share of the labour force increased from 11.0 per cent in 1970 to 15.0 per cent in 1983, after which, privatization saw it decrease to 10.0 per cent in 2012.

Table 3.1 Malaysia: Federal Government Finances, 1963–2015 (RM million)

	Revenue	Operating expenditure	Current balance	Development expenditure	Overall balance
1963–1965	4,188	3,959	229	1,527	-1,298
First Malaysia Plan, 1966–1970	9,897	9,309	588	3,187	-2,599
Second Malaysia Plan, 1971–1975	18,645	18,026	619	7,371	-6,752
Third Malaysia Plan, 1976–1980	47,189	38,199	8,990	20,659	-11,669
Fourth Malaysia Plan, 1981–1985	93,025	82,004	11,021	46,571	-35,550
Fifth Malaysia Plan, 1986–1990	114,422	109,480	4,942	28,738	-23,796
Sixth Malaysia Plan, 1991–1995	215,394	164,225	51,169	48,429	2,740
Seventh Malaysia Plan, 1996–2000	301,265	236,360	64,903	90,668	-25,764
Eighth Malaysia Plan, 2001–2005	461,391	397,222	64,668	162,452	-97,784
Ninth Malaysia Plan, 2006–2010	741,517	692,977	48,540	214,601	-166,061
Tenth Malaysia Plan, 2011–2015[a]	995,692	966,315	29,376	230,000	-200,624

Note: [a] Estimates.
Sources: Ministry of Finance, Malaysia, *Economic Report*, various issues; 10MP, Table 8.

Table 3.1 provides an overview of federal government finances over the last half century, including both revenue and expenditure. It shows federal government revenue and expenditure, and the overall fiscal deficit increasing very significantly in the 1970s until the mid-1980s, and then again after the 1997–1998 regional financial crisis. Figure 3.1 reflects spending on government services as a share of GDP, including changes in such government expenditure over the last four decades. While some big increases in spending, and corresponding fiscal deficits, were clearly counter-cyclical — e.g. in the mid-1970s, in the early 1980s and from 1998 — others are better understood in terms of securing political support, mainly before national general elections.

Before the 1990s, the Malaysian government fiscal rule was to ensure that government revenue exceeded operating or current expenditure to ensure a positive balance. Figure 3.2 shows the changing composition of

Figure 3.1 Government Sector, Malaysia: Services as a % of GDP and Annual Change in Total Expenditure, 1973–2012

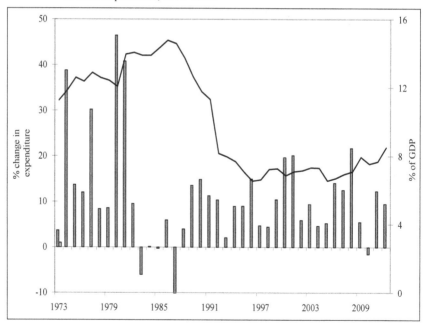

Note: GDP in constant 1987 prices for 1973–2004; in current prices for 2006–2012.
Sources: Calculated with data from Bank Negara Malaysia, *Monthly Bulletin of Statistics*, various issues.

Figure 3.2 Malaysia: Sources of Federal Government Revenue, 1970–2013
(RM million)

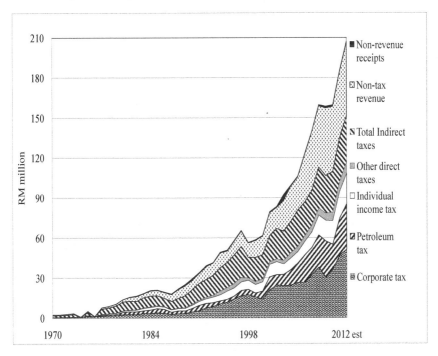

Sources: Bank Negara Malaysia, *Monthly Bulletin of Statistics*, various issues.

federal government revenue over a similar period. As Table 3.2 shows, development or capital expenditure was generally funded with government borrowings, largely from forced savings collected by the Employees Provident Fund (EPF), until the mid-1970s, when the government began borrowing from abroad with the availability of low real interest credit with the recycling of petrodollars following OPEC's success in raising petroleum prices in the mid- and late 1970s. Finance Ministers Daim Zainuddin and then Anwar Ibrahim ran an overall fiscal surplus from the late 1980s, and paid off much foreign government debt, especially during the decade-long boom from the late 1980s. However, the initially counter-cyclical fiscal deficits to address the 1997–1998 regional financial crisis has since become the 'new normal' although the government has paid down much of its crisis foreign debt.

Table 3.2 Malaysia: Overall Government Balance and Net Government Borrowings, 1970–2011 (RM million)

	1970	1975	1980	1985	1990	1995	2000	2005	2007	2008	2009	2010	2011
Balance (% of GNP)	-3.9	-8.8	-13.7	-7.9	-3.1	0.9	-6.0	-3.8	-3.3	-4.9	-7.1	-5.6	-4.9
External borrowings	-2	921	310	956	-767	-1,635	864	-3,503	-4,314	-474	-6,286	3,664	550
Domestic borrowings	365	1,210	2,311	3,591	3,793	–	12,714	12,700	25,800	35,879	56,879	36,456	45,069
Debt service (% of operating expenditure)	11.0	12.6	15.0	26.9	27.3	17.8	16.0	11.9	10.5	8.3	9.1	10.3	10.3
External debt service ratio (% of exports)	2.6	3.4	1.9	6.7	3.6	1.4	1.2	5.4	3.8	2.6	6.5	7.7	10.3

Sources: Bank Negara Malaysia, *Monthly Statistical Bulletin*, various issues; Ministry of Finance, Malaysia, *Economic Report*, various issues.

Taxation

Federal government taxes increased from RM915 million in 1963 to RM4,256 million in 1975, RM16,700 million in 1985, RM41,671million in 1995 and RM151,645 million in 2012 (Table 3.3). They increased from 15.2 per cent of GNP in 1967 to a peak of 23.5 per cent in 1980, dropped to 16.7 per cent during the recession of 1987, increased to 20.1 per cent in 1994, and fluctuated thereafter to 16.1 per cent in 2012.

Table 3.3 Malaysia: Federal Taxes, 1963–2012 (RM million)

Year	Federal Taxes	% of GNP	Year	Federal Taxes	% of GNP
1963	915	n.a.	1988	14,708	20.1
1964	1,049	n.a.	1989	16,774	20.2
1965	1,208	n.a.	1990	21,244	19.5
1966	1,343	n.a.	1991	25,830	20.1
1967	1,471	15.2	1992	28,772	19.6
1968	1,536	15.3	1993	31,900	19.5
1969	1,730	15.8	1994	37,487	20.1
1970	1,840	15.1	1995	41,671	16.9
1971	1,917	15.3	1996	47,272	16.2
1972	2,190	16.1	1997	53,627	13.2
1973	2,807	15.5	1998	45,346	17.4
1974	4,054	18.5	1999	45,346	17.4
1975	4,256	19.7	2000	47,173	15.5
1976	5,145	19.1	2001	61,492	15.2
1977	6,661	21.4	2002	66,860	15.5
1978	7,567	20.9	2003	64,891	14.9
1979	8,997	20.3	2004	72,050	14.6
1980	12,060	23.5	2005	80,594	15.1
1981	12,594	22.7	2006	86,630	15.2
1982	12,591	21.1	2007	95,168	14.2
1983	15,263	22.9	2008	112,897	15.6
1984	16,471	22.2	2009	106,504	20.1
1985	16,700	23.2	2010	109,516	20.2
1986	14,682	22.0	2011	134,885	19.5
1987	12,474	16.7	2012	151,645	16.1

Note: n.a. – not available

Sources: Calculated from Ministry of Finance, Malaysia, *Economic Report*, various issues.

Tax revenues increased from some 75 per cent of federal government revenue in 1963 to 94 per cent in 1973, and then fluctuated, declining to 81 per cent in 2011. Direct taxes increased from some 20 per cent of revenue in 1963 to 78 per cent in 1971, and fluctuated thereafter, falling to 70 per cent in 2011, while indirect taxes decreased from 60 per cent in 1963 to 15 per cent in 1971, and increased to 36 per cent in 1979 before decreasing to 11 per cent in 2011 (Figure 3.3). Much of the variation has been due to changes in petroleum prices and petroleum related revenues.

Tax coverage has been increasing over the years. As the economy grows, more businesses are subject to tax, and as personal incomes rise, more individuals are subject to personal income tax. Tax collection also improves with better administration, organization, technology and efficiency. Excise duties as well as sales and service taxes have been extended to more items, although some import duties have been reduced or abolished and export duties have declined in line with membership commitments of the World Trade Organization (WTO).

Figure 3.3 Malaysia: Direct Taxes, 1970–2012 (RM million)

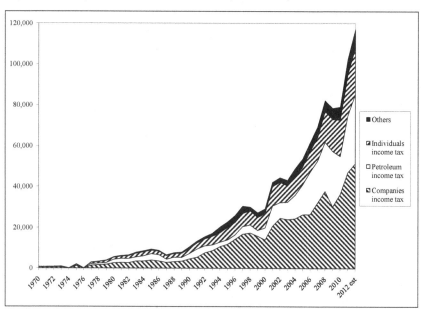

Sources: Bank Negara Malaysia, *Monthly Bulletin of Statistics*, various issues.

Direct Taxes

Direct taxes are levied on businesses and on personal incomes albeit at different rates. Direct taxes in Malaysia are generally presumed to be progressive mainly due to the (declining) progressivity of personal income tax. Businesses of different types are subject to different tax rates that tend to be flat for the category concerned. Some would argue that the tax incidence is generally higher on small and medium enterprises.

Taxes on Business

Corporate taxes other than tax on petroleum producing companies (petroleum tax) changed with the economic cycle, with a pre-financial crisis peak of 30.5 per cent in 1998 before dropping to 17 per cent in 2012. Petroleum tax increased from a low of 0.3 per cent in 1974 to 9.1 per cent in 1985, before decreasing to 2.3 per cent in 1996. Greater price volatility in recent years has caused this revenue source to fluctuate greatly, falling from 11.1 per cent in 2006 to 7.8 per cent in 2010, before increasing to some 10 per cent in 2011. Petroleum producing companies are generally assigned a generous 30 per cent of output value for cost recovery, though cost recovery rates increase with higher production costs and/or lower profitability (www.petronas.com.my).

The last five decades have seen overall personal income tax rates not only decline, but also become less progressive. The statutory corporate income tax rate was reduced from 40 per cent to 35 per cent in 1994, and then continuously reduced to the current 25 per cent. To justify this, the federal government has echoed the business community's argument that such tax rate reduction will encourage investments, although there is no strong evidence that this has been the case. In fact, domestic private investments have remained low for the last decade and a half since the 1997–1998 Asian crisis. However, in recent years, the government has suggested that tax reduction is secondary to political and exchange rate stability as well as provision of infrastructure, human resources and other inputs. As developing countries in general, and those in the region in particular have been involved in beggar thy neighbour tax rate competition resulting in reduced tax revenue from this source, it is difficult to raise corporate tax rates, especially on foreign investors.

Investment incentives in the form of tax exemptions further reduce the effective corporate tax rate. Hence, when the statutory tax rate was 40 per cent, the marginal effective tax rate (METR, i.e. the difference between pre-tax and post-tax rates of returns on investments[1]) was 32.0 per cent for all equities, and 20.5 per cent for 50 per cent debt equity[2] [Pellechio, Sirat and Dunn (1989), cited in Wee, 1997]. Further investment incentives in subsequent years would probably have caused taxes on investment incomes to be even more regressive.

Investment incentives in the form of tax exemptions usually follow a graduated schedule, where the exemption rate and period of exemption increase with the size of the capital invested and the number of fulltime workers employed. Needless to say, such a schedule favours large industries. Small and medium industries with paid-up capital of RM2.5 million or less have been taxed at a lower rate of 20 per cent only from 2003.

There have been taxes on 'excess profit' (for all businesses, e.g. for windfall gains in the tin and oil palm industries) while development tax has been imposed on income from business and from rental of property from the 1960s. Real property gains tax varied between 5 and 40 per cent in 1987, with the rate decreasing with a longer time lapse between the times of property acquisition and disposal. Over time, tax thresholds have been increased, tax rates reduced and some taxes even abolished, again generally reducing progressivity. The 2010 rate for property sold within the first five years of purchase was 5 per cent; since 2012, the rate for property held and disposed of within two years is 10 per cent, with the rate dropping to 5 per cent for property sold in the third to fifth year.

Taxes on business have also been used to control speculation. These include taxes on the transfer or disposal of shares exceeding RM1 million by companies with land assets. Following the 1997–1998 Asian financial crisis, a 30 per cent tax on profits repatriated within a month of capital transfer to Malaysia on or after 15 February 1999 and a 10 per cent tax on profits repatriated one year after capital transfer were introduced. Tax rates have also been reduced with some taxes abolished over time, ostensibly to encourage financial market growth (see Wee, 2006: Chapter 3).

Personal Income Taxes

Personal income tax revenue increased from 2.3 per cent of total revenue in 1970 to 7.2 per cent in 1979, fluctuated, rising to 12.2 per cent in 1999, and then decreased to 7.7 per cent in 2012. Generally, the tax reforms from the 1980s have reduced the progressivity of personal income tax incidence. The number of tax brackets was reduced from eleven in 1979 to eight by 2002. The combination of brackets means that those in the lower bracket are now taxed at the same rate as those in the higher bracket with whom they are combined. The highest tax rate for the highest income bracket was also reduced from 55 per cent in 1979 to 25 per cent in 2012, the same rate as the statutory corporate tax rate. Personal and family relief as well as exemptions for expenditure on health and education are provided. There has been no change in such relief since 2000. Comparing changes in the tax threshold for a four-member household with consumer price indices over time suggests considerable erosion of the real value of tax relief since 1991, especially with the consumer price index (CPI) increasing by 69 per cent during 1991–2000. For the first time in 2012, the tax relief is estimated to exceed the CPI increase (Table 3.4).

Estate duty is levied on the transfer of property from a deceased person to the beneficiaries. The exemption threshold was increased from RM10,000 to RM25,000 after 1965. Estate duties of 12–45 per cent were levied on property with a minimum value of RM100,000 for deaths occurring in Malaysia, and at 5–60 per cent on property with a minimum value of RM40,000 for deaths outside Malaysia. In 1984, the thresholds were increased to RM2 million and RM500,000 respectively, while the rates were reduced to 5–10 per cent. Estate duties for all deaths occurring on or after October 1991 were later abolished, eliminating the sole wealth tax in Malaysia.

The gross monthly household income of Malaysian citizens was RM1,563 in 1992. The abolition of estate duty with a threshold of RM2 million for death within Malaysia and RM500,000 for death outside Malaysia means that beneficiaries who inherit an amount equivalent to 106.6 years and 53.3 years of average household income respectively get them tax-free. The eventual abolition of estate duty effectively means that beneficiaries obtain even higher exemptions. The official argument for abolishing estate duties was that there were only a few who paid estate

Table 3.4 Malaysia: Tax Threshold for a Four-Member Household, 1980, 1991–1998, 2000–2012

	Non-working Spouse		Working Couple		Non-working Spouse		Working Couple		Non-working Spouse		Working Couple	
	1980	1991	1980	1991	1980	2000	1980	2000	1980	2012	1980	2012
Relief (RM)												
2 earners	10,000	10,000	10,000	10,000	10,000	16,000	10,000	16,000	10,000	18,000	10,000	18,000
Spouse	2,000	3,000	–	–	2,000	3,000	–	–	2,000	3,000	–	–
1st child	800	800	800	800	800	800	800	800	800	800	800	800
Total	12,800	13,800	10,800	10,800	12,800	19,800	10,800	16,800	12,800	21,800	10,800	18,800
Tax threshold	12,800[a]	18,800[b]	10,800[a]	15,800[b]	12,800[a]	24,300[b]	10,800[a]	21,800[b]	12,800[a]	26,800[b]	10,800[a]	26,800[b]
Increase (%)		47		46		82		102		109		148
Increase in consumer price index (%)		44		44		95		95		100		100

Notes: [a] The individual tax rate was 6 per cent for chargeable income (income less exemptions) of RM2,500.
[b] The individual tax rate was 0 per cent for chargeable income (income less exemptions) of RM2,500. Hence, the tax threshold for a household with a spouse not earning a cash income was the sum of the total exemptions plus RM2,500, while that for a household with a working couple was the sum of the total exemptions plus double RM2,500 or RM5,000.

Sources: Calculated with data from Inland Revenue Board, Malaysia; Bank Negara Malaysia, *Monthly Statistical Bulletin*, various issues; 2013 Budget.

duties. However, as the administrative mechanisms and arrangements had long existed, no additional burden was involved if estate duty continued to be imposed. Also, the number paying estate duty would be much more if the earlier threshold levels had been maintained.

Malaysian employers and employees are required by law to contribute to the Employees' Provident Fund (EPF) under the EPF Act, 1951. The contribution is effectively a production cost for employers, but constitutes deferred income for the employees in the form of forced savings for them. It reduces the take-home pay for employees, although their contributions are effectively forced savings for the future. The average income of employees is lower than that of employers or those involved in business (Inland Revenue Board, 2000). Hence, the EPF contribution constitutes a relatively greater current income loss for relatively low-income EPF contributors. Social security and payroll taxes as a proportion of household incomes decreased with household income for 1968, 1970, 1973 and 1979 (Ismail, 1980), suggesting greater current income loss among lower income contributors. The Gini ratio and Atkinson index for the distribution of income after paying EPF and for life insurance also increased during 1981–1998 (Wee, 2006a), implying greater income inequality post-payment.

Leaving aside EPF and SOCSO contributions, direct taxes on residents, such as income tax, development tax and excess profit tax, are progressive in impact. The Gini ratio and the Atkinson index for the distribution of income decline after these taxes are levied compared to before. However, the progressive impact of such taxes appears to have declined from the 1970s, as suggested by Wee (2006a).

Indirect Taxes

The major indirect taxes have been export duties, import duties, excise duties, sales taxes and service taxes. Export duties grew from RM259 million in 1970 to RM1,968 million in 2012, although their share of indirect taxes fell from 22.4 per cent to 5.7 per cent over this period. Meanwhile, import duties grew from RM558 million to RM2,282 million, declining from 48.3 per cent to 6.6 per cent of total indirect taxes over the same four decades. Excise duties grew from RM249 million (21.6 per

Figure 3.4 Malaysia: Indirect Taxes, 1970–2012 (RM million)

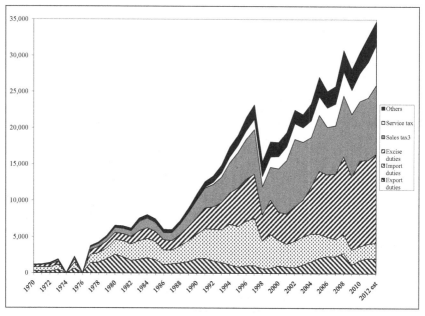

Sources: Bank Negara Malaysia, *Monthly Bulletin of Statistics*, various issues.

cent) in 1970 to RM112,187 million (35.1 per cent) in 2011, while sales and service taxes grew from insignificant amounts to RM8,171 million (26.8 per cent) and RM15,079 million (43.4 per cent) respectively over the same period (Figure 3.4).

Export Duties

Export duties have been levied on primary commodities such as rubber, palm oil, pepper, tin, iron ore, sawn timber and petroleum, as well as certain foodstuffs and manufactures. They were important sources of government revenue in colonial times and the early years after independence. It has been argued that export duties are essentially taxes on producers because Malaysia is a price taker internationally. The inelasticity of supply for both rubber and palm oil (0.00128, as estimated by Chow, 1975) further supports the argument. Some manufactured products were exempted from duties to encourage export-oriented industrialization.

Duty rates on rubber, palm oil, pepper and tin vary according to market prices. Hence, there is no consideration of producer taxpayers' incomes, which are also determined by volume of production. Narayanan (1986) estimated that in 1973, export duty on a four acre holding with a low-yielding rubber variety was 11.6 per cent of the net income of RM925.60, while that on a high yielding holding of the same size was 10.6 per cent of its net income of RM1,851.50. An urban worker earning the same income as the low yielding rubber smallholder would be below the income tax threshold level and only taxed at 12 per cent if his or her income was at least RM19,000. Ismail estimated that the incidence of export duties in 1968, 1970, 1973 and 1979 were U-shaped, i.e. regressive at low incomes and progressive at high incomes. However, they were highly regressive for those with low incomes, mainly rubber smallholders (Khoo, 1980), and also became more regressive over time (Ismail 1977: Table 5.6; 1980: Table 8; Wee, 2006a).

Smallholders have also been required to pay to the rubber replanting fund cess. Khoo (1980) estimated that the cess and export duty which smallholders paid was equivalent to about 40 per cent of smallholders' income. In the late 1970s, many smallholders had yet to use the replanting fund that had led to the creation of the Rubber Industry Smallholders Development Authority (RISDA). Nonetheless, long-term declines in commodity prices, especially for rubber, and better jobs available elsewhere have seen a significant decline in the number of smallholders, as the development of manufacturing and urban services have increased urban wage labour.

The tax rates seemed to favour the larger capital-intensive dredging companies, often owned by British corporations before they were bought over by Malaysians. Tax was a higher portion of producers' net returns for the mainly ethnic Chinese owned, less capital-intensive and lower net receipts gravel pump (tin) mining than for dredge mining in 1968 and 1975 (Narayanan, 1986: Table 5.2). Only when the tin price was highest, at RM1,140 per pikul[3] in 1976, was the tax on gravel pump mining a lower portion of producers' net receipts than for dredge mining.

Also, the highest marginal effective export duty rate was for tin (18.25 per cent), followed by processed rubber (7.61 per cent), sawn logs (7.26 per cent), rubber (2.24 per cent), rubber products (1.19 per cent), wearing apparel (18.1 per cent), (refined) oils and fats (0.74 per cent), sawn timber (0.39 per cent) and crude palm oil (0.25 per cent) (Boadway, Chua and Flatters, 1995). No clear policy stance emerges from these different rates. The much higher duty on tin may be due to it being a non-renewable mineral resource, but it is unusual for such a tax to be imposed in the form of an export duty. A higher duty on processed rubber than on rubber would have discouraged greater domestic value added, while the export duty on garments seemed to discourage such exports, thus contradicting the export-oriented industrialization policy.

The incidence of all export duties on the income distribution in 1968 and the 1970s was U-shaped, indicating a regressive impact at low-income levels (Wee, 2006a). In later years, lowering or eliminating export duties were presumed to benefit low-income workers seeking employment in export-oriented industries induced to invest in Malaysia by such tax reforms.

Import Duties

Besides generating government revenues, import duties were used to encourage and protect domestic industries. Some such duties have been abolished to promote tourism and shopping in Malaysia. In more recent years, import duties have been reduced or abolished on account of WTO obligations, although protection for heavy industries promoted in the 1980s remains, albeit at lower rates. Relatively high rates for import duties have been imposed on 'sinful' items such as alcoholic beverages and tobacco, but these have had regressive effects on low-income consumers. The incidence of import duties on households was found to be regressive in 1995 and 1999 (Wee, 2006a). However, Malaysia's membership of the WTO means that import duties are generally not high except for some favoured heavy industries.

Excise Duties

The first excise duties were levied on refined petroleum and heavy oils, sugar, liquor, tobacco and cigarettes. The rates for motor vehicles, levied from 1970, have been among the highest — 10–20 per cent for motorcycles and 30 per cent for vans were introduced in 1990; 5 per cent for passenger vehicles, which was increased to 45–60 per cent in 1991. The combined incidence of import duties and excise duties levied was regressive in 1968, 1970 and 1973, especially for low-income households (Wee, 2006a). The incidence of excise duties continued to be regressive in 1995 and 1999 (Wee, 2006a).

New arrangements were introduced in the 1980s, with excise duties levied on mass consumption goods, including aerated and non-aerated beverages, matches, cigarette lighters, playing-cards, some household equipment, plastic articles, inner tubes of motor vehicle tyres, electric machinery and cement. Excise duties were also levied to generate revenue until they were reduced or abolished to increase export competitiveness. In 1995, duties on kerosene and fuel were abolished. The abolition of duties on fuel aimed to reduce transport costs, ostensibly to augment growth. In 2000, the excise duty on petroleum was abolished in the ASEAN Free Trade Area as previously agreed (Bank Negara Malaysia, *Annual Report*, various issues).

Sales taxes

Sales taxes were imposed on businesses with annual sales over RM12,000 from 1972. The rates were 5 per cent for domestic manufactures, 4 per cent for imports and 10 per cent for luxuries, including cigars, cigarettes, alcoholic beverages, perfumery and jewellery. By 1978, coverage had broadened to include clothing and textiles, paper and paper products, metal and metal products, electrical parts, machinery, vehicles, as well as more alcohol, tobacco and luxury products, with more items taxed at 10 per cent and the others at 5 per cent. In 1985, taxed items included plastic products (30 per cent tax) and iron (5 per cent tax). By 1990, sales tax had been extended to food items, wood products and chemicals. In 2000, sales tax was extended to spare parts. In 2002, the rates were 5 per cent on fruits, certain foodstuffs and building materials, 15 per cent standard 'sin tax' on cigarettes, liquor and other alcoholic drinks, and a standard 10 per cent on all other items. The threshold for businesses subject to such taxes has been increased; currently, it is RM100,000 sales turnover in the preceding 12 months.

To reduce production costs, sales taxes on raw materials, components, as well as machinery and equipment for manufacturing were abolished in 1996, while exemption for other inputs was provided in 1997. There have been numerous exemptions — some 30 per cent of both locally produced and imported items were taxed up to the late 1980s (Randhawa, Onn, Khalid Ahmad, 1994). Taxes on many luxuries and consumer durables of interest to tourists — such as cameras, watches and fountain pens — were abolished in 1982, while a sales tax on petroleum replaced petroleum import and excise duties in 2000 (Department of Customs and Excise, Malaysia).

The incidence of sales taxes on food, beverages, tobacco and manufactured durables was regressive in 1973. As incomes increased, taxes as a proportion of income decreased (Ismail 1980). The regressive impact of the taxation of food (including sugar), tobacco and alcoholic beverages has been attributed to inelastic consumer demand (Kwok, 1979: Tables 1, 5, 8; Sritua Arief, 1983: Tables 1–4; Barjoyai Bardai, 1993: 100–101). Heavy fuels and oils are also believed to be characterized by inelastic demand. Petroleum, road transport and motor vehicles are also required for the transportation of persons and goods, implying the widespread effect of the taxation of such goods. The effect of all sales taxes was regressive — sales taxes as a proportion of household income decreased with income in 1973, 1979, 1995 and 1999 (Ismail, 1980; Wee, 2006a).

Service Taxes

A 5 per cent service tax was introduced in 1975. Service taxes have been levied on hotels, restaurants and establishments serving food and beverages, various entertainment centres, health services, transportation, communications and insurance services, security, parking and motor vehicle services, as well as the professional services of accountants, lawyers, engineers, architects, surveyors and accountants. In 1983, the rate was doubled to 10 per cent with the scope widened to establishments having annual sales turnovers of at least RM500,000. The scope was further widened every year from 1995 to 1998, and extended to institutions dealing with spare parts from 2000 (Department of Customs and Excise, Malaysia).

Table 3.5 Malaysia: Incidence of Indirect Taxes on Consumer Households, 1968, 1970, 1973, 1995, 1999

| | Gini Ratio | | | Atkinson Index (E = 2) | | |
	Before Taxes	After Taxes	Difference	Before Taxes	After taxes	Difference
1968	0.4583	0.4468	-0.0115	0.4727	0.4823	0.0096
1970	0.5139	0.5372	0.0233	0.5652	0.5784	0.0132
1973	0.5037	0.5285	0.0248	0.5413	0.5881	0.0468
1995	0.4543	0.4644	0.0101	0.5278	0.5537	0.0259
1999	0.4419	0.4585	0.0166	0.5093	0.5325	0.0232

Source: Wee (2006: Table 3.31).

As with sales taxes, the introduction and expansion of service taxes will provide an additional source of government revenue as the government continues to reduce the statutory direct tax rates and to abolish international trade taxes in line with WTO agreements. However, the government has postponed implementation an economy-wide general sales and services tax for fear of adverse public reaction following implementation. Services taxes were found to be regressive in 1995 and 1999, especially at the lower income levels (Wee, 2006a). The incidence of all indirect taxes has been regressive from the 1970s to the late 1990s (Wee, 2006a). Such taxation increased the Gini ratio and Atkinson index for household income inequality (Table 3.5). Except for informal labour and the top income bracket, indirect consumption taxes have been regressive (Barjoyai, 1993: Tables 2.8, 2.10).

There is insufficient information for detailed analysis of current tax incidence. Tax reforms from the mid-1980s have been pro-business; consequently, the incidence of taxation can be expected to be regressive. With taxation regressive in overall impact, a progressive redistributive fiscal impact can therefore only be achieved with sufficiently progressive government spending.

Government Expenditure

The incidence of government expenditure — in the form of public consumption, transfer payments and public investments — in Peninsular Malaysia was considered to be progressive in 1968 (Snodgrass, 1975:

Figure 3.5 Malaysian States: Development Allocation by Household Income, 1981–2010 (RM per household per month)

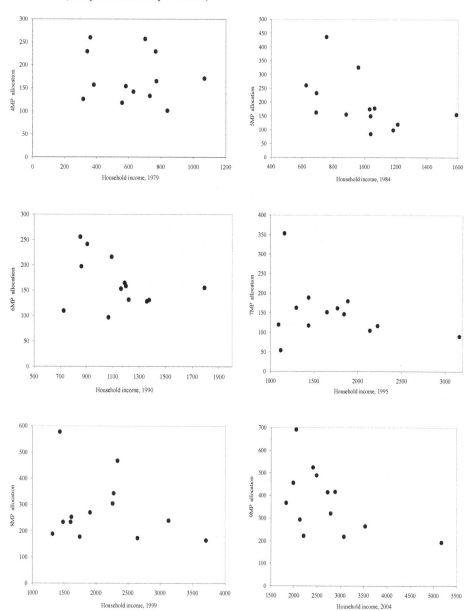

Sources: Various Malaysia plan documents.

Table III). However, the incidence of major government spending – such as on education, health, agriculture and pensions — was U-shaped by 1974, and slightly regressive for the fourth and fifth income quintiles in the peninsula (Snodgrass, 1980: Table 6.6). Further, development allocation per household by state has not been related to state household income (Figure 3.5). As government programmes have generally facilitated development (see Part 1), the pattern of development allocations has not been corrected for, but has probably exacerbated regional imbalances (Part 2).

Health Services

Malaysia has achieved significant improvements in the health status of its population. In 2009, life expectancy was 73, higher than most countries in the Association of Southeast Asian Nations (Table 3.6). In 2010, the infant mortality rate in 2010 was 5 per 1000, only higher than Singapore in ASEAN, while the maternal mortality rate was 29 per 100,000 live births, only higher than Brunei and Singapore in the region.

Health services have been growing, with health personnel more than doubling in the period 1990–2010 (Table 3.7); 60 per cent of doctors and 90 per cent of nurses served the government in 2006 (Department of Statistics, State/District Data Bank, 2007: Table 4.1). Government health

Table 3.6 Economic and Health Status in Selected Countries

	Life expectancy, 2009 (years)	*Infant Mortality, 2010 (per 1000 live births)*	*Maternal Mortality, 2010 (per 100,000 births)*
Singapore	82	2	3
Brunei	77	6	24
Malaysia	73	5	29
Thailand	70	11	48
Vietnam	72	19	59
Philippines	70	23	99
Indonesia	68	27	220
Myanmar	64	50	200

Source: World Health Organization.

Table 3.7 Malaysia: Number of Selected Medical and Allied Health Professionals, 1990, 2000, 2010

	1990	*2000*	*2010*
Doctors	7,012	16,468	22,979
Dentists	1,471	2,001	3,810
Pharmacists	1,239	2,801	7,750
Nurses	28,932	47,812	69,110
Medical assistants	4,903	8,287	10,350
Medical laboratory technologists			4,980[a]
Dental paramedics and auxiliaries	2,137	4,097	5,635
Occupational therapists	234	811	649[a]
Physiotherapists			807[a]
Radiographers	508	1,049	2,030[a]

Note: [a] Ministry of Health
Sources: 7MP, Table 17-2; MTR9MP, Table 4-1; Calculated with data from the Department of Statistics, Malaysia.

services are generally affordable as they are highly subsidized, that is, by over 95 per cent (see Wee and Jomo, 2007).

The poor were generally more likely to use government health services. The total number of visits per capita to government clinics or hospitals decreased with higher income (quintiles) in 1974/75, as in 1996. The poorest 20 per cent (quintile) in 1973/74 utilized about a fifth of government health services, the 6.8 per cent who were deemed poor utilized 19.4 per cent of government inpatient health services and 40.0 per cent of outpatient services in 1996 (Meerman, 1979: 80, 158–161; Abu Bakar and Jegathesan, 2000 [NHMS2 *The Second National Health and Morbidity Survey* 1996]: 20; *Third Outline Perspective Plan, 2001– 2010*, Table 2-6). Subsidization generally decreased — progressively — with income, but the trend is not consistent and strong; e.g. the third quintile appeared to enjoy more subsidization than the second quintile (Wee, 2006a; Meerman, 1979: 80, 158–161; Rozita Halina Hussein, 2000: Graph 8).

Greater use of public health services by the less well to do is principally due to affordability as the poor generally live further from health facilities, both public and private. Compared to the richest quintile, the poorest quintile was 1.5 to 2 times further from a government facility and 4 to 5 times further from a private facility in 1996 (Rozita Halina Hussein, 2000: Table 2). Eighty three per cent of the national population lived in Peninsular Malaysia in 1986–1987, with 74 per cent of the peninsular population living within 3 kilometres of a static health facility, and 89 per cent within 5 kilometres. By 1996, 81.1 per cent lived within 3 kilometres and 92.5 per cent within 5 kilometres (NHMS2). Ninety-two per cent of the urban population lived within 3 kilometres of a static health facility, compared to 69 per cent of the rural population. The largest and less developed states of Sarawak, Sabah and Pahang had lower shares of their populations within 5 kilometres, i.e. 60 per cent, 76 per cent and 79 per cent respectively (NHMS2). The rural populations in Sabah and Sarawak live even further from static health facilities, with 50 per cent and 62 per cent of their rural populations respectively living within 5 kilometres (NHMS2).

Greater distance from health facilities increases transportation costs and time with its associated opportunity costs. The average transport cost for seeking government health care and medical fees was RM0.41 in 1973/74, and increased to RM2.20–RM2.50 in 1986/87 and RM4.39 in 1996. The cost of transport and medical fees in 1986/87 was at least five times that in 1973/74, while average household income in 1986/87 was only 3.1 times that in 1973/74. Compared to 1973/74, the total cost for 1996 was more than ten times higher, while average monthly household income was only 6.7 times higher. Hence, government health service costs became relatively higher over this period (Wee, 2006a).

Greater distance, higher travel costs and the longer travel time involved have presumably reduced the demand for health services (Heller, 1976; Meerman, 1979; Ministry of Health, NHMS1, 1986/87; NHMS2). Waiting time is even more of a deterrent for many because of the opportunity costs incurred. Many can ill afford the cost of foregoing income to utilize health services. Hence, although low income earners are more likely to use (heavily subsidized) government health services, with relatively higher out of pocket expenses and opportunity costs as shares of personal or household income, it is not clear that public provision of health services has been significantly progressive.

Furthermore, the distributional impact of recently developed modern facilities, such as the government-owned National Heart Institute (NHI), is likely to benefit the better off more because of their better knowledge and ability to seek treatment in the capital city. For the period 1992–2001, only 6–14 per cent of subsidized NHI outpatients were categorised as low income, while 16–29 per cent of inpatients were thus classified. The proportions of subsidized government servants also exceeded their share of the workforce, which decreased from 15 per cent in 1983 to 10.2 per cent in 2010 (National Heart Institute, Malaysia, *Annual Report*, various issues).

Under-utilization of health services by the less well-off can be expected to worsen with government initiatives to privatize the health services. Although privatization was ostensibly meant to reduce the government's financial burden, it has increased various costs. For example, government medical stores used to produce or dispense drugs without profit or to buy drugs at bulk-discount. Privatization has increased costs

Table 3.8 Malaysia: Population per Doctor by State, 1980, 1990, 2000, 2010

	1980	*1990*	*2000*	*2010*
More developed states:				
Johor	4560	3130	1843	1229
Melaka	3840	2640	1174	721
N. Sembilan	3060	2604	1284	761
Perak	4430	2799	1406	912
Pulau Pinang	2780	1798	1077	741
Selangor	4420	2288	1839	915
Less developed states:				
Kedah	6980	4253	1967	1210
Kelantan	9970	3782	1569	1649
Pahang	4880	3509	2035	1125
Perlis	5090	3411	1704	772
Sabah	7830	5061	3325	2011
Sarawak	7230	4786	2719	1666
Terengganu	8340	4249	1835	1214
Malaysia	3800	2533	1490	1009

Sources: Calculated with data from Department of Statistics, Malaysia, *State/District Data Bank*, various issues.

without corresponding efficiency gains (Mohamed Izham, Dzulkifli and Zubaidah, 1997). Meanwhile higher remunerations prospect are attracting government health personnel into the private sector, especially in the more developed states, where higher income groups can better afford private health services. Hence, the less developed states are further disadvantaged, with higher population-doctor ratios (Table 3.8).

Education

Education has been associated with lower infant mortality rates and neo-natal death rates (Hill, 1975) as well as higher incomes — in the late 1960s (Hoerr, 1973), 1970s (Mazumdar, 1981; Anand, 1983) and the 1990s (Idrus and Cameroon, 2000). The increased education of Malays has also facilitated their movement into the modern urban sector and raised their incomes, narrowing inter-ethnic differences.

The government provides most education services (Wee, 2006), while education takes one of the largest shares of government expenditure. Over the years, literacy rates and education levels have increased (see Part 2). Free schooling for 11 years and subsidization of government schools increases absolutely — though not proportionately — with education level. For example, the government share of primary and secondary school operating costs increased from well over a third in 1973/74 to 97 per cent in 1996 (Meerman, 1979: Tables 4.5, 4.15). The ratio of subsidy per capita for secondary education increased from 28 per cent more than for primary education in 1975 to 76 per cent more in 1985.

Such subsidization has led to high private net internal rates of return (NIRR), which increased with the level of education, i.e. from 12.9 per cent for primary education to 17 per cent or more for secondary education (calculated using Hoerr, 1975). Comparison of the social NIRR with the private NIRR indicates that Malaysia had one of the highest rates of subsidization (per cent of the private NIRR over and above the social NIRR) (Harvard Institute for International Development, 1997: Table 2.14).

In spite of subsidization, the less well-off find it difficult to pay out-of-pocket expenses for schooling. School drop-out rates of the poor have also been higher because of less supportive household (e.g. lack of study facilities, work requirements to increase household income or welfare) and school conditions (e.g. poorer facilities in rural schools for students with lower household incomes). In 1973, the urban school enrolment rate was 47 per cent, while the rural rate was 28 per cent (Ministry of Education, 1973). The lower rate for rural households is presumably related to their lower household income of RM269 per month compared to RM570 for urban households in 1974. Taking into consideration the number of children per household and the enrolment rate by quintile, Meerman (1979) estimated that the unmet needs of the bottom 40 per cent of households was about 15.5 per cent, while the top fifth enjoyed 34.7 per cent in subsidies (Meerman, 1979). The lower enrolment rates for poorer households imply lower subsidization, with subsidization increasing from 15.1 per cent for the poorest quintile to 34.7 per cent for the richest quintile in 1975 (Mazumdar, 1981: Tables 11.5, 12.9).

Tertiary education is more costly, with government institutions of higher education even more highly subsidized (Bowman, Millot and Schiefelbein, 1986a). The better off are more likely to obtain tertiary education and hence enjoy the corresponding subsidies, with the average household subsidy increasing from less than RM77 for the poorest quintile to RM176 for the richest fifth in 1973/74. For example, students from the richest quintile of households accounted for 56.5 per cent of those in tertiary institutions in 1973 and 48 per cent in 1979 (Bowman, Millot and Schiefelbein, 1986b: Table 13-5; Jandhala, 1989: Table 11). Offers of places in public tertiary institutions are based on academic credentials within ethnic quotas (e.g. favouring Bumiputeras), i.e. meritocracies within segmented ethnic pools of applicants. Not surprisingly, the poor have been under-represented in tertiary education because of their poorer academic credentials probably due to their household circumstances, although the disparities may have narrowed over time (see Wee, 2006: 130–137).

Government subsidization of the better off is even higher if the award of government scholarships and loans at concessionary interest rates is considered. Lian (1976) found a fairly large number of children from well-to-do families receiving government scholarships for higher education. More than half the students in institutions of higher learning benefiting from state scholarships and loans in 1977/78 came from urban areas (Ministry of Education, Educational Planning and Research

Division 1981). As urban household incomes were about twice those of rural households (*4MP*, Table 3-9; *MTR4MP*, Table 3-8) and have become relatively higher, the imbalance is likely to have persisted (e.g. for 1982/1983, see Wee, 2006: Table 5-39).

Only MARA allocated slightly more than half its scholarships and loans to students from rural areas. MARA facilities have been reserved for Bumiputera, especially from the rural areas. However, Mehmet and Yip (1985, cited in Lee, 1999) found that a rich Bumiputera household was 21 times more likely than a poor Bumiputera household to be awarded a government scholarship.

The Sabah and Sarawak (State) Governments may have been more successful in reducing imbalances, with 70 per cent of scholarships going to low-income families. Poor Bumiputera families in rural Sabah and Sarawak got 50 per cent of scholarships, with their share increasing over time. However, among the non-Bumiputera in urban Sarawak, unlike the relatively poor, the better off had scholarships (Jasbir and Mehmet, 1991). The proportion of students receiving scholarships fell from 60 per cent in 1983 to 40 per cent in 1987. The National Higher Education Fund Corporation was established in 1997 to provide interest-free loans to students in institutions of higher learning, thus lowering the government financial burden by reducing scholarships and increasing loans, as the loan scheme requires repayment by students once they start working. The 2003 Budget established an initial RM1 billion grant to provide matching higher education grants for savings by children from low-income families. It appears to be an attempt to induce contributions from beneficiaries as well, with the focus on needy families.

However, growing graduate unemployment implies that the expectations of higher pay for higher education may not be realized. Hence, the expected contributions from targeted beneficiaries of both the higher education fund and the matching grant for poor families may not be forthcoming. The 2012 Budget abolished school fees for co-curriculum and internal examination and provides schooling assistance of RM100 for all students from Primary 1 to Form 5. Book vouchers of RM200 for students in higher institutions of learning are also provided. Tax exemption on expenses for higher education, including private education for those who can afford it, has also benefited the better-off.

Privatization

Public policy from the late colonial period, resulting in the emergence, growth and privatization of state-owned enterprises (SOEs) in Malaysia, involved a combination of developmental and distributional concerns. However, by the 1980s, it had become clear that many SOEs were poorly conceived and managed. Ineffective accountability and budget constraints as well as poor incentives to improve performance exacerbated the performance of many Malaysian SOEs.

The complex and varied circumstances of the emergence of SOEs meant that privatization was a rather blunt policy instrument for addressing the range of problems faced by Malaysian SOEs. There is uneven evidence suggesting some improvements in particular aspects of firm performance following privatization. This includes some efficiency gains accompanying, though not necessarily due to privatization. But such improved performance was often wrongly attributed to privatization, i.e. to changes in ownership *per se*, without any conclusive evidence of such causation. Thus, the uneven and modest overall efficiency gains *associated with* privatization have been misleadingly *attributed to* privatization. Efficiency gains, for instance, were often due to other changes coinciding with, but not caused by, the change in ownership associated with privatization. Actual efficiency gains ascribed to privatization had more to do with organizational, managerial and incentive reforms, which did not require privatization as a precondition.

In the Malaysian experience, the transfer of ownership from public to private hands did not reduce user charges or significantly enhance service quality cost-effectively. Improvements in efficiency as well as service quality were accompanied by disproportionately higher user charges, resulting in net consumer welfare losses. While there were undoubtedly improvements in the quality of services provided, user fees generally rose disproportionately more than additional costs, with obviously adverse implications for consumer welfare and distributional implications. This was largely due to the retained monopoly status and poor regulation of privatized entities. As with 'voucher privatization' elsewhere, the under-pricing of privatized SOE initial public offers (IPOs) also enhanced public support from direct beneficiaries, many of whom were politically well-connected, at the state's and the public's expense.

Hence, efficiency gains were not all that significant, but were exaggerated by privatization proponents. And in so far as there were some improvements, these were not the result of privatization *per se*, but were mainly due to incentive, managerial and organizational reforms which did not require privatization. Privatization advocates claimed that enhanced efficiency would be achieved as private owners respond better to competition. In the Malaysian context, however, privatization was not accompanied by significantly increased competition. For example, MAS, Pos Malaysia Berhad, Tenaga Nasional Berhad, Telekom Malaysia, and MISC remained virtual monopolies (Jomo [ed.], 1995).

While competition may induce more efficient behaviour among private — as well as public — entities, to achieve both productive and allocative efficiencies, increasing returns to scale and other factors may favour natural monopolies, especially in relatively small economies. Hence, competition policy must be mindful of such considerations that are important in pursuing developmental and progressive distributional objectives. After all, some of the privatized enterprises are natural monopolies. Thus, if privatization merely involves transforming a public monopoly into a private monopoly, consumer welfare may well be adversely affected. In such circumstances, even greater enterprise efficiency may not necessarily enhance consumer welfare, but only the monopoly profits accruing to a privatized enterprise.

Instead, the public sector, including statutory bodies and other SOEs, could be reformed to enhance efficiency, cost-effectiveness as well as dynamic, equitable, balanced and sustainable national economic development. Many SOEs were set up because the private sector was unable or unwilling to provide the services or produce the goods concerned at acceptable cost. Such claims may still be relevant in some cases, no longer relevant in other cases, and perhaps never even true or relevant in yet other cases. And regardless of the validity of the rationale for their establishment in the first place, many SOEs could have become problematic, often inefficient, frequently even failing to achieve their own original declared objectives, or abused by those who control them for their own ends, and draining scarce public resources due to their 'soft budget constraints' and the very inertia of their existence.

Clearly, privatization is not the universal panacea for the myriad problems of the public sector it is often touted to be. In many instances, the key problems of SOEs have not been due to state ownership *per se*, but rather, to the absence of clear, feasible or achievable objectives, or alternatively, to the existence of too many, often contradictory goals. In other cases, the absence of managerial and organizational systems (e.g. flexibility, autonomy) and cultures supportive of and encouraging fulfilment of these goals and objectives may be the key problem. Privatization may facilitate achievement of such organizational goals or objectives with the changes it may bring about in train, but this does not mean that privatization *per se* was responsible for the improvements concerned.

In such cases, managerial and organizational reforms may well achieve the same objectives and goals, or even do better, at lower cost, and thus, may be the superior option. However, the better option cannot be determined *a priori*, but should instead be the outcome of careful analysis of the roots of an organization's malaise. Such a critical review — with a view towards reform — should consider the variety of modes of privatization, marketization and other reform measures as alternative, sometimes complementary options in dealing with the public sector. With such an approach, privatization becomes one among several options available to the government for dealing with the undoubted malaise of many SOEs. This flexible approach is superior to the narrow dogmatic privatization fetish, which viewed it as the only solution to the complex variety of problems faced by public sectors.

A privatization fetish also neglects persistent problems faced by the rest of the public sector not targeted for privatization, which may, in fact, require more urgent attention. Ironically, their problems are probably more serious — which may explain the lack of private sector interest in privatizing them — and hence, in greater need of remedy.

Furthermore, if the privatization policy succeeds in selling off the public sector's most profitable enterprises and activities, it will be left with uneconomic, unprofitable, and unattractive enterprises and activities, thus only confirming prejudices and charges of public sector incompetence and inefficiency, besides worsening the public sector burden while reducing possibilities for cross-subsidization.

Significant increases in consumer prices for privatized or soon-to-be privatized utilities, services and infrastructure have been reluctantly accepted by consumers without much public dissent with some notable exceptions. The staggered nature of these price increases as well as of the privatizations themselves limited the likelihood of coordinated mass protests against privatization. The ruling coalition in Malaysia has successfully reshaped the political system and other rules, institutions and cultures to consolidate its continued incumbency, and to undermine political dissent and opposition.

It has been suggested that privatization has been an important means to enhance Bumiputera stock ownership, but there was little increase of the overall Bumiputera share of corporate wealth during the period of most privatizations. Rather, as Part 2 showed, privatization was an important means for enhancing the private wealth of the politically influential and well connected, especially, but not just among the Bumiputera elite.

There is also no evidence that privatization enhanced growth. In fact, financial resources — which may have gone into new productive capacities — were diverted to buy over assets from the government at discounted prices, i.e. at the expense of the state and the public. Some incentive reforms associated with privatization undoubtedly enhanced productivity, but these could have been introduced without privatization.

From the late 1980s until the mid-1990s, privatization proceeded rapidly, with well over 400 privatizations, ranging from power utilities, telecommunications, highways, ports, water, TV stations to rubbish disposal. Privatization reduced public sector employment, with over 97,000 employees, or 11.4 per cent of the total public sector workforce, transferred to the private sector by the end of 2000 (Matthias, 2000). Privatization also increased the capitalization of the Malaysian stock market and contributed to asset price bubbles, attracting massive inflows of foreign portfolio investments. The collapse of the ringgit — together with other regional currencies — from July 1997 accelerated the collapse of the stock market and property market bubbles, with tremendous negative 'wealth effects' and other adverse repercussions for financial institutions and other corporate interests.

The 1 September 1998 introduction of currency and capital controls provided the government with an opportunity to use macroeconomic policy to stimulate economic recovery. But this opportunity was abused, not only to bail out selected companies, but also certain well-connected individuals

(Johnson and Mitton, 2001). The bailout measures thus complemented the privatization policy to advance or protect crony business interests. Thus, the privatization policy was never meant to serve the public interest, but rather, to enrich a well-connected few at the expense of the public. With many of these beneficiaries in trouble due to the crisis, they lobbied senior government leaders to bail them out, by lowering interest rates, providing emergency credit facilities, ensuring less onerous emergency loan conditions, taking over debt and liabilities, and providing supplementary sources of revenue generation, while protecting the lucrative and profitable corporate assets and private wealth of the owners.

Ironically, the popular impression that the privatization policy in Malaysia was abused in practice to favour a few politically well-connected business interests was reinforced by its abandonment and virtual reversal in the aftermath of the 1997–1998 currency and financial crises. After some policy ambivalence between July 1997 and August 1998, the Mahathir administration undertook measures, especially those introduced in or implemented from September 1998, that disproportionately 'bailed out' and helped politically influential business interests popularly identified as 'cronies' (Johnson and Mitton, 2001).

Far from penalizing the businessmen who had been handed the privatized entities on a silver platter, several were 'rescued' from their failures with multi-billion ringgit bailouts at the expense of the government and. ultimately, the taxpayers. The bailouts often involved 'conversion of private debt to public debt'. Thus, nationalization via government bailouts, by taking over unprofitable privatized companies, seemed to confirm that the intent of the privatization policy was to 'privatize profits and socialize losses'.

Notes

1. Making the case for corporate tax reduction, the World Bank (1987) claimed that the METR would be zero if the statutory rate was 30 per cent (see Wee, 1997). To help make the case against government support for import-substitution, Boadway, Chua and Flatters (1995: Table 3) argued that tariff protection for import-substituting industries led to negative METR for over 20 industries in 1983.
2. Half of the investments with 50 per cent debt equity are financed by debt, e.g. sale of bonds by corporations to raise capital.
3. 1 pikul = 60.479 kilograms

Part 4

Federalism

Malaysia is a federation of 13 states with different human and natural resources. The Federal Constitution assigns jurisdictions over resources and various responsibilities to the different levels of government, i.e. the Federal Government and the State Governments. Federal and state government policies and development programmes as well as the different levels of government affect socio-economic development in the states. Malaysia is a centralized federation and the Federal Government has great influence on development at all levels. In particular, federal-state political relations have shaped socio-economic development at the state level.

This Part examines the powers of the federal and state governments, their respective fiscal capacities, federal-state financial relations as well as the regional and other spatial effects of various federal policies and governance arrangements. It reviews the Malaysian common market; trade between Peninsular Malaysia and Sabah as well as Sarawak reflects, but also shapes regional disparities in industrialization and development.

Formation of Malaysia

The different parties involved supported the Malaysia proposal for various reasons. The British wanted to disengage from Sabah (then British North Borneo) and Sarawak, while protecting their business interests in the region. Conservative leaders of the Malayan federation and Singapore wanted to contain the leftist ascendancy within and without. The new leaders of the People's Action Party (PAP) wanted to contain the party's left wing, access the larger Malaysian common market and become the major partner to UMNO in a new expanded ruling coalition.

Malayan leaders expected the indigenous populations in Sabah and Sarawak would offset Singapore's mainly Chinese population, and looked forward to commanding a larger population, territory and more resources. In less developed Sabah and Sarawak, some of the elite saw the formation of Malaysia as their best hope for decolonization to realize their own ambitions and expected more development funds, special rights and other privileges from the new Federal Government to be formed.

The Cobbold Commission on Sabah and Sarawak identified three groups, i.e. those in favour of joining Malaysia, those against, and those in favour in principle, but wanting more 'safeguards'. A fourth group appeared to 'know little or nothing about Malaysia but agreed to it because they have been told that Malaysia is good for them' (Milne and Ratnam, 1974: 23). The changing membership of the Malaysian federation has affected the legitimacy of the federation, e.g. with the legal challenge to the formation of Malaysia in 1963 and the withdrawal of Singapore from the federation in 1965.

On 10 September 1963 — six days before the formation of the Malaysian Federation — the Kelantan Government filed an action against the Government of the Malayan Federation and the Prime Minister to declare the Malaysia Act null and void or, alternatively, that it was not binding on Kelantan. The Court ruled that Parliament had acted within its constitutional power in forming Malaysia from the Malayan Federation, Sabah, Sarawak and Singapore (see also Jayakumar, 1971: 195–204; Hickling, 1978: 9; Salleh Abbas, 1978: 172; Shafruddin, 1988: 19–20).

The second challenge came when Singapore withdrew from the federation in August 1965, following acrimonious conflicts with Kuala Lumpur. The Sabah representatives discussed the matter and Chief Minister Donald (later Fuad) Stephens proposed discussing the matter among the remaining representatives of the federation. The Malaysian Prime Minister turned down the request, and Kelantan, Sabah and Sarawak have remained part of Malaysia since, although there have been occasional reports of these state governments having strained relations with the Federal Government even when belonging to the same ruling coalition.

Negotiations to form Malaysia had involved the Malayan federation (of 11 states), only represented by the federal government, Sabah, Sarawak and Singapore. Thus, three of the original four parties remained in the Malaysian Federation after Singapore left the federation on 9 August 1965. Official documents such as the Malaysian Constitution refer to the 'thirteen states', but Sabah and Sarawak have both insisted on the status of each being 'one of the three' equal founding parties.

Peninsular- and ethnic-based parties have dominated the ruling coalition since although the two Borneo states are 'over-represented' in Parliament, ostensibly because of the original 1963 understanding, their sparser population distributions in large states and the greater likelihood of their supporting the ruling coalition. The dominant United Malays National Organisation (UMNO), Malaysian Chinese Association (MCA), Malaysian Indian Congress (MIC) and the peninsular-based Gerakan have been prominent in the national ruling coalition, the Barisan Nasional (BN). Despite greater per capita parliamentary representation by state, the smaller BN parties of Sabah and Sarawak were relatively ineffective in ensuring more development funds for these less developed states until they became crucial to BN retention of power at the federal level following the March 2008 general election. However, alleged abuses of such resources and powers have limited the 'trickle-down' to the population.

Federal and State Government Jurisdictions

Malaysia is a centralized federation; the centralization provided for by the constitution was intended to facilitate national administration. Sovereign national government functions — such as external affairs, defence, internal security, federal citizenship and naturalization, federal government machinery, federal works and powers — are understandably vested with the Federal Government[1] (Table 4.1).

Macroeconomic functions — such as in finance, trade, commerce and industry — are also vested with the Federal Government. Functions with externalities — where benefits and costs spill over state boundaries[2] — are under federal jurisdiction. Functions of 'universal concern' — such as civil and criminal law, the administration of justice, labour and social security, the welfare of aborigines as well as co-operative societies — also come

Table 4.1 Malaysia: Federal and State Government Functions

Federal	State
1. External affairs	1. Muslim laws & customs
2. Defence	2. Land
3. Internal security	3. Agriculture & forestry
4. Civil & criminal law & the administration of justice	4. Local government
5. Federal citizenship & naturalization; aliens	5. Local public services: boarding houses, burial grounds, pounds & cattle trespass, markets & fairs, licensing of theatres & cinemas
6. Federal government machinery	6. State works & water
7. Finance	7. State government machinery
8. Trade, commerce & industry	8. State holidays
9. Shipping, navigation & fishery	9. Inquiries for state
10. Communication & transport	10. Creation of offences & indemnities related to state matters
11. Federal works & power	11. Turtles & riverine fishery
12. Survey, inquiries & research purposes	
13. Education	*Supplementary List for Sabah & Sarawak*
14. Medicine & health	1. Native laws and customs
15. Labour & social security	2. Incorporation of state authorities & other bodies
16. Welfare of aborigines	3. Ports & harbours other than those declared federal
17. Professional licensing	4. Cadastral land surveys
18. Federal holidays, standard of time	5. In Sabah, the Sabah Railway
19. Unincorporated societies	
20. Agricultural pest control	*Additional shared functions for Sabah and Sarawak*
21. Publications	1. Personal law
22. Censorship	2. Adulteration of foodstuff & other goods
23. Theatres & cinemas	3. Shipping under fifteen tons
24. Co-operative societies	4. Water power
25. Prevention & extinguishment of fires	5. Agricultural & forest research
	6. Charities & charitable trusts
Shared functions	7. Theatres, cinemas & other places of amusement
1. Social welfare	
2. Scholarship	
3. Protection of wild animals & birds, national parks	
4. Animal husbandry	
5. Town & country planning	
6. Vagrancy & itinerant hawkers	
7. Public health	
8. Drainage & irrigation	
9. Rehabilitation of mining land & land which has suffered soil erosion	
10. Fire safety measures	
11. Culture & sports	
12. Housing	

Source: Government of Malaysia, *Constitution of Malaysia*, Ninth Schedule.

under federal jurisdiction. This wide range of federal powers means that the welfare of peoples across the states depends heavily on the Federal Government, with the state governments left with residual functions.

Functions in land, agriculture and forestry as well as turtles and riverine fishery have been under state jurisdiction from pre-Malaysia days. Functions vested with the state governments include local government, local public services, licensing theatres and cinemas, state public works, water, land and other natural resources other than petroleum, state government machinery, state holidays, as well as legislation on offences and indemnities related to state matters. Muslim laws and customs as well as other native laws and customs in Sabah and Sarawak are vested with the state governments, as in pre-Malaysia days.

The administrative systems in Sabah and Sarawak were different from that of the Malayan Federation at the time of the formation of Malaysia. The supplementary lists for Sabah and Sarawak reflect some of these differences — the incorporation of state authorities and bodies, ports and harbours other than federal entities, cadastral land surveys and the Sabah Railway.

Both the Federal and all State Governments share functions such as for social welfare and scholarship provision; protection of wild animals and birds, animal husbandry, drainage and irrigation, rehabilitation of mining land and land which has suffered soil erosion; town and country planning, housing, vagrancy and itinerant hawkers, public health, fire safety measures as well as culture and sports. The Sabah and Sarawak State Governments have additional shared responsibilities for customary personal law (i.e. rooted in indigenous cultures), adulteration of foodstuff and other goods, shipping under fifteen tons, water power, agricultural and forestry research.

Federal law overrides state laws in the event of contradiction or inconsistency. The centralization of Malaysian federal arrangements has also increased over the years. Federal Government involvement and authority increased through federally financed and managed development projects (e.g. regional development schemes, the Muda irrigation scheme in Kedah and Perlis; land development schemes under the Federal Land Development Authority). The Federal Government also took over certain territories — the capital city, Kuala Lumpur, and the new administrative centre, Putrajaya, from Selangor, as well as Labuan from Sabah, though the federal takeovers of Kuala Lumpur, Putrajaya and Labuan were opposed by various quarters in Selangor and Sabah.

Federal-State Financial Relations

The constitution specifies government revenue sources and expenditure areas. Centralization is reflected in the allocation of federal and state government revenues and expenditures. In the period 1963–2011, the Federal Government got 76 to 93 per cent of consolidated federal and state government revenues, and spent 79 to 93 per cent of total government expenditure (Figure 4.1).

The major sources of revenue are assigned to the Federal Government. They include taxes on income, property and capital gains (classified as 'direct taxes') as well as taxes on international trade (export and import

Figure 4.1 Malaysia: Federal Government Finance and State Government Overall Balance, 1963–2012

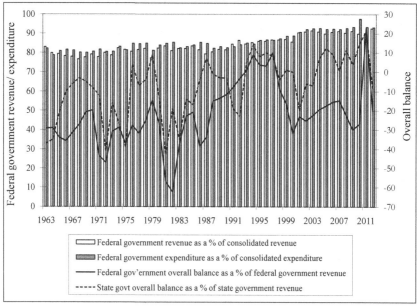

Sources: Calculated with data from Ministry of Finance, Malaysia, *Economic Report*, various issues.

Table 4.2 Malaysia: Federal and State Government Revenue

Federal	State
Tax Revenue	**Tax Revenue**
1. *Direct taxes*	1. Import & excise duties on petroleum products, export duties on timber & other forest products for Sabah & Sarawak, excise duty on toddy for all states
i. *Income taxes*:	
Individual	
Companies	
Co-operatives	2. Forests
Petroleum tax	3. Lands & mines
Development tax	4. Entertainment duties
Film hire duty	
ii. Taxes on property & capital gains:	**Other Receipts**
Real property gain tax	1. Licences & permits
Estate duty	2. Royalties
Share transfer tax on land-based companies	3. Service fees
	4. Commercial undertakings, e.g. water, gas, ports, etc.
2. *Indirect taxes*	5. Receipts from land sales
i. *Taxes on international trade*:	6. Rents on state property
Export duties	7. Proceeds, dividends & interest
Import duties	8. Federal grants & reimbursements
Surtax on imports	
ii. *Taxes on production & consumption*:	
Excise duties	
Sales taxes	
Service taxes	
iii. *Others*:	
Stamp duties	
Gaming tax	
Betting & sweepstakes	
Lotteries	
Casino	
Pool betting duty	
Non-Tax Revenue & Other Receipts	
1. Road tax	
2. Licences	
3. Service fees	
4. Fines & forfeitures	
5. Interests	
6. Contributions from foreign governments	
7. Revenues from Federal Territories	
8. Refund of expenditures	
9. Receipts from other government agencies	
10. Revenues from Federal Territories	
11. Royalties from oil/gas	

Source: Government of Malaysia, *Constitution of Malaysia*, Tenth Schedule.

duties), production (e.g. excise duties) and consumption (sales and services taxes). These taxes are related to administrative functions vested with the Federal Government. Other taxes, non-tax revenues and other receipts of the Federal Government are ostensibly related to other functions and investments, as with state government tax revenues and other receipts (Table 4.2).

As discussed elsewhere, the Malaysian tax system has become less progressive over time, especially since the tax reforms from the mid-1980s that reduced the progressive incidence of direct, notably income taxes. Direct taxes are generally progressively structured, and hence, more likely to be progressive than indirect taxes which are more likely to be 'flat' in impact. Direct taxes are imposed by the federal government and state governments but have not been well coordinated to ensure consistency and progressive outcomes.

The strongest argument for assigning production and consumption taxes to the federal government is that it has a better collection machinery. Centralized arrangements can help avoid 'beggar thy neighbour' competition among state governments to attract businesses into states with lower tax regimes. As state governments have no monetary and few fiscal instruments, it seems better for the Federal Government to collect taxes, and then transfer greater shares of the proceeds to State Governments, especially in the poorer states in order to help them close the gaps with the better off states.

Export duties, such as those on tin and rubber, are indirect taxes on the producers of these commodities. The regressive nature of export duties in the 1960s and 1970s (see Part 3) also undermined the presumably progressive incidence of Federal Government taxation, especially direct taxation. The Federal Government has increased the scope and rates of indirect taxes on sales and services (SST), generally considered regressive. The burden of such taxes can be shifted to consumers, especially where business interests have more market power. The Federal Government has delayed the economy-wide collection of SST several times, mainly for political considerations.

State governments have collected natural resource related taxes, such as revenue from land as well as forests, since colonial times. As land is a state matter, land-based property taxation has been handled by state

Table 4.3 Malaysia: Revenue Assignment under the Petroleum Development Act, 1974

Item	Distribution	Company	Government	
			Federal	State
Oil				
Cost recovery	20%	20%	–	–
Royalty	10%	–	5%	5%
Balance	70%	30% of 70% = 21%	70% of 70% = 49%	–
Tax	–	Tax on 21%	Tax on 21%	–
Total	100%	41% less tax on 21%	54% + tax on 21%	5%
Gas (liquefied natural gas or LNG)				
Cost recovery	25%	25%	–	–
Royalty	10%	–	5%	5%
Balance	65%	30% of 65% = 19.5%	70% of 65% = 45.5%	–
Tax	–	Tax on 19.5%	Tax on 19.5%	–
Total	100%	44.5% less tax on 19.5%	50.5% + tax on 19.5%	5%

Source: Petroleum Development Act, 1974.

administrations. Land-based property taxes — such as estate duty, real property gains tax and stamp duty on land transfers — can therefore be assigned to the states (Shahir, 1997). But as natural resources and real property values vary with location, this leads to rather different fiscal capacities among the states. The only natural resource under federal government jurisdiction is petroleum. Under the Petroleum Development Act (PDA, 1974), revenue assignment is allocated as in Table 4.3.

Oil and LNG royalties of 10 per cent are collected by the Federal Government, which transfers half (5 per cent) to the state governments entitled to these royalties. Only Sarawak, Terengganu, Sabah and Kelantan have petroleum resources; petroleum-related royalties have contributed greatly to the state coffers of Sarawak, Sabah and Terengganu. These royalties represent only 20 to 30 per cent of the petroleum tax assigned to the Federal Government, but the value of royalties and petroleum tax collected by the Federal Government represented at least half of the consolidated state government revenue (Table 4.4).

Table 4.4 Malaysia: Value of Petroleum Revenues as Percentages of Federal and State Government Revenues, 1981–2010

	Federal Government Revenue			State Government Revenue		
	Royalties	*Tax*	*Total*	*Royalties*	*Federal Government Tax*	*Total*
1981–1985	3.2	14.9	15.3	14.0	64.8	72.0
1986–1990	2.3	9.9	12.1	9.7	42.1	51.8
1991–1995	1.7	6.8	8.6	10.1	40.0	50.2
1996–2000	1.9	6.3	8.2	12.0	40.2	52.2
2001–2005	2.5	11.3	13.8	24.5	110.3	134.7
2006–2010	n.a.	14.7	n.a.	n.a.	139.1	n.a.

Sources: Calculated with data from Ministry of Finance, Malaysia, *Economic Report*, various issues.

Disputes over Petroleum Resources

There have been several disputes over petroleum royalties over the years. Most Malaysian oil is off the shore of Terengganu, while most gas is off the shore of Sabah and Sarawak. In 1969, the Sarawak Chief Minister claimed that the Federal Government had verbally assured Sarawak that it could have all the revenue from offshore petroleum in return for a lower grant to the state (Leigh, 1988: 133). Insofar as the Constitution was perceived to be silent on the matter then, the federal claim to offshore petroleum was construed as annexation (Reece, 1969, 1970, cited in Leigh, 1971: 233).

As colonial power, the United Kingdom had declared rights over the Malaysian continental shelf prior to the formation of Malaysia. Hence, the territories of the British North Borneo (later Sabah) and Sarawak at the time of the formation of Malaysia included the continental shelf. However, the related ownership rights of Sabah and Sarawak to offshore petroleum and natural (petroleum) gas have not provided these states with more than the 5 per cent royalty stipulated by the 1974 Petroleum Development Act. Management of petroleum resources is vested in the state owned company, PETRONAS, which pays taxes and royalties to the federal government.

In the 1990 election campaign, the Sabah Chief Minister called for oil royalties to the state to be increased to 50 per cent. There have been renewed calls to increase oil royalties to Sabah after the March 2008 election, as MPs from Sabah and Sabah together accounted for 54 of the 126 BN MPs after the election, and the BN could not form the ruling coalition without the Sabah and Sarawak BN MPs. The peninsular-based Prime Minister-cum-BN leader and the Parliamentary Opposition leader made several visits to the states, with the latter promising 20 per cent royalties to the states if he were to become PM. There has also been mention by the BN of increasing royalties to between 20 and 25 per cent.

After the March 2008 election, a forum on the formation of Malaysia was organized in Kuching, the capital city of Sarawak. James Wong, a former Sarawak Deputy Chief Minister, claimed that Tun Rahman Yaakub had agreed to the 5 per cent royalty rate when Rahman was Chief Minister of Sarawak. Rahman denied this, claiming that it was his deceased deputy, Stephen Yong, who had committed Sarawak to the deal (*Borneo Post*, 28 October 2008). The Sarawak United People's Party (SUPP), the BN component party that Yong had led, then issued its own denial, saying that Yong's memoirs had noted the inequity of the arrangements; in any case, as head of the coalition government, Rahman should be held responsible (*Borneo Post*, 1 November 2008). The then Sarawak Deputy Chief Minister from SUPP was later reported as saying that 'If the state government was unable to develop Sarawak by using developmental funds then perhaps it would think of increasing the oil royalty' (*Borneo Post*, 29 October 2008). Rahman also claimed that there was a provision to review the 5 per cent royalty rate every five years, but there is no public record of any such review, while the royalty to the state under PDA, 1974 has remained at 5 per cent.

Sabah and Sarawak BN MPs continue to form the majority in the ruling coalition after the May 2013 general election. In July 2013, the Office of the Minister of Finance organised a consultation on the 2014 budget, possibly the first such public consultation ever held in Kuching, the state capital of Sarawak. It was announced that another such consultation would be held in Sabah. The invited participants included government agencies and a limited range of non-government organizations.

Nonetheless, increased royalties would be preferable to development funds from the federal government, which usually come with conditions. The annual budget process requires State Governments to submit appli-

Table 4.5 Sarawak: Net Transfers of Public Funds, 1964–2010 (RM million)

	1964–70	*1971–80*	*1981–90*	*1991–2000*	*2001–10*
Federal funds to State Government	312	525	1,098	1,030	2,031
Federal operating & development expenditure	823	3,015	11,257	23,112	37,428
Total to state	1,135	3,530	12,355	24,825	39,459
Federal revenue	478	2,598	10,423	11,852	32,141
Petroleum royalties	–	464	1,627	11,379	11,456
Petroleum dividends[a]	–	–	4,163	9,024	n.a.
Total from state	478	3,062	16,213	32,255	n.a.
Net transfers to the state	657	468	-3,858	-7,430	n.a.

Note: [a] Apportioned according to the share of crude petroleum exports from Sarawak.

Sources: Department of Statistics, Malaysia, *Yearbook of Statistics, Sarawak*, various issues. Ministry of Finance, Malaysia, *Federal Public Accounts*, various issues.

cations for development funds to the Federal Government, which then decides on allocations from the federal coffers. Available data indicate the reversal of public funds from a net inflow into Sabah of RM784 million in 1966–1970 to net outflows from Sabah of RM350 million in 1971–1980 and RM3,515 million in 1981–1990 (Wee, 2006: Table 6.11). There has been a net transfer of funds from Sarawak to the federal coffers since the 1980s, as petroleum and gas revenues have mainly been appropriated by the Federal Government (Table 4.5).

After the opposition captured the Terengganu state government in the 1999 election, the Federal Government diverted its oil royalties to a discretionary fund under Federal Government control. In 2001, the Terengganu government filed a suit against the Federal Government for non-payment of (petroleum) royalties to the state. Without having declared territorial rights over the continental shelf, as in Sabah and Sarawak, the Terengganu government was said to have no right to royalties from offshore petroleum, and lost the case (Fong, 2008).

Currently, there are conflicts between the Kelantan State Government and the Federal Government over the state's right to revenue from petroleum resources offshore, where production since 2005 has been reported. As in the case of Terengganu, Kelantan had not declared territorial rights over the continental shelf before the formation of Malaysia. Tengku Razaleigh of UMNO[3], who was involved in federal-state negotiations over petroleum resources, has supported the payment of royalties to Kelantan. A Johor State Financial Officer has argued that the 5 per cent petroleum royalties should be shared with other states (Shahir, 1997).

Besides the dispute over petroleum revenue, there was another conflict with the Federal Government involving the Terengganu State Government's December 1999 proposal to collect *kharaj*, a Muslim agricultural land tax. The Federal Government disputed the proposal, although with the state having jurisdiction over Muslim law, and land being a state matter, *kharaj* should be under state government jurisdiction. The dispute fizzled out when the Terengganu State Government shelved its plans.

Federal Transfers to the States

Federal government transfers to the state governments take the form of grants and reimbursements. The Federal Constitution assigns a minimum of 10 per cent of the export duties on tin, iron and other minerals to the peninsular state governments as grants, based on a 'derivation principle'. There is no record of the Federal Government ever using its prerogative to increase this to more than 10 per cent to improve state government finances. The meagre value of this grant has declined with falls in output and price as well as the reduction or abolition of various export duties.

If the growth of federal revenue other than from export duty on tin and revenues under the Road Ordinance (1958) exceeds 10 per cent per annum, the increase will be assigned to the state governments, up to a maximum of RM150 million. Of this, RM25 million is to be equally shared by the states, another RM25 million is to be allocated by population, with the remaining RM100 million going to those with per capita GDP below the national average (Wilson and Sulaiman, 1997). This incremental arrangement takes annual revenue growth into consideration, but as such revenues sustained in subsequent years are no longer considered growth, they are no longer shared by the Federal Government with the state governments. Consequently, federal-state imbalances in revenue allocation have been aggravated over time as the economy grew and tax revenue increased.

The capitation grant is a relatively large general grant based on the state population size. Its regressive rate is justified by the scale economies associated with infrastructure provision and the greater likelihood of state government revenues from other sources in states with larger populations. Progressive rates beyond certain population thresholds from 1992 were justified by the diseconomies of scale beyond such thresholds (Government of Malaysia, *Constitution of Malaysia*, Tenth Schedule, Part I). With inter-state and international migration, accurate population estimates for the peninsular states during the usual 10-year intervals between censuses are difficult to make. The exclusion of illegal migrants from consideration also means that the capitation grant is even more inadequate for the states with the most illegal immigrants — a long standing issue in Sabah (Wilson and Sulaiman, 1997). The grant also ignores differences in infrastructure costs by state, which are generally higher in Sabah and Sarawak.

The state road grant is another relatively large grant for road maintenance, which may also be used by non-state residents for inter-state travel. The grant value is determined by road mileage and average maintenance costs, with the latter lagging behind inflation until appropriate adjustment (Wilson and Sulaiman, 1997). The service charge grant compensates state governments for involvement in federal projects implemented in the respective states, while the cost reimbursement grant covers projects under joint jurisdiction. Such federally determined grants have decreased over time as the Federal Government implements projects unilaterally, rather than in collaboration with the state governments.

Development grants may also be allocated from the State Reserve Fund to reduce inter-state social disparities, although evidence of growing regional inequalities suggests they have not been effective. The grants also come with project specifications, for the design, administration and control of programmes, further limiting state government autonomy. Contingencies Fund grants cover unforeseen needs, while State Advance Fund grants provide resources to cope with temporary cash-flow problems.

When recommended by the National Finance Council (NFC), the deficit grant is transferred from the State Reserve Fund to cover state current account deficits. Chaired by the PM, the Council consists of a representative from each state and Ministers designated by the PM; the PM is likely to appoint members reflecting his views. The Council acts in an advisory capacity without making binding decisions. Deficit grants have been minimal as state governments generally practise 'fiscal prudence' by limiting spending and handing some functions over to the Federal Government, thus further contributing to centralization (see also Umikalsum, 1991).

Special grants are given annually to the Governments of Kedah, Selangor, Sabah and Sarawak. The annual grant to Kedah of RM10,000 is in line with an 1869 agreement between Kedah and the British for territories handed over to Penang. The grant to Selangor is compensation for the Federal Territory of Kuala Lumpur (FTKL) and the Federal Territory of Putrajaya (FTP). The annual grant for FTKL was RM310.8 million before 1992 and RM18.3 million thereafter, while that for FTP is RM7.5 million. Sabah is similarly compensated for giving up the Federal Territory of Labuan (FTL) island.

When the vote for approval of the Federal Territory of Putrajaya Bill 2000 was taken in the Selangor State Assembly, all six opposition members of the 48-member House walked out in protest against the hasty handling of the matter, including the failure to consult 'the people, non-government organisations and the State Assembly itself'. The Selangor Mentri Besar (MB or chief minister) replied that the matter had been discussed with the State Executive Council fourteen months earlier. He added that the Selangor Government had also received RM200 million besides a RM62.3 million premium for private land acquired by the Federal Government for development. However, the MB did not dispute the opposition's claim of failure to consult the State Assembly. The opposition also referred to the four-year long discussion between the Federal Government and the Selangor Government on the FTKL proposal (*Daily Express, Sabah*, 2000) — much longer than for the Federal Territory of Putrajaya.

The special grants for Sabah and Sarawak, as part of the Malaysia Agreement, were to be reviewed. Sabah received growth revenue grants of RM67 million for 1964–68. The 1969 review replaced the growth revenue grants with reduced grants of RM20 million in 1969, RM21.5 million in

1970, RM23.1 million in 1971, RM24.8 million in 1972 and RM26.7 million in 1973. This happened despite Sabah's hope for more federal funds for development by joining the Malaysian federation.

Sarawak's special annual grant of RM5.8 million for 1964–1968 was abolished from 1969. There is an escalating grant, which rose from RM3.5 million in 1964 to RM7.0 million in 1965, RM11.5 million in 1966, RM16.0 million in 1967 and RM21.0 million in 1968. The escalating grant dropped to RM12.0 million in 1969, then increased to RM12.9 million in 1970, RM13.9 million in 1971, RM14.9 million in 1972 and RM16 million in 1973. The grant has remained at RM16 million since then.

The Federal Government reimburses the state governments for projects that they jointly implement. Over time, Federal grants and reimbursements as a proportion of state government revenue decreased while Federal government support for state governments has shifted to loans (Figure 4.2). Federal grants to the States decreased from 37.0 per

Figure 4.2 Malaysia: Consolidated State Government Revenue, 1963–2011 (RM million)

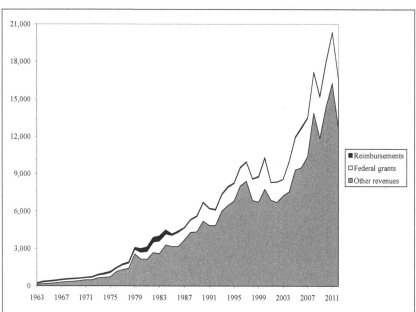

Sources: Ministry of Finance, Malaysia, *Economic Report*, various issues.

cent of consolidated state government revenue in 1963 to 15.2 per cent in 1996, before increasing to 24.7 per cent in 2006 and decreasing to 19.7 per cent in 2011. Meanwhile, federal reimbursements as a proportion of consolidated state government revenue declined from 23.0 per cent in 1963 to 13.6 per cent in 1967, and fluctuated between 4.7 and 11.6 per cent until 1981, before declining to 0.4 per cent in 1997. It has been less than 1.0 per cent since 1994.

Deficit grants and contingency grants increased in the aftermath of the 1997–1998 financial crisis (Wee, 2006b). The increased grants for contingencies following the 1997–1998 crisis reflected the dire situation of the state governments. After the NFC meeting in August 2011, the PM announced an increase of grants based on level of development amounting to RM10 million for 2012 and RM288 million for 2013. Another RM30 million was to be added for grants to states with government account deficits (Bernama, 2011).

Loan Financing for Development

The Federal Government borrows from both domestic and foreign sources for capital expenditure or development spending. Peninsular state governments can only borrow from the Federal Government or, with federal authorization, from other domestic sources for five years or less (Article 111, Malaysian Constitution), while the Sabah and Sarawak State Governments may freely borrow from within their respective states (Article 112B). The Federal Government provides loan guarantees for state government borrowing, having to pay up if the state governments cannot repay the loans. But the inability of state governments to repay their loans and their very need to borrow in the first place are due to shortfalls in state government revenues.

In 1968, the Federal Government took the opposition Kelantan Government to court for borrowing without approval by receiving mining and logging royalties from a private corporation before they were due. The Kelantan Government got the advance royalty payments with the intention of building a bridge, as it had promised to in the 1964 election campaign. However, the Court ruled that the royalty advances did not constitute borrowing, thus finding in favour of the Kelantan Government.

Subsequently, the Federal Government amended the Constitution to define 'borrowing' to include entering into an 'agreement requiring payment before any taxes, rates, royalties, fees or any other payments are due' (Jayakumar, 1971: 206–225; Shafruddin, 1987: 66–67).

Net federal loans to state governments increased from RM26 million in 1966 to RM908 million in 1983, then decreased to minus RM91 million due to repayments in 1990, before increasing again to RM940 million in 1992–1993, and rising thereafter to RM1,757 million in 2011 (Ministry of Finance, Malaysia). Outstanding loans increased from RM142 million in 1965 to RM18,482 million in 2009.

Public Accounts

As noted earlier, the Federal Government collects more revenues and spends more than all the state governments together. Federal government expenditure exceeded revenue by 5 per cent or less during 1963–2011 (Figure 4.1). The federal budgetary deficit increased from RM337 million in 1963 to RM10,421 million in 1982, then decreased with its new stance of 'austerity' and 'fiscal prudence', eventually achieving a surplus of RM6,626 million in 1997. Deficits have been consistently incurred since the 1997–1998 Asian financial crisis, in the region of RM18,000–21,000 million during 2000–2007 before ballooning to RM47,424 million in 2009 and then declining to RM43,338 million in 2010. Deficits fell from 31.9 per cent of revenue in 2000 to 14.8 per cent in 2007 before rising in response to the global financial crisis. Nonetheless, debt-servicing fell from a peak of 27.3 per cent of federal government operating expenditure in 1990 to 10.3 per cent in 2011 (see Part 3).

Federal government debts increased from RM5,019 million in 1970 to RM456,128 million in 2011. Most of the debts are from domestic sources. Domestic debts fell from 85.2 per cent of total debt in 1970 to 61.7 per cent in 1986, and then increased to 96.0 per cent in 2011. Some 42 to 60 per cent of domestic debt in the period 1970 to 2007 was from the EPF (Bank Negara Malaysia). However, borrowings from the EPF fell to 18.5 per cent in 2011. At the same time, there have been increasing issues of Islamic debt instruments to raise funds from banking institutions, insurance companies and individuals.

Malaysian government outstanding external debt maturing beyond one year — mainly borrowed by the Federal Government — has mainly been used to finance development expenditure. After reaching a peak of 39.5 per cent of GDP in 1986, these debts were reduced to 4.1 per cent of GDP in 1996, before increasing to 10.0 per cent of GDP in 2002, and then declining to 1.1 per cent of GDP in 2011. Similarly, its external debt service ratio peaked at 7.2 per cent in 1986, before falling to 0.7 per cent in 1997, then increasing to 1.3 per cent in 2003, and then declining again to 0.2 per cent in 2010.

Government Finance by State

State government finance has paralleled the trend of Federal Government finance. State government spending has increased over the years, with high deficits since the 1970s (Figures 4.1, 4.3). The major sources of state government revenues are from land, mines, forestry and water sale. Sabah, Sarawak and Terengganu have also had significantly higher revenues

Figure 4.3 Malaysia: Consolidated State Government Accounts, 1963–2011 (RM million)

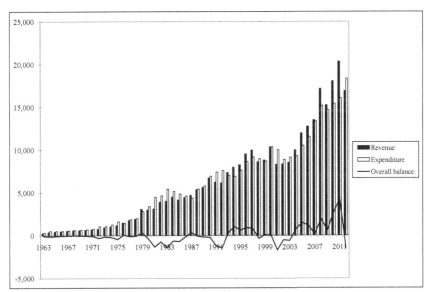

Sources: Ministry of Finance, Malaysia, *Economic Report*, various issues.

from petroleum royalties, although there have been disputes over resource rights. Moreover, federal government revenue is 4.5 to 5.5 times state government revenue from petroleum (Table 4.4).

Forestry is under state jurisdiction, but timber exports and industries are under federal jurisdiction. The federal Minister of Primary Industries proposed to ban log exports from Sabah from 1992 'to encourage the growth of wood-based industries'. The Sabah Government argued that such a ban would protect inefficient industries and also appealed for compensation for the revenue loss due to the ban as its revenue from log exports was substantial. The Minister agreed to the compensation, but changed his stand after the Sabah ruling party Parti Bersatu Sabah (PBS) defected to the opposition during the 1990 election campaign. After drastic increases in log prices in 1992, the Minister lifted the ban at the behest of Japanese importers in spite of Sabah Government protests at the policy reversal, which adversely affected timber prices.

The Federal Government has never proposed any ban on log exports from Sarawak despite efforts by indigenous peoples groups and others to prevent logging in certain areas. Timber depletion in Sarawak was not as advanced as in Sabah, but the Federal Government was also less sympathetic to Sabah. Historically, there have been more federal ministers and assistant ministers appointed from among Sarawak MPs, and these ministers have allocated more development funds from their ministries to Sarawak. The greater degree of autonomy enjoyed by Sarawak is also reflected in the timing of its state elections which have long been held at different times from the federal parliamentary elections, unlike the concurrent state and parliamentary elections in other states, especially in the peninsula.

In fact, Sarawak has ranked among the top three states in terms of state development allocations since the 1990s (Table 4.6). However, Sarawak has one of the poorest road systems in the federation (Table 4.7). The poor road system limits access to government health and education services as well as markets for agricultural produce. And despite being more favoured than Sabah, Sarawak has also experienced more net outflows of public funds (Table 4.5).

When Mahathir was Prime Minister, development allocations favoured his home state, Kedah, which some observers suggest is the basis for his

Table 4.6 Malaysia: Development Allocations by State, 1976–2010 (RM million)

	3MP 1976–80	4MP 1981–85	5MP[a] 1986–90	6MP[b] 1991–95	7MP[b] 1996–2000	8MP[b] 2001–05	9MP[b] 2006–10
More developed states:							
Johor	1,832 (2)	2,929 (4)	4,529 (1)	3,794 (2)	3,613 (4)	5,937 (4)	10,200 (4)
Melaka	328 (12)	940 (12)	520 (13)	924 (11)	1,191 (12)	2,465 (11)	3,686 (12)
N. Sembilan	617 (11)	1,131 (11)	1,302 (10)	1,548 (10[a])	1,801 (11)	5,221 (5)	5,884 (10)
Perak	1,792 (3)	2,834 (6)	3,738 (6)	2,563 (7)	3,216 (6)	4,849 (7)	7,614 (7)
P. Pinang	894 (9)	1,236 (10)	1,257 (11)	1,548 (10[b])	1,968 (9)	4,040 (8)	6,152 (9)
Selangor	1,413 (6)	3,677 (1)	4,365 (2)	4,295 (1)	4,296 (3)	7,848 (3)	15,539 (2)
Less developed states:							
Kedah	854 (10)	2,389 (8)	2,659 (9)	2,826 (5)	3,341 (5)	5,180 (6)	7,817 (6)
Kelantan	1,019 (7)	2,848 (5)	3,621 (7)	2,064 (9)	1,850 (10)	2,905 (10)	6,651 (8)
Pahang	2,054 (1)	2,944 (3)	4,118 (3)	2,837 (4)	3,090 (7)	3,821 (9)	9,851 (5)
Perlis	156 (13)	304 (13)	560 (12)	505 (12)	953 (13)	1,581 (13)	2,201 (13)
Sabah	1,452 (5)	3,172 (2)	3,913 (4)	2,307 (8)	4,495 (2)	7,990 (2)	15,658 (1)
Sarawak	1,657 (4)	2,608 (7)	3,464 (8)	3,209 (3)	4,548 (1)	8,676 (1)	13,437 (3)
Terengganu	911 (8)	2,023 (9)	3,790 (5)	2,729 (6)	2,553 (8)	2,443 (12)	5,806 (11)

Notes: Figures in brackets indicate ranking from highest to lowest.
[a] Federal Government and Non-Financial Public Enterprise (NFPE) development allocations only.
[b] Federal government development allocations only.

Sources: Various Malaysia plan documents.

Table 4.7 Malaysia: Road Distribution by State, 1985–2010

	Km per sq km			% paved			
	1985	*2002*	*2010*	*1985*	*1990*	*2002*	*2010*
More developed states:							
Johor	0.23	0.37	0.74	81.9	80.8	87.2	79.0
Melaka	0.59	1.15	1.40	95.9	71.4	81.5	74.9
N. Sembilan	0.37	0.60	1.56	75.2	82.0	90.0	76.4
Perak	0.16	0.31	0.43	93.3	89.6	97.4	75.2
P. Pinang	1.28	1.95	2.53	89.8	97.0	94.6	89.2
Selangor	0.54	1.39	1.88	81.7	85.9	91.2	86.9
Less developed states:							
Kedah	0.34	0.59	0.81	69.5	76.5	88.6	80.8
Kelantan	0.14	0.18	0.93	66.6	76.6	79.8	78.7
Pahang	0.12	0.22	0.37	67.3	70.9	82.4	63.0
Perlis	0.60	0.77	2.29	89.7	92.2	96.6	65.1
Sabah	0.10	0.15	0.29	33.3	30.0	35.0	36.8
Sarawak	0.04	0.05	0.20	32.3	30.3	61.1	62.2
Terengganu	0.16	0.34	0.53	85.2	82.0	83.8	70.3
Malaysia	0.13	0.22	0.44	66.3	70.0	77.7	68.5

Sources: 5MP, Table 16-2; 7MP; Department of Statistics, Malaysia, *Social Statistical Bulletin*, various issues.

son's current political ambitions. The state now has better roads than most other less developed states (Table 4.7). Meanwhile, the BN Federal Government succeeded in denying the Parti Islam (PAS) Terengganu State Government petroleum revenues after the opposition party gained control of the state government for one term from the late 1990s. Terengganu's ranking in development allocations deteriorated from 5th during the 5MP (1986–1990) to 6th (6MP, 1991–1995), 8th (7MP, 1996–2000), 12th (8MP, 2001–2005) and 11th (9MP, 2006–2010) during the subsequent five-year development plan periods — just ahead of Perlis, the smallest state with 23.0 per cent of its population and 6.1 per cent of its land area.

After the Terengganu State Government lost the court case to get royalties for its offshore petroleum, the BN recaptured and then held the state government in the 2004 and 2008 elections. The BN Federal

Government paid royalties of RM408.6 million to the Terengganu State Government in December 2008, a month before a by-election for a Terengganu parliamentary constituency. The Terengganu Chief Minister also announced that PETRONAS would resume paying royalties to the Terengganu Government from March 2009, and argued that it was unnecessary for the opposition to raise the royalty issue in future, as it had in the 2004 and 2008 general elections (*Borneo Post*, 3 January 2009).

Under a PAS government for a long time, Kelantan has had modest and deteriorating development allocations except when it was ruled by the BN. Delays in disbursing federal grants to the Kelantan Government have also jeopardized its administrative functions. Following its legal success in the late 1960s, advance receipt of revenues due is now outlawed as 'borrowing', further constraining its already modest fiscal capacity. As is the case for Terengganu, loans to Kelantan from the Federal Government have been decreasing relatively (Figure 4.4).

State governments' traditional revenues from forest or tin exports have been deteriorating with forest depletion and the collapse of the tin industry in the 1980s. State governments' limited sources of revenue are said to have caused over-exploitation of forest resources, with forest degradation adversely affecting water sources. Hence, states have become increasingly dependent on federal funds. The less developed states of Kedah and Sabah have increased their relative shares of loans from the Federal Government throughout, while Sarawak and the more developed states of Melaka and Negri Sembilan have been increasing their relative shares of loans from 1990.

State government debts may not have been settled due to limited state government fiscal capacities. The Federal Government has written off some loans that could not be serviced as bad debts after failed attempts to reschedule repayment. Selangor had one of the highest share of loans from the federal government up to 2000. Unlike other states, however, it reduced its outstanding loans from 2007 to 2009. Perak has also reduced its relative loans over the years, while Penang has had one of the lowest shares (Figure 4.4). These three more developed states as well as Kelantan and Kedah fell under opposition control in the 2008 elections, although the ruling coalition recaptured Perak when two members of the state assembly defected to the Barisan Nasional.

Figure 4.4 Malaysia: Outstanding Federal Loans by State, 1965–2009 (RM '000 million)

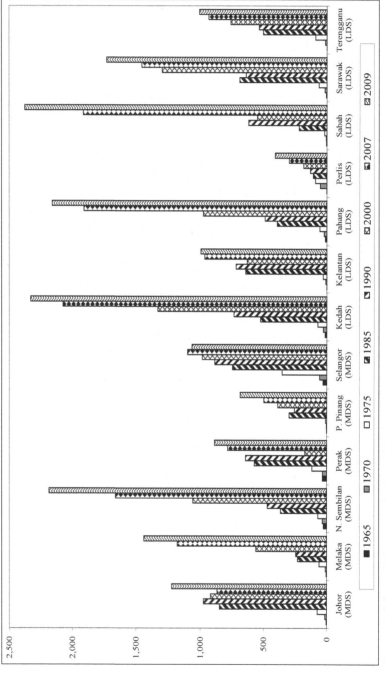

Sources: Ministry of Finance, Malaysia, *Public Accounts*, various issues.

Meanwhile, the Federal Government has started taking over water supply, which eliminates a major state government revenue source. The Federal Government proposes to privatise water supply but has not agreed to privatise that in Penang to the opposition state government, which indicated its interest. There have also been conflicts between the opposition Selangor Government and the water concessionaries in the state, which the Selangor Government is interested in taking over.

Soon after the 8 March 2008 12th General Election, the federal Minister of Tourism also announced that the ministry's memorandums of understanding (MOUs) with new opposition states (including Kedah and Selangor) would be terminated, as state-level Tourism Action Councils would no longer be chaired by BN state executive councillors in the four newly opposition-run states. The Minister proposed establishing committees with members from those involved in tourism to develop tourism in the four states, as in the case of the longstanding opposition-held State of Kelantan (*Star*, 3 April 2008). The Minister later said that tourism programmes in these states would continue to be implemented as before, but financial management would be under the ministry's Secretary-General instead of the state financial controllers (Bernama, 2008). This new *modus operandi* would deprive the opposition state governments of tourism promotion funds, as with the oil royalties for Terengganu while it was ruled by the opposition.

In December 2008, a Deputy Minister in the PM's Department told reporters that co-ordination officers would be appointed for 11 parliamentary constituencies and 22 state constituencies in the newly opposition-held State of Kedah. The officers' main duty would be 'to ensure that development in the constituencies … proceeded smoothly' (*Borneo Post*, 8 December 2008). Clearly, fiscal federalism has become an important Federal Government tool to control the state governments and to limit their ability to gain credit for achievements requiring federal government funding.

Until today, Sabah and Sarawak receive among the highest federal grants, historically introduced to induce them to accept the Malaysia Agreement to join the new federation in 1963. Selangor receives huge grants for handing over territories to the Federal Government. Densely populated Selangor, Johor and Perak also have large capitation grants, while Selangor, Johor, Kedah, Pulau Pinang, Perak and Pahang get substantial grants for their long or heavily used state roads.

The natural resource revenues and grants described above have to be considered in light of state needs. Sabah, Sarawak and Pahang are the largest states in terms of area, for which the governments incur higher travel, transport and other administrative costs. Sabah and Sarawak also rank among the four poorest states, together with Terengganu and Kelantan, which both suffer from low state revenues.

Overall, assigning more revenues to state governments would be appropriate for meaningful decentralization expected of a federation. In addition, appropriate auditing and accountability are also necessary to ensure efficiency in spending across the board without favouring any particular state. For example, the Sarawak State Government is investigating the claim, by the Malaysian Anti-Corruption Commission, that up to 60 per cent of government allocations for vital infrastructure projects in the state during 2002–2008 had been misappropriated by certain quarters responsible for handling these projects.

External Trade

High growth in the Malaysian economy has been attributed to the growth of exports, first primary commodities, and then manufactures as well. As trade statistics measure the total value of exports and imports, rather than manufacturing value-added in Malaysia, the disparity between national income and trade data has become quite considerable. Hence, trade trends poorly reflect the actual growth of manufacturing value-added in so-called 'global value chains' as the international division of labour in manufacturing involves more country locations while reported trade data increasingly reflects transfer pricing responding to differential tax rates.

Malaysia's export earnings increased from about half of GDP around 1980 to about the value of its GDP in this century (Figure 4.5). Sabah and Sarawak contributed substantially more to national export earnings in the 1970s and the 1980s, mainly in the form of pepper, timber, petroleum, gas, cocoa and palm oil. As export-oriented manufacturing and related trade grew in the peninsula from the 1970s, using imported raw materials and intermediate goods, its share of international trade rapidly outpaced those

Figure 4.5 Malaysia: Merchandise Imports and Exports by Region, 1980, 1990, 2000, 2005 (% of GDP)

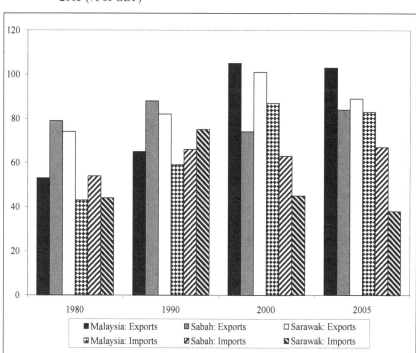

Sources: Calculated with data from Department of Statistics, Malaysia, *Yearbook of Statistics, Malaysia*, various issues; *Yearbook of Statistics, Sabah*, various issues; *Yearbook of Statistics, Sarawak*, various issues.

of Sabah and Sarawak whose share of exports fell with the exhaustion of timber resources.

Malaysia has registered significantly trade surpluses, doubling from 10 per cent of GDP in 1980 to 20 per cent in 2005 (Table 4.8). Until the 1990s, Sabah's trade surplus as a proportion of its GDP exceeded the national average. Meanwhile, Sarawak's trade balance as a proportion of its GDP has continued to exceed the national average, at least since 1980. Hence, Sabah and Sarawak have contributed significantly to Malaysia's favourable trade balance; unlike raw material or processed raw material exports, manufactured exports from the peninsular states often have a high import content of raw materials or intermediate goods.

Sabah and Sarawak petroleum, timber and agricultural resources have contributed much to Malaysian exports (Table 4.9). However, the dominance of such primary commodities in exports indicates failure to generate greater value added from natural resources by processing and manufacturing in these two states. Conversely, exports from the peninsula have been much more diversified with most industrialization, whether import-substituting or export-oriented, located there.

Table 4.8 Malaysia: Balance of Trade, 1980, 1990, 2000, 2005, 2010

	1980	*1990*	*2000*	*2005*	*2010*[a]
Malaysia: Balance as % of GDP	10	6	17	20	15
Sabah: Balance as % of GDP	25	22	11	17	n.a.
Sarawak: Balance as % of GDP	30	43	56	56	n.a.
Malaysia: Per capita balance	399	83	2,781	3,819	4,712
Sabah: Per capita balance	1,460	861	791	1,680	5,036
Sarawak: Per capita balance	1,411	2,820	8,590	13,038	20,245

Note: [a] Estimate.
Sources: Calculated with data from Department of Statistics, Malaysia, *Yearbook of Statistics, Malaysia*, various issues; *Yearbook of Statistics, Sabah*, various issues; *Yearbook of Statistics, Sarawak*, various issues.

Table 4.9 Malaysia: Exports by Region, 2010 (%)

	Malaysia	*Sabah*	*Sarawak*
Pepper			0.3
Rubber	1.4	1.2	0.4
Palm oil		34.7	7.5
Palm kernel cake	9.7	0.4	
Palm kernel oil		4.7	0.9
Cocoa beans		0.1	
Sago flour & starch			0.1
Tin	0.3		
Crude petroleum	4.8	35.4	20.9
Petroleum products	4.0		1.2
LNG	6.1		50.9
Urea			0.6
Ammonia			
Sawlogs	0.3	0.5	2.5

Table 4.9 (continued)

	Malaysia	Sabah	Sarawak
Sawn timber	0.4	1.6	1.1
Plywood	0.8	2.9	4.6
Veneer sheets		0.4	0.4
Laminated wood		0.2	
Wood moulding		0.4	
Sanded/finger-joined wood		0.1	
Other timber-based product	1.7		
Tiles			0.1
Lime, cement & fabricated building materials	0.2		
Fresh & frozen prawns	0.2	0.5	0.1
Organic chemicals	0.1	2.4	
Cocoa butter, fats & oils	0.3		
Coated printed paper		0.8	
Hot briquetted iron	0.1	2.5	
Iron & steel bars, rods, etc.	0.3		
Heating & cooling equipment & parts	0.7		
Thermionic valves & tubes, photocells, etc.	15.3		
Electronic integrated circuits	10.5		
Parts & accessories for office machines & automatic data processing equipment	5.4		
Telecommunications equipment, parts & accessories	2.7		
Electrical power machinery & parts	2.5		1.0
Electronic integrated circuits	1.9		
Other electrical & electronic products	16.1		
Professional, scientific & controlling instruments & apparatus	2.3		
Ships, boats & floating structures	0.3		0.7
Motorcars	0.1		
Aircraft & associated equipment	0.3		
Excavators, levellers, bulldozers			0.1
Sulphates of nickel			0.1
Articles of apparel & clothing accessories	0.6		
Rubber gloves	1.4		
Footwear	0.1		
Other articles of aluminium			0.3
Total	90.9	88.7	94.3
No. of items	31	17	20
Average	2.9	5.2	4.7

Sources: Calculated with data from Department of Statistics, Malaysia, *Yearbook of Statistics, Malaysia*, various issues; *Yearbook of Statistics, Sabah*, various issues; *Yearbook of Statistics, Sarawak*, various issues.

Malaysian Common Market

Before the formation of Malaysia in 1963, the peninsula, Sabah and Sarawak had different foreign trade profiles, including trade with one another. The Malaysian common market was formed with the establishment of the Malaysian federation in 1963. In 1965, Malaysia harmonized tariffs on goods imported from outside the Malaysian common market, with all domestic trade, including that among the three regions, exempt from duty. Import duties increased from 10.9 per cent of imports in 1963 to 13.3 per cent in 1970, before declining to 8.8 per cent in 1980, 4.3 per cent in 1990, less than 1.0 per cent from 2004, to 0.4 per cent in 2011.

Before its commitment to reduce tariffs in line with its World Trade Organization (WTO) commitments, the Malaysian Government reduced various tariffs for some industries that had been induced from the 1960s to set up in the country to compete with imports. While many of these earlier tariffs have been reduced, there has been greater reluctance to reduce tariffs for the heavy industries promoted by Prime Minister Mahathir in the early and mid-1980s; hence, they continue to receive considerable protection despite their limited prospects for ever achieving international competitiveness in light of their track records since. With some notable exceptions, most such industries have located in the relatively more developed west coast states to gain greater access to better infrastructure, support services and human resources. Meanwhile, the less developed states continue to serve as captive markets for protected import-substituting industries and as sources of raw materials for export processing.[4]

The effective rate of tariff protection increased from the 1960s to peak in the early 1970s (Part 1); during this period, exports from the peninsula to Sabah and Sarawak grew fastest, increasing to almost ten times from 0.5 per cent to 4.9 per cent (Table 4.10). Without uniform national import tariffs, consumers in Sabah and Sarawak might have opted for more competitively priced goods from sources other than the peninsula, or peninsular goods might have to be sold in Sabah and Sarawak at more competitive prices. In fact, consumers in Sabah and Sarawak have been paying higher prices than their counterparts in the peninsula due to higher transport charges from factories to consumers in these states.

Table 4.10 Malaysia: Intra-Regional Trade, 1960–2010 (%)

	1960	1964	1970	1980	1985	1990	1995	2000	2005	2010
Sabah's exports to:										
Peninsula	n.a.	0.3	0.9	1.1	10.0	12.5	19.5	15.1	13.2	11.5
Sarawak	n.a.	1.5	1.4	2.4	9.4	7.6	6.4	4.5	7.5	5.0
Total	n.a.	1.8	2.2	3.5	19.4	20.1	26.0	19.7	20.7	16.5
Sarawak's exports to:										
Peninsula	–	4.3	1.8	18.8	7.3	7.0	13.6	12.8	24.1	14.5
Sabah	0.2	1.1	0.9	5.8	5.7	8.0	5.9	2.8	0.6	0.5
Total	0.2	5.4	2.7	24.6	13.0	15.0	19.6	15.7	24.7	15.0
Peninsula's exports to:										
Sabah	–	0.3	2.4	4.6	5.0	4.5	2.8	1.7	0.2	–
Sarawak	–	0.2	2.4	3.7	5.1	4.5	3.2	2.0	2.6	–
Total	0.1	0.5	4.9	8.3	10.2	9.1	5.9	3.6	2.8	–

Sources: Calculated with data from Department of Statistics, Malaysia, *Yearbook of Statistics, Malaysia*, various issues; *Yearbook of Statistics, Sabah*, various issues; *Yearbook of Statistics, Sarawak*, various issues; *External Trade Statistics, Malaysia*, various issues.

Trade Items

Thus, tariff protection for the Malaysian common market led to trade diversion. Sabah imported increasing proportions of cigarettes, vehicles and petroleum products from the peninsula (Table 4.11). At least 70 per cent of Sabah's imports of cigarettes, on which high import duties are imposed (see Part 3), are from the peninsula. Sabah's increasing imports of vehicles from the peninsula are also in line with the heavy industrialization policy (see Part 1).

Notably, Sabah is exporting crude petroleum, but importing petroleum products from the peninsula. Sabah's exports of petroleum to the peninsula grew from 0.7 per cent of all its exports (from the state) in 1975 to 10.0 per cent in 2010. While facilitating the development of petroleum industries elsewhere, the federal government owned PETRONAS has yet to locate further processing of Sabah's petroleum resources within the state.

Instead, the Federal Government is building a pipeline to supply gas from Sabah to the LNG plant in Bintulu, Sarawak. Some Sabah politicians objected to the project, saying that the gas was needed for development projects and downstream industries in Sabah. A Sabah minister, Bernard Dompok, brought up the matter in the Federal Cabinet. The cabinet responded with an announcement to build a petrochemical industry in Sabah. The government subsequently announced that the pipeline project

Table 4.11 Sabah: Import Shares of Selected Manufactures from Peninsular Malaysia, 1980–2010 (%)

	1980	1990	1995	2000	2005	2010
Cigarettes	71.1	87.2	82.5	76.4	79.5	94.7
Vans & 4-wheel drive vehicles, CBU	22.7	83.4	71.9	86.3	65.8[a]	81.4[b]
Petroleum products	0.3	31.2	31.3	28.1	66.0	37.3
Fertilisers	23.2	37.1	19.1	15.0	16.9	12.1

Notes: [a] For 4-wheel drive vehicles only.
　　　　　 [b] For vehicles.
Sources: Calculated with data from Department of Statistics, Malaysia, *Yearbook of Statistics, Sabah*, various issues.

would continue, but that only excess gas would be piped to Sarawak for the LNG plant in Bintulu (*Borneo Post*, 30 December 2008). Sabah's fertilizer imports from the peninsula increased from 23.2 per cent in 1980 to 37.1 per cent in 1990 before decreasing to 12.1 per cent in 2010.

PETRONAS has sited various petrochemical industries in Sarawak, including the Asean Bintulu Fertilizer project and the LNG plant, for which the pipeline from Sabah was proposed. PETRONAS' profits from petroleum resources in Sabah and Sarawak (or Terengganu and now Kelantan) are not known as it is registered as a company not answerable to Parliament.

Within the Malaysian common market, Sarawak's exports increased from 5.4 per cent in 1964 to 15.1 per cent in 2010. Exports to the peninsula grew from 4.3 per cent to 14.5 per cent. While contributing 44 per cent of Malaysian crude petroleum exports for the period 1965–2006, and about half during 1996-2010, its imports of mineral fuels and lubricants from the peninsula increased from 0.5 per cent in 1965 to 35.4 per cent in 2010.

Sarawak's share of imported manufactures as well as machinery and transport equipment from the peninsula increased from less than 3 per cent in 1965 to at least 50 per cent from 1980 (Table 4.12). Sarawak is also dependent on the peninsula for food (with its imported share increasing from 6.7 per cent in 1965 to over 50 per cent by 1985), beverages and tobacco (from 0.4 per cent in 1965 to over 70 per cent from 1970) as well as animal and vegetable fats and oils (from a negligible amount to over 70 per cent by 1975). Currently, over 40 per cent of its chemical imports and 17.3 per cent of its inedible crude material imports are imported from the peninsula.

Thus, the growth of inter-regional trade has been unfavourable to Sabah and Sarawak. Sabah's trade deficit with the peninsula deteriorated from RM11.6 million in 1964 to RM8,550.5 million in 2010 (Table 4.13), while Sarawak's trade balance deteriorated from a surplus of RM7.8 million to a deficit of RM3,109.5 million over this period.

After the 1960s, manufacturing in the peninsula has been more export-oriented. Malaysian exports have become more diversified to involve more industrial goods. While the Malaysian government has promoted more export diversification and higher value-added manufacturing for the country, Sabah and Sarawak continue to rely on a handful of primary

Table 4.12 Sarawak: Import Shares from Peninsular Malaysia by Commodity Section, 1965–2010 (%)

	1965	1970	1975	1980	1985	1990	1995	2000	2005	2010
Manufactures	2.5	55.1	60.0	51.5	80.3	95.1	93.9	95.3	64.0	65.6
Machinery, transport equipment	1.0	10.6	29.8	25.2	23.7	31.2	42.3	50.8	51.2	50.2
Mineral fuels, lubricants	0.5	1.2	1.3	4.8	63.4	57.5	38.3	50.3	69.3	34.5
Food	6.7	23.6	50.9	48.1	52.8	59.0	59.1	54.3	53.7	52.4
Beverages & tobacco	0.4	74.6	88.3	92.0	94.2	98.4	98.5	87.0	98.9	96.4
Animal & vegetable oils & fats	–	3.0	77.5	86.9	78.1	90.1	70.6	70.5	36.3	–
Chemicals	13.0	41.9	60.4	60.1	66.7	68.2	64.0	47.8	43.6	43.7
Inedible crude material	0.4	15.3	3.2	5.2	20.8	31.7	22.3	20.7	17.3	–

Sources: Calculated with data from Department of Statistics, Malaysia, *Yearbook of Statistics, Sarawak*, various issues.

Table 4.13 Malaysia: Sabah and Sarawak Trade with Peninsular Malaysia, 1960–2010 (RM million)

	1960	1964	1970	1980	1985	1990	1995	2000	2005	2010
Sabah's trade with the peninsula										
Exports	n.a.	0.7	4.6	50.9	553.5	1169.6	2080.9	1998.0	3157.2	4,994.2
Imports	n.a.	12.3	101.7	809.7	1359.2	3201.4	4703.1	5918.0	1,000.7	13,544.8
Balance	n.a.	-11.6	-97.1	-758.8	-805.7	-2031.9	-2622.2	-3920.0	-7843.5	-8,550.5
Sarawak's trade with the peninsula										
Exports	20.0	16.4	12.1	759.1	615.9	792.6	2131.2	3993.5	8594.0	11,083.0
Imports	n.a.	8.6	45.3	725.4	1270.8	2622.7	5154.3	6883.8	12644.5	14,192.5
Balance	n.a.	7.8	-33.2	33.7	-654.9	-1830.1	-3023.1	-2890.3	-4,050.5	-3,109.5

Sources: Calculated with data from Department of Statistics, Malaysia, *Yearbook of Statistics, Sabah*, various issues; *Yearbook of Statistics, Sarawak*, various issues.

commodity exports with their (narrow) manufacturing bases. The primary sectors in Sabah and Sarawak have been larger than the national average (at current estimates of 25 per cent, 15 per cent and 7 per cent respectively). The manufacturing sector in Sabah (9 per cent) is smaller than the national average (27 per cent). While the manufacturing sector in Sarawak (27 per cent) is as large, it is overwhelmingly concentrated in petroleum industries, which do not contribute much employment; 28.8 per cent of Malaysia's exports in 2010 comprised 31 major export items, with the degree of export concentration much higher in Sabah and Sarawak (Table 4.9).

The Malaysian Government implemented a cabotage policy from 1980 under the Merchant Shipping Act (1952), by which only Malaysian shipping companies are allowed to carry Malaysian goods between the peninsula, Sabah and Sarawak. The Federation of Sabah Manufacturers complained that the policy reduced competition, increasing shipping charges and consumer prices in Sabah. Hence, it welcomed allowing foreign container ships to compete from June 2010. It also proposed that the Federal Government support the development of ports and shipping in Sabah to encourage shipping manufactured goods directly to foreign countries, thus facilitating industrial development in the state (*Daily Express*, 11 June 2009).

The Malaysian Shipowners' Association (MASA) argued that shipping costs account for 46 per cent of transportation and logistical costs for goods exported from the peninsula to Sabah. Other related cost components include port charges, forwarding, trucking, storage and terminal handling charges. The MASA Chairman further argued that 'the larger national interest of Malaysia as a Maritime Nation must also be served with the Cabotage Policy'. However, the Federal Government's Cabotage Policy has undoubtedly burdened residents of Sabah and Sarawak with higher prices exacerbated by higher transport charges. Compensatory and corrective measures have to be designed and implemented to reduce such differences in the interest of equity. Lower prices for liquefied natural (petroleum) gas in the petroleum producing states of Sabah and Sarawak from 2008 has helped to compensate for higher prices for other items. A nationwide standard pricing policy would ease the burden of higher consumer prices in the two Borneo states.

The Federal Government allocated RM386 million in its 2013 budget to reduce the higher costs of delivery to Sabah and Sarawak to achieve price uniformity throughout the nation. This is to be conducted by opening 57 retail shops known as 'Kedai Rakyat 1Malaysia' (KR1M) offering goods at lower prices. However, the Federation of Sabah Manufacturers complained that prices in KR1M were 30 per cent higher than in Kuala Lumpur. As Sabah and Sarawak together account for about 60 per cent of the national area but have poorer road systems, KR1M may not achieve its intended impact in the states (Thilaganathan, 2012).

Notes

1. National political and administrative concerns, such as decisions over matters such as federal holidays and standard time, are also vested in the Federal Government. Authority over unincorporated societies, publications, censorship as well as theatres and cinemas are vested with the Federal Government, which may thus influence and shape culture.
2. Such as shipping, navigation and fisheries; communication and transport; survey, inquiries and research purposes; education; medicine and health; professional licensing; agricultural pest control; prevention of and extinguishing fires.
3. Tengku Razaleigh of UMNO, Kelantan, unsuccessfully challenged Dr Mahathir in the 1987 UMNO election, after which UMNO was declared illegal by the court. UMNO was then re-established as UMNO Baru (the new UMNO) by Mahathir, while Razaleigh formed Semangat 46 in 1989 (the number 46 refers to 1946, the year UMNO was originally formed) after failing to re-establish UMNO with the support of two former presidents, Tunku Abdul Rahman and Hussein Onn. Razaleigh disbanded Semangat 46 and re-joined UMNO seven years later.
4. Protected manufacturers in Peninsular Malaysia thus enjoyed 'the benefits of an all-Malaysia market' (Lee, 1978: 613).

Part 5

Lessons?

This book has sought to summarize and reconsider Malaysian economic history of the last half century. Viewing the present as history in the making underscores the importance of viewing Malaysian economic development in terms of reproduction as well as transformation. Such a perspective on economic growth and distribution offers a different lens not only for understanding the past, but also for anticipating the near future. It tries to go beyond received ethnic and other stereotypes and related prejudices to deepen Malaysian economic analysis.

Development Stages

Part One has reviewed economic growth and structural change in Malaysia since the formation of the federation. The changing role of the federal or central government — particularly in policy, planning, public finances and public enterprises — is central to this narrative. The country's generally impressive economic development has been partly due to government interventions and reforms responsive to changing circumstances and challenges.

The five periods of the first four decades of post-colonial economic development are explained and distinguished in such terms. The greatly increased role of the state during the 1970s succeeded in inducing greater private investments in both plantation agriculture as well as export-oriented manufacturing besides expanding state-owned enterprises in primary production, both agriculture and mining. However, the greater role of the state since the 1997–1998 regional financial crisis has not been matched by a corresponding expansion of private investments, raising questions about the sustainability of fiscal deficits for over a decade and a half, recently articulated in terms of an ostensibly 'middle income (country) trap'.

Economic policy regime changes in Malaysia have generally responded to major political crises and developments. Thus, policy changes responded to previous problems, but rarely anticipated future challenges. The catalysts of change were thus often political, rather than economic. Ironically, all this has often been obscured by the political longevity of the ruling coalition, which has held on to political power at the crucial federal level since the first ever general elections in 1955 just before Malayan independence on 31 August 1957. Post-colonial development has therefore been chequered, with no unqualified successes or failures.

Thus, prior conditions are important, but not in a mechanical or deterministic way. Rather, policy interventions invariably sought to overcome constraints and difficulties inherited from the past. Options and choices were not unlimited, but very much constrained by available human, natural, financial and other resources. Over time, some of these resources could be increased and — arguably — transformed into other types of resources, e.g. natural resources, can be more or less efficiently sold for financial resources. One could argue that the starting point for Malaysian development was to utilize natural resources to augment other productive resources for development; or to use the World Bank's language, to transform natural capital into financial or productive physical capital. However, other factors determine how effectively such resources are invested and deployed for economic development (Khan and Jomo [eds], 2000). But as is generally acknowledged, only a small fraction of the rents from such resource extraction, except possibly in the case of petroleum resources, has been effectively mobilized and deployed for developmental purposes.

Part One has therefore emphasized the political economy of policy making and change. However, this does not mean that path dependence is 'over-determined', and there is no one explanation, let alone a single cause, for all successes or failures. Incentives are needed to induce needed investments and learning for rapid technical progress. Such inducements are needed for primary, as well as for secondary and tertiary economic activities. Development and employment generation require such industrial and advanced service activities. Private agents are unlikely to undertake the needed initiatives and activities without state interventions to create the inducements for needed activities. Fiscal resources are also needed to provide necessary infrastructure as well as other long term investments needed for development.

Malaysia was among the 'early birds' in developing export processing zones, but has been facing growing competition with others since. China's emergence as the 'manufacturing workshop' of the world continues to transform the dynamics international economic specialization and location in the last two decades — to which Malaysia has yet to respond successfully. Unlike the Republic of Korea or Taiwan Province of China, relatively few Malaysian industrial entrepreneurs have emerged to become internationally competitive in export manufacturing. Likewise, little was gained by Malaysia in development terms from being an early bird in privatization or stock market promotion.

The main advantage of a 'latecomer' is the ability to learn from earlier experiences. Unfortunately, Malaysia did not learn much from the Northeast Asian success with effective protection conditional on export promotion — combining import substitution with export orientation — or even heavy industrialization. And while it has made impressive gains with its affirmative action policies, it is hardly a model for emulation in terms of efficient or well-targeted policies, let alone improved inter-ethnic relations, or even sustained, comprehensive social policy gains.

With its relatively high per capita income compared to other developing countries and sustained growth over the decades, Malaysia has not needed significant foreign capital to augment domestic private or public financial resources. Nevertheless, Malaysia continued to receive financial aid from abroad until the 1980s, although the nature of this assistance changed significantly over time. FDI has long been sought, although FDI priorities have changed over time. Many believe such FDI has been encouraged to offset primarily ethnic Chinese domestic private investment, which has been unevenly mobilized for private investment and economic growth over the decades. Besides capital, however, FDI has also brought access to technology, markets and relevant managerial expertise.

Some recent economic literature has claimed that trade liberalization or trade openness has been good for growth and development although many such claims have been challenged on theoretical and methodological grounds. Malaysia has undoubtedly grown more than most other developing countries, with much of this growth involving exports, initially of tin, then rubber and other primary commodities, most notably palm oil, wood, petroleum and gas. Manufactured exports began with processed primary commodities, with assembly and testing of intermediate manufactured imports more important from the 1970s.

However, trade openness and other liberalization measures have greatly limited the options for developing new productive capacities and capabilities. Regaining trade policy space is thus crucial for development. As there is nothing intrinsically developmental about free trade or trade liberalization, without appropriate trade and other 'distortions', it is difficult to create the conditions necessary for starting or accelerating development by prioritizing trade openness.

The modest Malaysian value addition to considerable intermediate goods imports has meant that trade or openness measures greatly exaggerate such growth — unlike domestic resource processing, where export values reflect the full value added. Clearly, such aggregate measures offer little useful guidance to successful development policies or strategy. In recent years, there has been greater recognition of how gross trade figures greatly exaggerate the value addition of particular economic activities to national economies. This problem has been compounded by 'transfer pricing' accounting or book-keeping, often to minimize corporate tax liabilities.

Various policy interventions may be said to have addressed market failures. But some interventions cannot be honestly justified in such terms although they were nonetheless crucial to Malaysia's developmental success. After all, development is not an automatic outcome of market processes or even equilibrium. Hence, the criterion of market failure is hardly adequate to determine needed interventions to achieve economic development. Efforts to identify and overcome 'binding constraints' are essential. However, conventional economic wisdom is problematic, as the notion of 'market failure' provides a very limited basis for analysis to identify appropriate developmental policy innovation and initiatives.

This is not to suggest that all policy interventions have been developmental or that they have necessarily been intended to promote economic development. Some of those meant to be developmental have been poorly conceived, badly implemented, abused by politically influential business interests, or inappropriate for other reasons. Others, e.g. privatization in Malaysia, have been politically driven for aggrandizement and ideological reasons. They have served to disguise rent-seeking behaviour in terms of new international policy fads.

Such actions have been portrayed as instances of 'policy capture' as if such policies were well intended, but subsequently captured and abused for self-aggrandizement by the politically well-connected. Such a view presumes that the policy making process is generally benign and technocratic, rather than the outcome of the contestation of rival interests, ideologies and policies. The last three decades since the mid-1980s have seen economic liberalization on some fronts, implying some different conditions and constraints. Earlier, protectionism had successfully promoted several import-substituting industries.

Distributional Struggles

Although the rationale for much government intervention in Malaysia is ostensibly either developmental or redistributive, one can distinguish those with positive externalities in terms of contributing to growth and structural change from those with simply redistributive motives. The political legitimacy, acceptability and priority of inter-ethnic economic redistributive measures in Malaysia have been especially important in shaping perceptions of government intervention, especially along ethnic lines. Proponents of redistribution not only emphasize its progressive aspects, e.g. 'compensating for historical (colonial) neglect or underdevelopment', but also its alleged politically stabilizing consequences, so crucial for sustained economic growth. Critics emphasize various abuses which have arisen, particularly in implementing ostensibly ethnic redistributive measures.

Most importantly, perhaps, the priority given to such measures has tended to compromise and undermine the efficacy of interventions with other objectives, e.g. privatization. It is therefore quite feasible to distinguish between redistributive measures that also enhance productivity and those that merely involve transfers. Thus, somewhat ironically, both the NEP's ethnic 'restructuring' agenda as well as subsequent economic liberalization, especially privatization, have facilitated significant private capture of rents by the politically well connected, presumably with some sharing of the rents captured with those in a position to allocate them as well as others whose support is necessary to retain positions of political privilege.

Such appropriation and transfer of rents may well violate notions of fairness, including those deemed desirable for healthy competition, but may not, in themselves, be socially wasteful since they only involve transfers. However, in so far as expenses may be incurred to secure such rents (e.g. bribery or election campaign expenses), they would be wasteful, constituting dissipation of the rents created. Their respective proportions would be largely determined by the nature of the rent-seeking regime created by the intervention, and would have considerable bearing — together with other relevant factors — on the efficiency of the new rights created by the intervention.

Meanwhile, accumulation in the 'internationalized' sectors of the economy may not be significantly undermined by the magnitude and nature of these rents, and may instead ensure growth and dynamism. The allocation of rents in favour of industrialization, especially of the export-oriented variety, ensured rapid growth for many years, albeit mainly under foreign auspices — which raises doubts about its sustainability, as has become more evident in recent years. Rents effectively served as incentives for foreign investors to relocate export-oriented production to Malaysia, which was responsible for the rapid growth of most such manufacturing in the 1970s and 1990s. Some government policy reforms — including a more efficient implementation and enforcement (e.g. with the introduction of 'one-stop agencies') — also reduced clientelist pay-offs to government officials and politicians by such firms, which essentially operate in the global, rather than the national economy.

Discussion of economic distribution in Malaysia has tended to focus on inter-ethnic disparities. In addition to the New Economic Policy (NEP) poverty reduction and wealth redistribution objectives, attention is given in Part Two to some social dimensions of the structural transformation of the national economy. Forming the rural majority, Bumiputeras have generally had lower household incomes and a higher incidence of poverty. Inter-ethnic disparities decreased with the New Economic Policy, increasing with economic liberalization. However, the Gini coefficient for household income distribution among citizens has only decreased a little while intra-ethnic inequality has worsened, especially for Bumiputeras.

Part Two has also considered the changing spatial, gender and ethnic distribution of the population, household income, employment, education levels, wages, economic sector and occupation. The less developed states, with larger rural sectors, have lower household incomes and higher levels of poverty. Wage rates are generally related to industries, while poorer economic conditions in the less developed states have accounted for their lower household incomes. Differing costs of living have further influenced real wage rates and household incomes across states.

Employment, the major source of income, is often influenced by access to education and occupational opportunities in varying economic conditions over time and spatially, e.g. by region or state. Higher incomes appear to be associated with industrialization and the corresponding expansion of modern, high value-added services (Khong with Jomo, 2010) while low incomes appear to be associated with agriculture, fisheries and other low-skill occupations.

Better access to education in urban areas has contributed to higher household incomes and lower incidences of poverty as new industries also require appropriate education and training. Expansion of government education programmes has increased the education level of the labour force, especially for Bumiputeras, thanks to the government's affirmative action policies. However, historically, the poor have generally had less access to such opportunities because of unaffordable out-of-pocket expenses and the option for their children to work for income, rather than attend school. Owing to cultural prejudices across most of the ethnic communities in multicultural Malaysia, more schooling opportunities have been given to boys rather than to girls. Gender stereotyping in education and occupational status has also lowered the incomes of women workers while women's greater family and social care work commitments have also limited their participation in wage labour.

Differing access to land and capital, educational opportunities as well as employment opportunities in the private sector — as regulated by the government affirmative action policy and employment opportunities in the public sector — have led to ethnic patterns of employment. Private sector employees have generally been more susceptible to economic volatility. As more Chinese are self-employed, compared to Bumiputeras and Indians, their unemployment rates are generally lower. Influenced by business interests wanting 'cheaper' immigrant labour, the government has also used immigration policy as a blunt instrument to control Malaysian workers, besides using them for political advantage.

Public Finances

Against this complex backdrop, the distributional consequences of federal government finance, including both taxation and spending, have been considered in Part Three. Most Malaysian government revenue is from taxation, although revenue from state-owned enterprises — especially PETRONAS, the relatively well-run national petroleum corporation — has been very significant.

In Malaysia, the federal government receives at least three quarters of all government revenue and accounts for over four-fifths of total government spending. On the other hand, State government revenues vary significantly, largely reflecting their varied prerogatives and revenue streams. The main sources of State government revenue — largely linked to land and other natural resources — have declined relatively over time, increasing the central government's leverage over the State authorities, with its now exclusive control of petroleum-related revenues. Consequently, most State governments rely on federal government grants and loans to supplement their own limited revenue sources. Through such means, the federal government exerts considerable control over State governments, even if held by rival political parties.

With the declining progressivity of taxation from the 1980s, decreasing redistribution following the privatization of health services, and the likely regressive impact of government education spending, public finance has become more regressive in terms of redistribution over time. Indirect taxation in Malaysia has generally been regressive. The increase in its scope and coverage, especially the sales and services taxes, has increased regressivity. Although direct taxation of income has generally been progressive, its progressivity has decreased with tax reforms from the mid-1980s.

Part Three also considers social expenditure, such as health and education spending, as well as the changing incidence and distributional impacts of various taxes. Malaysian government health services have probably been progressive in impact, but the privatization of health services and increased user costs have probably reduced its progressivity. The better-off can, of course, better afford private health services. Tax exemption for expenses on health services also benefits the better-off. Growing private health services compete for health personnel, reducing their availability to public health services, and thus, to the poor. Health services have also been less accessible to those in the large, less developed states because of the distance of health facilities from rural communities and uneven transport infrastructure and facilities.

Government education services have tended to perpetuate inequality, rather than facilitate progressive redistribution. More from better off households have enjoyed more highly subsidized tertiary education, which provides higher private internal rate of returns. Tax exemptions on expenses for higher education have also benefited the better-off more. Although free schooling is widely available, out-of-pocket costs render schooling less accessible to the poor. As the labour force becomes more educated, returns to higher levels of schooling have not brought the expected returns. Meanwhile, increasing unemployment also means that higher incomes from graduate employment after higher education are less likely to be realized.

Privatization was supposed to accelerate growth, improve efficiency and productivity, trim the public sector, and reduce the government's financial and administrative role. But the reality was quite different. Privatization did not provide a miracle cure for the problems of the public sector. Nor has private enterprise, left to its own devices, enhanced the public interest. By diverting private capital from productive new investments to buy public sector assets, economic growth was probably retarded, rather than encouraged. Greater public accountability and transparency could ensure greater efficiency in achieving the public and national interest while limiting public sector waste and borrowing. Privatization may temporarily reduce fiscal deficits, but in the process, the public sector loses income from profitable activities, and is stuck with financing unprofitable ones, undermining the potential for cross-subsidization within the public sector.

Privatization in Malaysia came to an abrupt end barely a dozen years after it began in the mid-1980s when the 1997–1998 financial crisis exposed the vulnerabilities of the privatized SOEs. Many were 'renationalized' at considerable public expense. Many are appreciative of improvements in the operation of these SOEs, which could well have been achieved through SOE reform, rather than through the dubious and expensive process of privatization and then renationalization.

Malaysian Federalism

Part Four of this book has considered some consequences of common market expansion following the formation of Malaysia. It reviews trade between Peninsular Malaysia on the one hand and Sabah as well as Sarawak on the other. The new context has shaped the uneven nature of industrialization and development since, reshaping regional disparities in the new federation. The respective powers of the federal and State governments, including their respective fiscal capacities, as well as consequent federal-state financial relations have also been considered. Some spatial consequences of particular policies and arrangements are also considered.

Except for some limited concessions to Sabah and Sarawak, Malaysia began as a centralized federation, and centralization has generally advanced with political, administrative and socio-economic changes since 1963. The Malaysian Constitution was intended to facilitate centralized national administration, but legal and fiscal constraints faced by State governments have also strengthened the various powers of the federal government. Over time, the federal government has taken over and implemented development projects which could and should be undertaken by less fiscally constrained State governments, e.g. Federal Government financed and controlled (sub-) regional development authorities.

The Malaysian federal system provides the opportunity for the federal government to reduce inter-state and inter-regional disparities. For example, the Federal Government can increase financial allocations to the poorer states. But despite the longevity of the BN ruling coalition since 1955, its record in this regard has been chequered and uneven. Instead, Federal Government development priorities and allocations often appear to have been politically motivated. Opposition-run states have been discriminated against, while preferential treatment has favoured BN ruled states, while powerful State chief ministers have been able to exercise some degree of independence to ensure long-lasting personalized rule.

Federal powers, conferred by the Constitution and other laws, can also be used to expand the fiscal capacities of state governments, but these have not been deployed for this purpose. Instead, federal government discretion has generally been used to limit the fiscal space of state governments, especially those held by the opposition. For example, the federal government has not increased grants from mineral export taxes to more than the 10 per cent assigned to the States.

Instead, legal ambiguities and federal government political advantages have been used to limit and undermine opposition-held State governments. These include delaying grants to Kelantan and banning log exports from Sabah in the early 1990s. When Terengganu fell under opposition control, offshore petroleum royalties were diverted from the opposition-held State government to a BN-controlled federal government fund, ostensibly for the people of the state. While encouraging the private sector takeover of government assets and projects in line with its privatization policy, the federal government has ignored the opposition Penang and Selangor State governments' interest in regaining government control of water supply in their states.

Coordination and cooperation among various levels of government are required for a meaningful and viable federalism to maximize the public good. The federal government could design and implement corrective programmes to reduce national level disparities among States and regions. The devolution of financial and administrative powers would facilitate greater development roles for all State governments. The devolution of powers can be achieved through constitutional and legal changes supported by MPs from all political parties. However, such changes can only be initiated by the ruling coalition, which has increased centralization over the years. Thus, Malaysian economic liberalization has not been accompanied by serious efforts to achieve devolution and a more equitable federalism.

Concluding Remarks

This volume has revisited several less explored dimensions of Malaysian economic history with a view to considering economic development and distribution issues, particularly in relation to the role of the federal state. Three themes were given special attention in the preceding, namely public finances, fiscal federalism and the privatization of state-owned enterprises. To provide an overview of the larger context, the first part identified and reviewed five stages of economic development over the first four decades of Malaysian economic development. Similarly, population and income distribution by ethnicity, location, employment status, occupation and gender over the last half century were summarized in Part Two. The third part focused on some distributional and other related implications of public taxation and other revenue sources as well as government spending patterns, especially for ostensibly social ends. Finally, the fourth part reviewed the major economic dimensions of the unique Malaysian experience of federalism, which has changed significantly over the decades. While the emphasis is on economic relations between the peninsula and the Borneo States of Sabah and Sarawak, some aspects of the uneven development of the peninsula are also considered.

Considered as a whole, this volume seeks to challenge several dominant narratives. First, it challenges the laissez faire conventional economic wisdom by underscoring how certain developmental state economic interventions have been crucial for addressing and at least partially overcoming certain economic challenges. Second, it challenges a simple *dirigiste* narrative which would claim that the state has been progressive and developmental throughout. Third, while it acknowledges that outcomes do not necessarily flow from motives, it insists on a much more nuanced and dialectical understanding of the present as history. Fourth, it also rejects the various ethno-populist narratives so influential in Malaysia. Finally, it also raises difficult questions for those who would take comfort in simplistic solutions such as democracy, devolution or good governance.

Bibliography

Abu Bakar bin Suleiman and M. Jegathesan [eds] (2000). *Health in Malaysia: Achievements and Challenges*. Ministry of Health, Kuala Lumpur.

Alavi, Rokiah (1996). *Import-Substitution Industrialisation: Infant Industries in Malaysia*. Routledge, London.

Anand, Sudhir (1983). *Inequality and Poverty in Malaysia: Measurement and Decomposition*. Oxford University Press, Oxford.

Arief, Sritua (1983). "Household Consumption Patterns in Peninsular Malaysia: A Household Budget Survey". In Sritua Arief and Jomo K.S. [eds]. *The Malaysian Economy and Finance*. Rosecons, Australia.

Bacon, Robert, and Walter Eltis (1979). "The Measurement of the Growth of the Non-Market Sector and its Influence: A Reply to Hadjimatheou and Skouras". *Economic Journal*, 89, June.

Bank Negara Malaysia. *Annual Report*, various issues. Bank Negara Malaysia, Kuala Lumpur.

Bank Negara Malaysia. *Monthly Statistical Bulletin*, various issues. Bank Negara Malaysia, Kuala Lumpur.

Barjoyai Bardai (1993). *Malaysian Tax Policy: Applied General Equilibrium Analysis*. Pelanduk Publications, Kuala Lumpur.

Bernama (2008). "Tourism Excos in Opposition States Should be Sincere, Says Azalina". 29 May.

Bernama (2011). "Najib Announces Additional Grants for States". 28 August.

Boadway, Robin, Dale Chua and Frank Flatters (1995). "Investment Incentives and the Corporate Tax System in Malaysia". In Anwar Shah [ed.]. *Fiscal Incentives for Investment and Innovation*. Oxford University Press, Oxford: 341–397.

Borneo Post (2008a). "5 per cent Royalty Not My Decision". 28 October.

Borneo Post (2008b). "Devt Funds as Good as Increased Royalty". 29 October.

Borneo Post (2008c). "Unacceptable to Make Yong Scapegoat: SUPP". 1 November.

Borneo Post (2008d). "Kedah Appoints Coordination Officers as People's Reps". 8 December.

Borneo Post (2008e). "SAPP Creates Political Ripples in Year of the Rat". 30 December.

Borneo Post (2009). "Oil Royalty No Longer an Issue, Says MB". *Borneo Post*, 3 January.

Bowman, Mary Jean, Millot, Benoit, and Ernesto Schiefelbein (1986a). *The Political Economy of Public Support of Higher Educational Studies in Chile, France and Malaysia*. Research Division, Education and Training Department, World Bank, Washington, D.C.

Bowman, Mary Jean, Millot, Benoit, and Ernesto Schiefelbein (1986b). "An Adult Life Cycle Perspective on Public Subsidies to Higher Education in Three Countries". *Economics of Education Review*, 5 (2): 135–145.

Chee Peng Lim (1994). "Heavy Industrialisation: A Second Round of Import Substitution". In Jomo K.S. [ed.]. *Japan and Malaysian Development: In the Shadow of the Rising Sun*. Routledge, London.

Chow C.S. (1975). "Some Aspects of Price Elasticity of Rubber Production in Peninsular". In *International Rubber Conference, Kuala Lumpur, 20–25 October 1975*. Vol. 3. Rubber Research Institute of Malaysia, Kuala Lumpur: 350–369.

Daily Express, Sabah (2000). "Putrajaya FT: S'gor to Get RM200m Plus RM7.5m Yearly". 17 November.

Daily Express, Sabah (2009). "Cabotage Policy should be Liberalised Further". 11 June.

Department of Customs and Excise, Malaysia. *Annual Report*, various issues. Department of Customs and Excise, Kuala Lumpur.

Department of Statistics, Malaysia. www.statistics.gov.my

Department of Statistics, Malaysia. *External Trade Statistics, Malaysia*, various issues. Department of Statistics, Kuala Lumpur.

Department of Statistics, Malaysia. *Household Expenditure Survey, Malaysia*, various issues. Department of Statistics, Kuala Lumpur.

Department of Statistics, Malaysia. *Labour Force Survey Report*, various issues. Department of Statistics, Kuala Lumpur.

Department of Statistics, Malaysia. *Labour and Manpower Report*, various issues. Department of Statistics, Kuala Lumpur.

Department of Statistics, Malaysia. *Population Census*, various years. Department of Statistics, Kuala Lumpur.

Department of Statistics, Malaysia. *Social Statistics Bulletin*, various issues. Department of Statistics, Kuala Lumpur.

Department of Statistics, Malaysia (2009). *Report on the Annual Survey of Manufacturing Industries, 2008*. Department of Statistics, Kuala Lumpur.

Department of Statistics, Malaysia. *State/District Data Bank, Malaysia*, various years. Department of Statistics, Kuala Lumpur.

Department of Statistics, Malaysia. *Yearbook of Statistics, Malaysia*, various issues. Department of Statistics, Kuala Lumpur.

Department of Statistics, Malaysia. *Yearbook of Statistics, Sabah*, various issues. Department of Statistics, Kuala Lumpur.

Department of Statistics, Malaysia. *Yearbook of Statistics, Sarawak*, various issues. Department of Statistics, Kuala Lumpur.

Drabble, John (2000). *An Economic History of Malaysia, 1800–1900*. Macmillan, London.

Fong, J.C. (2008). *Constitutional Federalism in Malaysia*. Sweet and Maxwell Asia, Petaling Jaya.

Gomez, E.T. and Jomo K.S. (1999). *Malaysia's Political Economy*. 2nd Edition, Cambridge University Press, Cambridge.

Heller, Peter S. (1976). "A Model of the Demand for Medical and Health Services in West Malaysia". Discussion Paper No. 62, Centre for Research on Economic Development, University of Michigan, Ann Arbor, Michigan.

Heller, P.S. and A.A. Tait (1984). "Government Employment and Pay: Some International Comparisons". Occasional Paper 24, International Monetary Fund, Washington, DC.

Hickling, R.H. (1978). "An Overview of Constitutional Changes in Malaysia: 1957–1977". In Mohamed Suffian, H.P. Lee and F.A. Trindade [eds]. *The Constitution of Malaysia — Its Development: 1957–1977*. Oxford University Press, Kuala Lumpur: 1–26.

Hill, Kim Quile (1975). "Public Expenditure and Services as Policy Outcome Predictors: A Two Nation Analysis for Health and Education". Paper No. 65, Programme of Development Studies, Rice University, Houston.

Hoerr, O.D. (1973). "Education, Income and Equity in Malaysia". *Economic Development and Cultural Change*, 21 (2). Reprinted in David Lim [ed.]. (1975). *Readings in Malaysian Economic Development*. Oxford University Press, Kuala Lumpur.

Idrus, A. and S. Cameron (2000). "Returns to Education between the Self-employed and Employed Sectors: Evidence from Malaysia". *The Pakistan Development Review*, 39 (4), Autumn: 263–268.

ILO (1988). *World Labour Report*. Volume 3. International Labour Office, Geneva.

Inland Revenue Board, Malaysia. *Annual Report*, various issues. Inland Revenue Board, Kuala Lumpur.

Ismail Muhammad Salleh (1977). "Tax Incidence and Income Distribution in West Malaysia". PhD thesis, University of Illinois, Urbana-Champaign.

Ismail Muhammad Salleh (1980). "Redistributional Impact of Taxation on the Peasant Household". Paper for the Conference on "Development: The Peasantry and Development in the ASEAN Region", 26–29 May, Universiti Kebangsaan Malaysia, Bangi.

Jandhala, Tilak B.G. (1989). "Education and Its Relationship to Economic Growth, Poverty and Income Distribution". Discussion Paper, World Bank, Washington, DC.

Jasbir Sarjit Singh and Ozay Mehmet (1991). *Human Capital Formation in East Malaysia: A Socio-Economic Profile of Graduates in Sabah and Sarawak*. Institute for Advanced Studies, University of Malaya, Kuala Lumpur.

Jayakumar, S. (1971). *Constitutional Law Cases for Malaysia and Singapore*. Malayan Law Journal, Singapore.

Johnson, Simon and Todd Mitton (2001). "Cronyism and Capital Controls: Evidence from Malaysia". Processed, 20 August. National Bureau of Economic Research, Cambridge, MA.

Jomo K.S. (1990). *Growth and Structural Change in the Malaysian Economy*. Macmillan, London.

Jomo K.S. (2001). *Malaysian Eclipse: Economic Crisis and Recovery*. Zed Books, London.

Jomo K.S. (2004). *M Way: Mahathir's Economic Legacy*. Forum, Kuala Lumpur.

Jomo K.S. [ed.] (1985). *The Sun Also Sets: Lessons in 'Looking East'*. 2nd edition. Institute of Social Analysis, Kuala Lumpur.

Jomo K.S. [ed.] (1994). *Japan and Malaysian Development: In the Shadow of the Rising Sun*. Routledge, London.

Jomo K.S. [ed.] (1995). *Privatizing Malaysia: Rents, Rhetoric, Realities*. Westview Press, Boulder.

Jomo K.S. [ed.] (1998). *Tigers in Trouble*. University of Hongkong Press, Hong Kong.

Jomo K.S. [ed.] (2002). *Ugly Malaysians? — South-South Investments Abused*. Institute for Black Research, Durban.

Jomo K.S. [ed.] (2003). *Manufacturing Competitiveness in Asia: How Internationally Competitive National Firms and Industries Developed in East Asia*. RoutledgeCurzon, London.

Jomo K.S. [ed.] (2004). *After The Storm: Crisis, Recovery and Sustaining Development in East Asia*. Singapore University Press, Singapore.

Jomo K.S. [ed.] (2007). *Malaysian Industrial Policy*. Singapore University Press, Singapore, and University of Hawaii Press, Honolulu.

Jomo K.S. and Wee Chong Hui (2013). "Lessons from Post-Colonial Malaysian Economic Development". In Augustin K. Fosu [ed.]. *Achieving Development Success: Strategies and Lessons from the Developing World*. Oxford University Press, Oxford: 50–71.

Khalid Ibrahim (1987). "Monitoring Government Companies: Central Information Collection Unit (CICU) Findings". *Ilmu Masyarakat* 13 (October–December): 49–58.

Khan, Mushtaq and Jomo K.S. [eds] (2000). *Rents, Rent-Seeking and Economic Development: Theory and the Asian Evidence*. Cambridge University Press, Cambridge.

Khong How Ling (1986). "Export-orientated Industrialization, Employment and Real Wages in Malaysia". *Kajian Ekonomi Malaysia*, 23 (2), December: 1–30.

Khong How Ling (1991). "Service Employment in the Malaysian Economy: Structure and Change". PhD thesis, Cambridge University, Cambridge, UK.

Khong How Ling with Jomo K.S. (2010). *Labour Market Segmentation in Malaysian Services*. National University of Singapore Press, Singapore.

Khoo Khay Jin (1980). "The Marketing of Smallholder Rubber". In Kamal Salih [ed.]. *Rural-Urban Relations, Special Studies in the Malaysian Case*. UNCRD Project 50R, Study No. 6, School of Comparative Social Studies, Universiti Sains Malaysia, Penang.

Khor, K.P. (1987). *Malaysian Economy in Decline*. Consumers Association of Penang, Penang.

Kwok Kwan Kit (1979). "An Analysis of Household Demand in Peninsular Malaysia". Research Paper No. 15, Department of Statistics, Malaysia, Kuala Lumpur.

Lee Hock Lock (1978). *Public Policies and Economic Diversification in West Malaysia, 1957–1970*. Penerbit Universiti Malaya, Kuala Lumpur.

Lee, Molly (1999). "Public Policies on Private Education in Malaysia". In *Private Higher Education in Malaysia*. Monograph Series No. 2/1999, School of Educational Studies, Universiti Sains Malaysia, Penang: 21–34.

Leeds, Roger S. (1989). "Malaysia: Genesis of a Privatization Transaction". *World Development*, 17 (5): 741–756.

Leigh, Michael Bechett (1971). "The Development of Political Organizations and Leadership in Sarawak, East Malaysia". PhD thesis, Cornell University, Ithaca, New York.

Leigh, Michael Bechett (1988). *The Rising Moon: Political Change in Sarawak*. Sydney University Press, Sydney.

Lian Teck Jin (1976). "Financing Higher Education: An Examination of the Rationale for Subsidising Malaysian Higher Education and the Alternative to Traditional Policy". PhD thesis, University of Chicago, Chicago.

Lim Kit Siang (1987). *The $62 Billion North-South Highway Scandal*. Democratic Action Party, Kuala Lumpur.

Mahathir Mohamad (1970). *The Malay Dilemma*. Donald Moore for Asia Pacific Press, Singapore.

Mahathir Mohamad (1976). *Menghadapi Cabaran*. Penerbit Utusan Melayu, Kuala Lumpur.

Mahathir Mohamad (1984). "Malaysia Incorporated and Privatization: Its Rationale and Purpose". In Mohd Nor Abdul Ghani, Bernard T.H. Wang, Ian K.M. Chia and Bruce Gale [eds]. *Malaysia Incorporated and Privatisation: Towards National Unity*. Pelanduk Publications, Petaling Jaya: 1–8.

Malaysia. *Constitution of Malaysia*. Percetakan Nasional Malaysia Berhad, Kuala Lumpur.

Malaysia. *Malaysian Government Gazette*, various issues. Percetakan Nasional Malaysia Berhad, Kuala Lumpur.

Malaysia. *Petroleum Development Act, 1974*.

Malaysia, Economic Planning Unit. http://www.epu.gov.my

Malaysia (1971). *The Second Malaysia Plan, 1971–1975*. Economic Planning Unit, Kuala Lumpur.

Malaysia (1973). *Mid-Term Review of the Second Malaysia Plan, 1971–1975*. Economic Planning Unit, Kuala Lumpur.

Malaysia (1976). *The Third Malaysia Plan, 1976–1980*. Economic Planning Unit, Kuala Lumpur.

Malaysia (1979). *Mid-Term Review of the Third Malaysia Plan, 1976–1980*. Economic Planning Unit, Kuala Lumpur.

Malaysia (1981). *The Fourth Malaysia Plan, 1981–1985*. Economic Planning Unit, Kuala Lumpur.

Malaysia (1984). *Mid-Term Review of the Fourth Malaysia Plan, 1981–1985*. Economic Planning Unit, Kuala Lumpur.

Malaysia (1985). *Guidelines for Privatisation*. Economic Planning Unit, Kuala Lumpur.

Malaysia (1986). *The Fifth Malaysia Plan, 1986–1990*. Economic Planning Unit, Kuala Lumpur.

Malaysia (1989). *Mid-Term Review of the Fifth Malaysia Plan, 1986–1990*. Economic Planning Unit, Kuala Lumpur.

Malaysia (1991a). *The Sixth Malaysia Plan, 1991–1995*. Economic Planning Unit, Kuala Lumpur.

Malaysia (1991b). *The Second Outline Perspective Plan, 1991–2000*. Economic Planning Unit, Kuala Lumpur.

Malaysia (1994). *Mid-Term Review of the Sixth Malaysia Plan, 1991–1995*. Economic Planning Unit, Kuala Lumpur.

Malaysia (1996). *The Seventh Malaysia Plan, 1996–2000*. Economic Planning Unit, Kuala Lumpur.

Malaysia (1999). *Mid-Term Review of the Seventh Malaysia Plan, 1996–2000*. Economic Planning Unit, Kuala Lumpur.

Malaysia (2001a). *The Third Outline Perspective Plan, 2001–2010*. Economic Planning Unit, Kuala Lumpur.

Malaysia (2001b). *The Eighth Malaysia Plan, 2001–2005*. Economic Planning Unit, Kuala Lumpur.

Malaysia (2003). *Mid-Term Review of the Eighth Malaysia Plan, 2001–2005*. Economic Planning Unit, Kuala Lumpur.

Malaysia (2006). *The Ninth Malaysia Plan, 2006–2010*. Economic Planning Unit, Kuala Lumpur.

Malaysia (2008). *Mid-Term Review of the Ninth Malaysia Plan, 2006–2010*. Economic Planning Unit, Kuala Lumpur.

Malaysia (2010). *The Tenth Malaysia Plan, 2011–2015*. Economic Planning Unit, Kuala Lumpur.

Malaysia, State Government. *Financial Statement*, various issues.

Malaysian Shipowners' Association, http://www.malaysianshippingopwners.org/chairmsg. html (downloaded 21 May 2010)

Matthias, John (2000). "Malaysia's Privatization Mess". *Asiafeatures.com*, 31 December.

Mazumdar, Dipak (1981). *The Urban Labour Market and Income Distribution: A Study of Malaysia*. Oxford University Press, New York.

Meerman, Jacob (1979). *Public Expenditure in Malaysia: Who Benefits and Why*. Oxford University Press, New York.

Mehmet, Ozay (1988). *Development in Malaysia: Poverty, Wealth and Trusteeship*. Institute of Social Analysis, Kuala Lumpur.

Milne, R.S., and K.J. Ratnam (1974). *Malaysia — New States in a New Nation*. Frank Cass, London.

Ministry of Education, Malaysia (1973). *Dropout Study*. Ministry of Education, Kuala Lumpur.

Ministry of Education, Malaysia: Educational Planning and Research Division (1981). *A Summary Report for Higher Education Study, 1977/78*. Ministry of Education, Kuala Lumpur.

Ministry of Finance, Malaysia. *Federal Public Accounts*, various issues. Ministry of Finance, Kuala Lumpur.

Ministry of Finance, Malaysia. *Economic Report*, various issues. Ministry of Finance, Kuala Lmpur

Ministry of Health. (1987). *The First National Health and Morbidity Survey*. Ministry of Health, Kuala Lumpur.

Ministry of Health. (1996). *The Second National Health and Morbidity Survey*. Ministry of Health, Kuala Lumpur.

Ministry of Health, Malaysia: National Heart Institute. *Annual Report*, various issues. Ministry of Health, Kuala Lumpur.

Mohamed Izham, M.I., A.R. Dzulkifli, and C.E. Zubaidah (1997). "Drug Distribution System in Malaysia: The Privatization of the General Medical Store". Paper presented at the "National Conference on Privatization and Health Care Financing in Malaysia: Emerging Issues and Concerns", organized by Universiti Sains Malaysia, Malaysian Medical Association and Consumers' Association of Penang, 5–6 April.

Murthi Semudram (1988). "The Services Sector of the Malaysian Economy: Macro-economic Issues". In Sieh M.L. [ed.]. *Services in Development: An Agenda for Research in ASEAN*. International Development Research Centre, Ottawa.

Narayanan, Suresh (1986). "Sectoral Tax Incidence in an Open Economy: A Study of Peninsular Malaysia". PhD thesis, Boston University, Boston.

NEAC (2010a). *New Economic Model for Malaysia: Part I*. National Economic Advisory Council, Putrajaya.

NEAC (2010b). "New Economic Model for Malaysia — Part II: Market Friendly and Transparent Affirmative Action". Processed. National Economic Advisory Council, Putrajaya.

NECC (1990). *Laporan Majlis Perundingan Ekonomi Nasional*. Economic Planning Unit, for Majlis Perundingan Ekonomi Nasional (National Economic Consultative Council), Kuala Lumpur.

New Straits Times, various issues.

PETRONAS. www.petronas.com.my (accessed on 30 June 2010).

Poulgrain, Greg (1998). *The Genesis of Konfrontasi: Malaysia, Brunei, Indonesia, 1945–1965.* Crawford House Publishing, Bathurst.

Randhawa, Inderjit Singh, Oon Seang Boon, Khalid Ahmad (1994). *Taxes in Malaysia: Towards a Value-Added Tax.* Pelanduk Publications, Petaling Jaya.

Rasiah, Rajah (2002). "Manufactured Exports, Employment, Skills and Wages in Malaysia". Processed, International Labour Office, Geneva.

Rasiah, Rajah, H. Osman-Rani and Rokiah Alavi (2000). "Changing Dimensions of Malaysian Trade: Beyond Neoliberal and Dirigiste Approaches". *International Journal of Business and Society*, 1 (1).

Rozita Halina Hussein (2000). "Financing Health Care Through General Taxation in Malaysia". In *Proceedings on Internal Conference on Evidence-based Practice: Towards Evidence-based Policy Making in Health and Development, 4–6 September 2000, organized by Institute of Public Health, National Institutes of Health, Ministry of Health, Malaysia; World Health Organization; Academy of Medicine, Malaysia; ASEM Trust Fund and World Health Organization Collaboration Centre for Health System Research, Malaysia*, Ministry of Health, Malaysia, Kuala Lumpur.

Salleh Abbas, Mohd (1978). "Federalism in Malaysia — Changes in the First Twenty Years". In Mohamed Suffian, H.P. Lee and F.A. Trinidade [eds]. *The Constitution of Malaysia — Its Development: 1957–1977.* Oxford University Press, Kuala Lumpur: 163–191.

Shafruddin, B.H. (1987). *The Federal Factor in the Government and Politics of Peninsular Malaysia.* Oxford University Press, Singapore.

Shafruddin, B.H. (1988). "Malaysia Centre-State Relations by Design and Process". In Shafruddin B.H. and Iftikhar A.M.Z. Fadzil [eds]. *Between the Centre and State.* Institute of Strategic and International Studies, Malaysia, Kuala Lumpur: 3–29.

Shahir bin Nasir (1997). Discussion of "Issues in the Evolution of the Malaysian Federal System: The Changing Role of the State and Local Governments". In Sulaiman Mahbob, Frank Flatters, Robin Boadway, Sam Wilson and Elayne Yee Siew Lin [eds]. *Malaysia's Public Sector in the Twenty-First Century: Planning for 2020 and Beyond.* Queen's University, Kingston, Ontario and Malaysian Institute of Economic Research, Kuala Lumpur: 184–185.

Shamsulbahriah, Ku Ahmad (1988). "Stratification and Occupational Segmentation in the Peninsular Malaysia Labour Force: A Case for Gender Oriented Development Planning". In "Colloquium on Women and Development in Malaysia — Implications for Planning and Population Dynamics", 10–12 January 1989, Kuala Lumpur.

Snodgrass, Donald R. (1975). "The Fiscal System as an Income Redistributor". In David Lim [ed.]. *Readings on Malaysian Economic Development.* Oxford University Press, Kuala Lumpur: 269–291.

Snodgrass, Donald R. (1980). *Inequality and Economic Development in Malaysia.* Oxford University Press, Kuala Lumpur.

Sritua Arief (1983). "Household Consumption Patterns in Peninsular Malaysia: A Household Budget Survey". In Sritua Arief and Jomo K.S. [eds]. *The Malaysian Economy and Finance.* Rosecons, Australia: 329–342.

Star (2008). "Azalina: Tourism MoUs with Opposition-ruled States to be Terminated". 3 April.

Supian Ali (1988). "Malaysia". In Gus Edgren [ed.]. *The Growing Sector: Studies in Public Sector Employment in Asia*. ILO-ARTEP, New Delhi.

Tan Tat Wai (1982). *Income Distribution and Determination in West Malaysia*. Oxford University Press, Singapore.

Tan, Jeff Wooi Syn (2008). *Privatization in Malaysia: Regulation, Rent-Seeking and Policy Failure*. Routledge, London.

The Star, various issues.

Thilaganathan, Pushparani. "No Major Budget Cheer for Sabah, Sarawak". http://freemalaysiatoday.com/category/nation/2012/09/28/no-budget0cheer-for-sabah -and-sarawak/ (accessed on 21 October 2012)

Umikalsum Haji Mohd Noh (1991). "Fiscal Federalism in Malaysia". PhD thesis, Faculty of Economics and Administration, University of Malaya, Kuala Lumpur.

UNIDO (United Nations Industrial Development Organisation) (1985). "Industrialisation and Employment Generation in the Services Sector of Developing Countries". *Industry and Development*,15.

Waldinger, R. (1985). "Immigrant Enterprise and the Structure of the Labour Market". In B. Roberts, R. Finnegan and D. Gullie [eds]. *New Approaches to Economic Life*. University of Manchester Press, Manchester: 213–228.

Wee Chong Hui (1995). *Sabah and Sarawak in the Malaysian Economy*. Institute of Social Analysis, Kuala Lumpur.

Wee Chong Hui (2006a). *Fiscal Policy and Inequality in Malaysia*. Universiti Malaya Press, Kuala Lumpur.

Wee Chong Hui (2006b). *Regional Disparities and Federalism in Malaysia*. Universiti Malaya Press, Kuala Lumpur.

Wee Chong Hui and Jomo K.S. (2007). "Equity in Malaysian Health Care: An Analysis of Public Health Expenditure and Health Care Facilities". In Chee Heng Leng and Simon Barracough [eds]. *Health Care in Malaysia: The Dynamics of Provision, Financing and Access*. Routledge, London: 102–116.

Wee, Victor Eng Lian (1997). "An Analysis of Tax Reform in Malaysia". PhD thesis, University of Bristol, Bristol.

Wilson, Sam, and Sulaiman Mahbob (1997). "Decentralisation and Fiscal Federalism in Malaysia". In Sulaiman Mahbob, Frank Flatters, Robin Boadway, Sam Wilson and Elayne Yee Siew Lin [eds]. *Malaysia's Public Sector in the Twenty-First Century: Planning for 2020 and Beyond*. Queen's University at Kingston, Ontario and Malaysian Institute of Economic Research, Kuala Lumpur: 46–66.

Wong Sook Ching and Jomo K.S. with Chin Kok Fay (2005). *Malaysian "Bail-Outs"? Capital Controls, Restructuring & Recovery in Malaysia*. Singapore University Press, Singapore.

World Bank (1983). *Malaysia: Structural Change and Stabilization*. World Bank, Washington, DC.

World Health Organization. http://www.who.org.int/research/en

Index